Also edited by Lamar Underwood

Classic Hunting Stories
Classic War Stories
The Greatest Adventure Stories Ever Told
The Greatest Disaster Stories Ever Told
The Greatest Fishing Stories Ever Told
The Greatest Flying Stories Ever Told
The Greatest Hunting Stories Ever Told
The Greatest Survival Stories Ever Told
The Greatest War Stories Ever Told
The Quotable Soldier
The Quotable Writer
Basic Wilderness Survival Skills
Bowhunting Tactics of the Pros
Into the Backing
Man Eaters
Theodore Roosevelt on Hunting
Tales of the Mountain Men
Whitetail Hunting Tactics of the Pros

CLASSIC SURVIVAL STORIES

THIRTEEN TALES OF STRENGTH,
DETERMINATION, AND THE WILL TO LIVE

———————————

EDITED BY LAMAR UNDERWOOD

———————————

MJF BOOKS
NEW YORK

Published by MJF Books
Fine Communications
322 Eighth Avenue
New York, NY 10001

Classic Survival Stories
LC Control Number 2005938782
ISBN-13: 978-1-56731-792-3
ISBN-10: 1-56731-792-8

Manufactured in the United States of America.

MJF Books and the MJF colophon are trademarks of Fine Creative Media, Inc.

QM   10 9   8 7 6 5 4 3 2 1

Contents

Introduction   VII

To Build a Fire
by Jack London   1

The Great Unknown
by John Welsey Powell   29

*The Battle of the Marten and the
Porcupine*
by Mayne Reid   67

Robinson Crusoe
by Daniel Defoe   77

Love of Life
by Jack London   143

Shipwreck of the Whaleship Essex
by Owen Chase   175

CONTENTS

An Adventure with a Dog and a Glacier
by John Muir   217

The Boat Journey
by Sir Ernest Shackleton   243

Battle with the Giant Octopus
by Victor Hugo   303

Encounter with the Blackfeet
by Osborne Russell   321

Around the Horn
by Richard Henry Dana Jr.   333

The Worst Journey in the World
by Apsley Cherry-Garrard   351

On Dangerous Ground
by Lamar Underwood   391

Introduction

For this reader, the word "survival" in a story or book title jump-starts a great deal of anticipation and interest about what I expect to find in the pages ahead. There should not be any dreaded "slow parts" in the prose, no meandering passages about settings, characters, and back-story. I wish to quite literally "cut to the chase"—immerse myself in the situation and action where fate or blunders have gotten some luckless chap or critter into one hell of a mess. Will they live or die? What would I have done under the same circumstances?

The word "survival," of course, can mean something as ordinary as holding on to your job during a particularly grueling session in the corporate board room, or keeping a small business afloat anytime. Our interests in the places the word takes us here are more primitive, however. They are the same as when our ancient kinfolk first left the caves and tried to pick up the trail of a wooly mammoth to get something for supper. The stakes are much higher in this kind of survival story than the television programs where they kick you off the show. Here failure serves up a nightmarish list of miseries—starvation, freezing to death, drowning, thirst, attacks by Indians, and being bitten or even eaten by wild creatures and insects.

As your Editor of *Classic Survival Stories*, I consider my mission to be one of pleasure and privilege: To serve up in the pages of this little book some of the most engaging and exciting stories of battles for survival ever told. If you like books that "take you somewhere" (to use one story-telling benchmark), you've come to the right stand. Whether you're reading while hanging on a subway strap, waiting for a plane that should have been there two hours ago, or cushioned in your favorite easy chair, you'll soon be transported to other worlds where the threat of an agonizing death is always but a heartbeat away.

I personally have neither the interest nor the appropriate degrees from academia to attach the word "Classic" to any story in such a way as to be meaningful in the dusty halls of literature. When a tale has been around a very long time and is still being read with a great deal of interest…well, that's a "Classic" in my library. Books like *Robinson Crusoe* come to mind. I also reserve the privilege of using the word "Classic" for books and stories that are personal favorites that I rank among the most enjoyable and interesting reading experiences I have ever known.

I have a great deal of confidence in the reading reward you're going to enjoy in the tales presented here. Whether or not you consider them to be "Classic" in a more-traditional sense, or just darn good "Reads" (to use the modern expression), you'll find engaging prose about situations when, indeed, the chips are down, the cards on the table, and desperation is in command.

The fact that I have chosen a story of my own—a selection from my novel *On Dangerous Ground* (Doubleday, 1989)—may seem to be an arrogant, free-handed act for an editor working under the "Classic" title. Forgive me, if you feel that way, for I have not included the tale for any personal gain or satisfaction but for one reason only: I think most readers will enjoy it a great deal. If that explanation is not good enough, then perhaps one of today's common quips will suffice: I did it because I *could*.

For many readers, certainly in my own case, between the lines of every survival tale lurks the unwritten question, "What if I had been there?"

Could I hack it? Would I collapse, weak and trembling? Or would I put up a damn good fight?

One wonders about the huge audiences attracted to the television "Survivor" series and its spin-offs. Did the viewers picture themselves in the situation? Or were they merely interested in who would win the game?

The "survivalists" here are not playing games. Call their predicaments fate or plain old bad luck, they face doom in a variety of circumstances. Expeditions to the blank spaces on the maps—like Scott's and Shackleton's in the Antarctic or John Wesley Powell's on the Colorado—evolve from being heroic bold ventures into savage struggles to stay alive. Disasters at sea are the catalyst of adventures like Robinson Crusoe and the story of the Whaleship *Essex*. Some tales, like Jack London's classic "To Build a Fire," begin with the protagonist being naive about the unusual dangers of his surroundings and situation—on the trail, alone, with the temperature seventy-five degrees below zero. He will face the ultimate test—as do the participants in all of these stories. Some make it back, some don't.

Whatever happens, *you* will be there.

Lamar Underwood
Winter, 2003

To Build a Fire

JACK LONDON

Day had broken cold and gray, exceedingly cold and gray, when the man turned aside from the main Yukon trail and climbed the high earth-bank, where a dim and little-travelled trail led eastward through the fat spruce timberland. It was a steep bank, and he paused for breath at the top, excusing the act to himself by looking at his watch. It was nine o'clock. There was no sun nor hint of sun, though there was not a cloud in the sky. It was a clear day, and yet there seemed an intangible pall over the face of things, a subtle gloom that made the day dark, and that was due to the absence of sun. This fact did not worry the man. He was used to the lack of sun. It had been days since he had seen the sun, and he knew that a few more days must pass before that cheerful orb, due south, would just peep above the skyline and dip immediately from view.

The man flung a look back along the way he had come. The Yukon lay a mile wide and hidden under three feet of ice. On top of this ice were as many feet of snow. It was all pure white, rolling in gentle undulations where the ice jams of the freeze-up had formed. North and south, as far as his eye could see, it was unbroken white, save for a dark hairline that curved and twisted from around the spruce-covered island to the south, and that curved and twisted away into the north, where it disappeared behind another spruce-covered island. This dark hairline was the trail—the main trail—that led south five hundred miles to the Chilcoot Pass, Dyea, and salt water; and that led north seventy miles to Dawson, and still on to the north a thousand miles to Nulato, and finally to St. Michael, on Bering Sea, a thousand miles and half a thousand more.

But all this—this mysterious, far-reaching hairline trail, the absence of sun from the sky, the tremendous cold, and the strangeness and weirdness of it all— made no impression on the man. It was not because he was long used to it. He was a newcomer in the land, a *chechaquo,* and this was his first winter. The trouble with him was that he was without imagination. He was quick and alert in the things of life, but only in things, and not in the significances. Fifty degrees below zero meant eighty-odd degrees of frost. Such fact impressed him as being cold and uncomfortable, and that was all. It did not lead him to meditate upon his frailty as a creature of temperature, and upon man's frailty in general, able only to live within certain narrow limits of heat and cold; and from there on it did not lead him to the conjectural field of immortality and man's place in the universe. Fifty degrees below zero stood for a bite of frost that hurt and that must be guarded against by use of mittens, ear flaps, warm moccasins, and thick socks. Fifty degrees below zero was to him just precisely fifty degrees below zero. That there should be anything more to it than that was a thought that never entered his head.

As he turned to go, he spat speculatively. There was a sharp, explosive crackle that startled him. He spat again. And again, in the air, before it could fall to the snow, the spittle crackled. He knew that at fifty below spittle crackled on the snow, but this spittle had crackled in the air. Undoubtedly it was colder than fifty below—how much colder he did not know. But the temperature did not matter. He was bound for the old claim on the left fork of Henderson Creek, where the boys were already. They had come over across the divide from the Indian Creek country, while he had come the roundabout way to take a look at the possibilities of getting out logs in the spring from the islands in the Yukon. He would be in to camp by six o'clock; a bit after dark, it was true, but the boys would be there, a fire would be going, and a hot supper would be ready. As for lunch, he pressed his hand against the protruding bundle under his jacket. It was also under his shirt, wrapped up in a handkerchief and lying against the naked skin. It was the only way to keep the biscuits from freezing. He smiled agreeably to himself as he thought of those biscuits, each cut open and sopped in bacon grease, and each enclosing a generous slice of fried bacon.

He plunged in among the big spruce trees. The trail was faint. A foot of snow had fallen since the last sled had passed over, and he was glad he was without a sled, travelling light. In fact, he carried nothing but the lunch wrapped in the handkerchief. He was surprised, however, at the cold. It certainly was cold, he concluded, as he rubbed his numb nose and cheekbones with his mittened hand. He was a warm-whiskered man, but the hair on his face did not protect the high cheekbones and the eager nose that thrust itself aggressively into the frosty air.

At the man's heels trotted a dog, a big native husky, the proper wolf dog, gray-coated and without any visible or temperamental difference from its brother, the wild wolf. The animal was depressed by the tremendous cold. It knew that it was no time for travelling. Its instinct told it a truer tale than was told to the man by the man's judgment. In reality, it was not merely colder than fifty below zero; it was colder than sixty below, than seventy below. It was seventy-five below zero. Since the freezing point is thirty-two above zero, it meant that one hundred and seven degrees of frost obtained. The dog did not know anything about thermometers. Possibly in its brain there was no sharp consciousness of a condition of very cold such as was in the man's brain. But the brute had its instinct. It experienced a vague but menacing apprehension that subdued it and made it slink along at the man's heels, and that made it question eagerly every unwonted movement of the man as if expecting him to go into camp or to seek shelter somewhere and build a fire. The dog had learned fire, and it wanted fire, or else to burrow under the snow and cuddle its warmth away from the air.

The frozen moisture of its breathing had settled on its fur in a fine powder of frost, and especially were its jowls, muzzle and eyelashes whitened by its crystalled breath. The man's red beard and mustache were likewise frosted, but more solidly, the deposit taking the form of ice and increasing with every warm, moist breath he exhaled. Also, the man was chewing tobacco, and the muzzle of ice held his lips so rigidly that he was unable to clear his chin when he expelled the juice. The result was that a crystal beard of the color and solidity of amber was increasing its length on his chin. If he fell down it would shatter itself, like glass, into brittle fragments. But he did not mind the appendage. It was the penalty all tobacco chewers paid in that country, and he had been out before in two cold snaps. They had not been so cold as this, but by the spirit thermometer at Sixty-Mile he knew that they had been registered at fifty below and at fifty-five.

He held on through the level stretch of woods for several miles, crossed a wide flat of nigger heads, and dropped down a bank to the frozen bed of a small stream. This was Henderson Creek, and he knew he was ten miles from the forks. He looked at his watch. It was ten o'clock. He was making four miles an hour, and he calculated that he would arrive at the forks at half-past twelve. He decided to celebrate that event by eating his lunch there.

The dog dropped in again at his heels, with a tail drooping discouragement, as the man swung along the creek bed. The furrow of the old sled trail was plainly visible, but a dozen inches of snow covered the marks of the last runners. In a month no man had come up or down that silent creek. The man held steadily on. He was not much given to think-ing, and just then particularly he had nothing to think about save that he would eat lunch at the forks and that at six o'clock he would be in camp with the boys. There was nobody to talk to; and, had there been, speech would have been impossible because of ice muzzle on his mouth. So he continued monot-onously to chew tobacco and to increase the length of his amber beard.

Once in a while the thought reiterated itself that it was very cold and that he had never experienced

such cold. As he walked along he rubbed his cheekbones and nose with the back of his mittened hand.
He did this automatically, now and again changing
hands. But, rub as he would, the instant he stopped
his cheekbones went numb, and the following
instant the end of his nose went numb. He was sure
to frost his cheeks; he knew that, and experienced a
pang of regret that he had not devised a nose strap
of the sort Bud wore in cold snaps. Such a strap
passed across the cheeks, as well, and saved them. But
it didn't matter much, after all. What were frosted
cheeks? A bit painful, that was all; they were never
serious.

Empty as the man's mind was of thoughts, he was
keenly observant, and he noticed the changes in the
creek, the curves and bends and timber jams, and
always he sharply noted where he placed his feet.
Once, coming around a bend he shied abruptly, like
a startled horse, curved away from the place where
he had been walking, and retreated several paces
back along the trail. The creek he knew was frozen
clear to the bottom—no creek could contain water
in that arctic winter—but he knew also that there
were springs that bubbled out from the hillsides and
ran along under the snow and on top the ice of the
creek. He knew that the coldest snaps never froze
these springs, and he knew likewise their danger.
They were traps. They hid pools of water under the
snow that might be three inches deep, or three feet.

Sometimes a skin of ice half an inch thick covered them, and in turn was covered by the snow. Sometimes there were alternate layers of water and ice skin, so that when one broke through he kept on breaking through for a while, sometimes wetting himself to the waist.

That was why he had shied in such panic. He had felt the give under his feet and heard the crackle of a snow-hidden ice skin. And to get his feet wet in such a temperature meant trouble and danger. At the very least it meant delay, for he would be forced to stop and build a fire, and under its protection to bare his feet while he dried his socks and moccasins. He stood and studied the creek bed and its banks, and decided that the flow of water came from his right. He reflected awhile, rubbing his nose and cheeks, then skirted to the left, stepping gingerly and testing the footing for each step. Once clear of the danger, he took a fresh chew of tobacco and swung along at his four-mile gait.

In the course of the next two hours he came upon several similar traps. Usually the snow above the hidden pools had a sunken, candied appearance that advertised the danger. Once again, however, he had a close call; and once, suspecting danger, he compelled the dog to go on in front. The dog did not want to go. It hung back until the man shoved it forward, and then it went quickly across the white, unbroken surface. Suddenly it broke through, floundered to one side, and got away to firmer footing. It had wet its forefeet and legs, and almost immediately the water that clung to it turned to ice. It made quick efforts to lick the ice off its legs, then dropped down in the snow and began to bite out the ice that had formed between the toes. This was a matter of instinct. To permit the ice to remain would mean sore feet. It did not know this. It merely obeyed the mysterious prompting that arose from the deep crypts of its being. But the man knew, having achieved a judgment on the subject, and he removed the mitten from his right hand and helped tear out the ice particles. He did not expose his fingers more than a minute, and was astonished at the swift numbness that smote them. It certainly was cold. He pulled on the mitten hastily, and beat the hand savagely across his chest.

At twelve o'clock the day was at its brightest. Yet the sun was too far south on its winter journey to clear the horizon. The bulge of the earth intervened between it and Henderson Creek, where the man walked under a clear sky at noon and cast no shadow. At half-past twelve, to the minute, he arrived at the forks of the creek. He was pleased at the speed he had made. If he kept it up, he would certainly be with the boys by six. He unbuttoned his jacket and shirt and drew forth his lunch. The action consumed no more than a quarter of a minute, yet in that brief moment the numbness laid hold of the exposed fingers. He did not put the mitten on, but, instead, struck the fingers a dozen sharp smashes against his leg. Then he sat down on a snow-covered log to eat. The sting that followed upon the striking of his fingers against his leg ceased so quickly that he was startled. He had had no chance to take a bite of biscuit. He struck the fingers repeatedly and returned them to the mitten, baring the other hand for the purpose of eating. He tried to take a mouthful, but the ice muzzle prevented. He had forgotten to build a fire and thaw out. He chuckled at his foolishness, and as he chuckled he noted the numbness creeping into the exposed fingers. Also, he noted that the stinging which had first come to his toes when he sat down was already passing away. He wondered whether the toes were warm or numb. He moved them inside the moccasins and decided that they were numb.

He pulled the mitten on hurriedly and stood up. He was a bit frightened. He stamped up and down until the stinging returned into the feet. It certainly was cold, was his thought. That man from Sulphur Creek had spoken the truth when telling how cold it sometimes got in the country. And he had laughed at him at the time! That showed one must not be too sure of things. There was no mistake about it, it *was* cold. He strode up and down, stamping his feet and threshing his arms, until reassured by the returning warmth. Then he got out matches and proceeded to make a fire. From the undergrowth, where high water of the previous spring had lodged a supply of seasoned twigs, he got his firewood. Working carefully from a small beginning, he soon had a roaring fire, over which he thawed the ice from his face and in the protection of which he ate his biscuits. For the moment the cold of space was outwitted. The dog took satisfaction in the fire, stretching out close enough for warmth and far enough away to escape being singed.

When the man had finished, he filled his pipe and took his comfortable time over a smoke, then he pulled on his mittens, settled the ear flaps of his cap firmly about his ears, and took the creek trail up the left fork. The dog was disappointed and yearned back towards the fire. This man did not know cold. Possibly all the generations of his ancestry had been ignorant of cold, of real cold, of cold one hundred and seven degrees below freezing point. But the dog knew; all its ancestry knew, and it had inherited the knowledge. And it knew that it was not good to walk abroad in such fearful cold. It was the time to lie snug in a hole in the snow and wait for a curtain of cloud to be drawn across the face of outer space whence this cold came. On the other hand, there was no keen intimacy between the dog and the man. The one was the toil slave of the other, and the only caresses it had ever received were the caresses of the whip lash and of harsh and menacing throat sounds that threatened the whip lash. So the dog made no effort to communicate its apprehension to the man. It was not concerned in the welfare of the man; it was for its own sake that it yearned back toward the fire. But the man whistled, and spoke to it with the sound of whip lashes, and the dog swung in at the man's heels and followed after.

The man took a chew of tobacco and proceeded to start a new amber beard. Also, his moist breath quickly powdered with white his mustache, eyebrows, and lashes. There did not seem to be so many springs on the left fork of the Henderson, and for half an hour the man saw no signs of any. And then it happened. At a place where there were no signs, where the soft, unbroken snow seemed to advertise solidity beneath, the man broke through. It was not deep. He wet himself halfway to the knees before he floundered out to the firm crust.

He was angry, and cursed his luck aloud. He had hoped to get into camp with the boys at six o'clock, and this would delay him an hour, for he would have to build a fire and dry out his footgear. This was imperative at that low temperature—he knew that much; and he turned aside to the bank, which he climbed. On top, tangled in the underbrush about the trunks of several small spruce trees, was a high-water deposit of dry firewood—sticks and twigs, principally, but also larger portions of seasoned branches and fine, dry, last year's grasses. He threw down several large pieces on top of the snow. This served for a foundation and prevented the young flame from drowning itself in the snow it otherwise would melt. The flame he got by touching a match to a small shred of birch bark that he took from his pocket. This burned even more readily than paper. Placing it on the foundation, he fed the young flame with wisps of dry grass and with the tiniest dry twigs.

He worked slowly and carefully, keenly aware of his danger. Gradually, as the flame grew stronger, he increased the size of the twigs with which he fed it. He squatted in the snow, pulling the twigs out from their entanglement in the brush and feeding directly to the flame. He knew there must be no failure. When it is seventy-five below zero, a man must not fail in his first attempt to build a fire—that is, if his feet are wet. If his feet are dry, and he fails, he can run along the trail for half a mile and restore his circulation. But the circulation of wet and freezing feet cannot be restored by running when it is seventy-five below. No matter how fast he runs, the wet feet will freeze the harder.

All this the man knew. The old-timer on Sulphur Creek had told him about it the previous fall, and now he was appreciating the advice. Already all sensation had gone out of his feet. To build the fire he had been forced to remove his mittens, and the fingers had quickly gone numb. His pace of four miles an hour had kept his heart pumping blood to the surface of his body and to all the extremities. But the instant he stopped, the action of the pump eased down. The cold of space smote the unprotected tip of the planet, and he, being on that unprotected tip, received the full force of the blow. The blood of his body recoiled before it. The blood was alive, like the dog, and like the dog it wanted to hide away and cover itself up from the fearful cold. So long as he walked four miles an hour, he pumped the blood, willy-nilly, to the surface; but now it ebbed away and sank down into the recesses of his body. The extremities were the first to feel its absence. His wet feet froze the faster, and his exposed fingers numbed the faster, though they had not yet begun to freeze. Nose and cheeks were already freezing, while the skin of all his body chilled as it lost its blood.

But he was safe. Toes and nose and cheeks would be only touched by the frost, for the fire was beginning to burn with strength. He was feeding it with twigs the size of his finger. In another minute he would be able to feed it with branches the size of his wrist, and then he could remove his wet footgear, and, while it dried, he could keep his naked feet warm by the fire, rubbing them at first, of course, with snow. The fire was a success. He was safe. He remembered the advice of the old-timer on Sulphur Creek, and smiled. The old-timer had been very serious in laying down the law that no man must travel alone in the Klondike after fifty below. Well, here he was; he had had the accident; he was alone; and he had saved himself. Those old-timers were rather womanish, some of them, he thought. All a man had to do was to keep his head, and he was all right. Any man who was a man could travel alone. But it was surprising, the rapidity with which his cheeks and nose were freezing. And he had not thought his fingers could go lifeless in so short a time. Lifeless they were, for he could scarcely make them move together to grip a twig, and they seemed remote from his body and from him. When he touched a twig, he had to look and see whether or not he had hold of it. The wires were pretty well down between him and his finger ends.

All of which counted for little. There was the fire, snapping and crackling and promising life with every dancing flame. He started to untie his moccasins. They were coated with ice; the thick German socks were like sheaths of iron halfway to the knees; and the moccasin strings were like rods of steel all twisted and knotted as by some conflagration. For a moment he tugged with his numb fingers, then, realizing the folly of it, he drew his sheath knife.

But before he could cut the strings, it happened. It was his own fault or, rather, his mistake. He should not have built the fire under the spruce tree. He should have built it in the open. But it had been easier to pull the twigs from the brush and drop them directly on the fire. Now the tree under which he had done this carried a weight of snow on its boughs. No wind had blown for weeks, and each bough was full freighted. Each time he had pulled a twig he had communicated a slight agitation to the tree—an imperceptible agitation, so far as he was concerned, but an agitation sufficient to bring about the disaster. High up in the tree one bough capsized its load of snow. This fell on the boughs beneath, capsizing them. This process continued, spreading out and involving the whole tree. It grew like an avalanche, and it descended upon the man and the fire, and the fire was blotted out! Where it had burned was a mantle of fresh and disordered snow.

The man was shocked. It was as though he had just heard his own sentence of death. For a moment he sat and stared at the spot where the fire had been. Then he grew very calm. Perhaps the old-timer on Sulphur Creek was right. If he had only had a trail mate he would have been in no danger now. The trail mate could have built the fire. Well, it was up to him to build the fire over again, and this second time there must be no failure. Even if he succeeded, he would most likely lose some toes. His feet must be badly frozen by now, and there would be some time before the second fire was ready.

Such were his thoughts, but he did not sit and think them. He was busy all the time they were passing through his mind. He made a new foundation for a fire, this time out in the open, where no treacherous tree could blot it out. Next he gathered dry grasses and tiny twigs from the high-water flotsam. He could not bring his fingers together to pull them out, but he was able to gather them by the handful. In this way he got many rotten twigs and bits of green moss that were undesirable, but it was the best he could do. He worked methodically, even collecting an armful of larger branches to be used later when the fire gathered strength. And all the while the dog sat and watched him, a certain wistfulness in its eyes, for it looked upon him as the fire provider, and the fire was slow in coming.

When all was ready, the man reached in his pocket for a second piece of birch bark. He knew the bark was there, and though he could not feel it with his fingers, he could hear its crisp rustling as he fumbled for it. Try as he would, he could not clutch hold of it. And all the time, in his consciousness, was the knowledge that each instant his feet were freezing. This thought tended to put him in a panic, but he fought against it and kept calm. He pulled on his mittens with his teeth, and threshed his arms back and forth, beating his hands with all his might against his sides. He did this sitting down, and he stood up to do it; and all the while the dog sat in the snow, its wolf brush of a tail curled around warmly over its forefeet, its sharp wolf ears pricked forward intently as it watched the man. And the man, as he beat and threshed with his arms and hands, felt a great surge of envy as he regarded the creature that was warm and secure in its natural covering.

After a time he was aware of the first faraway signals of sensations in his beaten fingers. The faint tingling grew stronger till it evolved into a stinging ache that was excruciating, but which the man hailed with satisfaction. He stripped the mitten from his right hand and fetched forth the birch bark. The exposed fingers were quickly going numb again. Next he brought out his bunch of sulphur matches. But the tremendous cold had already driven the life out of his fingers. In his effort to separate one match from the others, the whole bunch fell into the snow. He tried to pick it out of the snow, but failed. The dead fingers could neither clutch nor touch. He was very careful. He drove the thought of his freezing feet, and nose, and cheeks, out of his mind, devoting his whole soul to the matches. He watched, using the sense of vision in place of that of touch, and when he saw his fingers on each side the bunch, he closed them—that is, he willed to close them, for the wires were down, and the fingers did not obey. He pulled the mitten on the right hand, and beat it fiercely against his knee. Then, with both mittened hands, he scooped the bunch of matches, along with much snow, into his lap. Yet he was no better off.

After some manipulation he managed to get the bunch between the heels of his mittened hands. In this fashion he carried it to his mouth. The ice crackled and snapped when by a violent effort he opened his mouth. He drew the lower jaw in, curled the upper lip out of the way and scraped the bunch with his upper teeth in order to separate a match. He succeeded in getting one, which he dropped on his lap. He was no better off. He could not pick it up. Then he devised a way. He picked it up in his teeth and scratched it on his leg. Twenty times he scratched before he succeeded in lighting it. As it flamed he held it with his teeth to the birch bark. But the burning brimstone went up his nostrils and into his lungs, causing him to cough spasmodically. The match fell into the snow and went out.

The old-timer on Sulphur Creek was right, he thought in the moment of controlled despair that ensued: after fifty below, a man should travel with a partner. He beat his hands, but failed in exciting any sensation. Suddenly he bared both hands, removing the mittens with his teeth. He caught the whole bunch between the heels of his hands. His arm muscles not being frozen enabled him to press the hand heels tightly against the matches. Then he scratched the bunch along his leg. It flared into flame, seventy sulphur matches at once! There was no wind to blow them out. He kept his head to one side to escape the strangling fumes, and held the blazing bunch to the birch bark. As he so held it, he became aware of sensation in his hand. His flesh was burning. He could smell it. Deep down below the surface he could feel it. The sensation developed into pain that grew acute. And still he endured it, holding the flame of the matches clumsily to the bark that would not light readily because his own burning hands were in the way, absorbing most of the flame.

At last, when he could endure no more, he jerked his hands apart. The blazing matches fell sizzling into the snow, but the birch bark was alight. He began laying dry grasses and the tiniest twigs on the flame. He could not pick and choose, for he had to lift the fuel between the heels of his hands. Small pieces of rotten wood and green moss clung to the twigs, and he bit them off as well as he could with his teeth. He cherished the flame carefully and awkwardly. It meant life, and it must not perish. The withdrawal of blood from the surface of his body now made him begin to shiver, and he grew more awkward. A large piece of green moss fell squarely on the little fire. He tried to poke it out with his fingers, but his shivering frame made him poke too far, and he disrupted the nucleus of the little fire, the burning grasses and the tiny twigs separating and scattering. He tried to poke them together again, but in spite of the tenseness of the effort, his shivering got away with him, and the twigs were hopelessly scattered. Each twig gushed a puff of smoke and went out. The fire provider had failed. As he looked apathetically about him, his eyes chanced on the dog, sitting across the ruins of the fire from him, in the snow, making restless, hunching movements, slightly lifting one forefoot and then the other, shifting its weight back and forth on them with wistful eagerness.

The sight of the dog put a wild idea into his head. He remembered the tale of the man, caught in a blizzard, who killed a steer and crawled inside the carcass, and so was saved. He would kill the dog and bury his hands in the warm body until the numbness went out of them. Then he could build another fire. He spoke to the dog, calling it to him; but in his voice was a strange note of fear that frightened the animal, who had never known the man to speak in such a way before. Something was the matter, and its suspicious nature sensed danger—it knew not what danger, but somewhere, somehow, in its brain arose an apprehension of the man. It flattened its ears down at the sound of the man's voice, and its rest-less, hunching movements and the liftings and shift-ings of its forefeet became more pronounced; but it would not come to the man. He got on his hands and knees and crawled toward the dog. This unusu-al posture again excited suspicion, and the animal sidled mincingly away.

The man sat up in the snow for a moment and struggled for calmness. Then he pulled on his mit-tens, by means of his teeth, and got upon his feet. He glanced down at first in order to assure himself that he was really standing up, for the absence of sensa-tion in his feet left him unrelated to the earth. His erect position in itself started to drive the webs of suspicion from the dog's mind; and when he spoke peremptorily, with the sound of whip lashes in his voice, the dog rendered its customary allegiance and came to him. As it came within reaching distance, the man lost his control. His arms flashed out to the dog, and he experienced genuine surprise when he discovered that his hands could not clutch, that there was neither bend nor feeling in his fingers. He had forgotten for the moment that they were frozen and that they were freezing more and more. All this happened quickly, and before the animal could get away, he encircled its body with his arms. He sat down in the snow, and in this fashion held the dog, while it snarled and whined and struggled.

But it was all he could do, hold its body encircled in his arms and sit there. He realized that he could not kill the dog. There was no way to do it. With his helpless hands he could neither draw nor hold his sheath knife nor throttle the animal. He released it, and it plunged wildly away, with tail between its legs, and still snarling. It halted forty feet away and surveyed him curiously, with ears sharply pricked forward.

The man looked down at his hands in order to locate them, and found them hanging on the ends of his arms. It struck him as curious that one should have to use his eyes in order to find out where his hands were. He began threshing his arms back and forth, beating the mittened hands against his sides. He did this for five minutes, violently, and his heart pumped enough blood up to the surface to put a stop to his shivering. But no sensation was aroused in his hands. He had an impression that they hung like weights on the ends of his arms, but when he tried to run the impression down, he could not find it.

A certain fear of death, dull and oppressive, came to him. This fear quickly became poignant as he realized that it was no longer a mere matter of freezing his fingers and toes, or of losing his hands and feet, but that it was a matter of life and death with the chances against him. This threw him into a panic, and he turned and ran along the old, dim trail. The dog joined in behind and kept up with him. He ran blindly, without intention, in fear such as he had never known in his life. Slowly, as he plowed and floundered through the snow, he began to see things again—the banks of the creek, the old timber jams, the leafless aspens, and the sky. The running made him feel better. He did not shiver. Maybe, if he ran on, his feet would thaw out; and, anyway, if he ran far enough, he would reach camp and the boys. Without doubt he would lose some fingers and toes and some of his face; but the boys would take care of him, and save the rest of him when he got there. And at the same time there was another thought in his mind that said he would never get to the camp and the boys; that he would soon be stiff and dead.

This thought he kept in the background and refused to consider. Sometimes it pushed itself forward and demanded to be heard, but he thrust it back and strove to think of other things.

It struck him as curious that he could run at all on feet so frozen that he could not feel them when they struck the earth and took the weight of his body. He seemed to himself to skim along above the surface, and to have no connection with the earth. Somewhere he had once seen a winged Mercury, and he wondered if Mercury felt as he felt when skimming over the earth.

His theory of running until he reached camp and the boys had one flaw in it: he lacked the endurance. Several times he stumbled, and finally he tottered, crumpled up, and fell. When he tried to rise, he failed. He must sit and rest, he decided, and next time he would merely walk and keep on going. As he sat and regained his breath, he noted that he was feeling quite warm and comfortable. He was not shivering, and it even seemed that a warm glow had come to his chest and trunk. And yet, when he touched his nose or cheeks, there was no sensation. Running would not thaw them out. Nor would it thaw out his hands and feet. Then the thought came to him that the frozen portions of his body must be extending. He tried to keep this thought down, to forget it, to think of something else; he was aware of the panicky feeling that it caused, and he was afraid of the panic. But the thought asserted itself, and persisted, until it produced a vision of his body totally frozen. This was too much, and he made another wild run along the trail. Once he slowed down to a walk, but the thought of the freezing extending itself made him run again.

And all the time the dog ran with him, at his heels. When he fell down a second time, it curled its tail over its forefeet and sat in front of him, facing him, curiously eager and intent. The warmth and security of the animal angered him, and he cursed it till it flattened down its ears appeasingly. This time the shivering came more quickly upon the man. He was losing in his battle with the frost. It was creeping into his body from all sides. The thought of it drove him on, but he ran no more than a hundred feet, when he staggered and pitched headlong. It was his last panic. When he had recovered his breath and control, he sat up and entertained in his mind the conception of meeting death with dignity. However, the conception did not come to him in such terms. His idea of it was that he had been making a fool of himself, running around like a chicken with its head cut off—such was the simile that occurred to him. Well, he was bound to freeze anyway, and he might as well take it decently. With this newfound peace of mind came the first glimmerings of drowsiness. A good idea, he thought, to sleep off to death. It was like taking an anesthetic. Freezing was not so bad as people thought. There were lots worse ways to die.

He pictured the boys finding his body the next day. Suddenly he found himself with them, coming along the trail and looking for himself. And, still with them, he came around a turn in the trail and found himself lying in the snow. He did not belong with himself any more, for even then he was out of himself, standing with the boys and looking at himself in the snow. It certainly was cold, was his thought. When he got back to the States he could tell the folks what real cold was. He drifted on from this to a vision of the old-timer on Sulphur Creek. He could see him quite clearly, warm and comfortable, and smoking a pipe.

"You were right, old hoss; you were right," the man mumbled to the old-timer of Sulphur Creek.

Then the man drowsed off into what seemed to him the most comfortable and satisfying sleep he had ever known. The dog sat facing him and waiting. The brief day drew to a close in a long, slow twilight. There were no signs of a fire to be made, and, besides, never in the dog's experience had it known a man to sit like that in the snow and make no fire. As the twilight drew on, its eager yearning for the fire mastered it, and with a great lifting and shifting of forefeet, it whined softly, then flattened its ears down in anticipation of being chidden by the man. But the man remained silent. Later the dog whined loudly. And still later it crept close to the man and caught the scent of death. This made the animal bristle and back away. A little longer it delayed, howling under the stars that leaped and danced and shone brightly in the cold sky. Then it turned and trotted up the trail in the direction of the camp it knew, where there were other food providers and fire providers.

The Great Unknown

JOHN WESLEY POWELL

From Exploration of the Colorado River and Its Tributaries, *Powell's account of his epic journey running the Green and Colorado rivers in 1869. Powell's journey in wooden boats with nine other men took him into places where no white man had ever made a footprint, including the Grand Canyon.*

*A*ugust 13.—We are now ready to start on our way down the Great Unknown. Our boats, tied to a common stake, chafe each other as they are tossed by the fretful river. They ride high and buoyant, for their loads are lighter than we could desire. We have but a month's rations remaining. The flour has been resifted through the mosquito-net sieve; the spoiled bacon has been dried and the worst of it boiled; the few pounds of dried apples have been spread in the sun and reshrunken to their normal bulk. The sugar has all melted and gone on its way down the river. But we have a large sack of coffee. The lightening of the boats has this advantage: they will ride the waves better and we shall have but little to carry when we make a portage.

We are three quarters of a mile in the depths of the earth, and the great river shrinks into insignificance as it dashes its angry waves against the walls and cliffs that rise to the world above; the waves are but puny ripples, and we but pigmies, running up and down the sands or lost among the boulders.

We have an unknown distance yet to run, an unknown river to explore. What falls there are, we know not; what rocks beset the channel, we know not; what walls rise over the river, we know not. Ah, well! we may conjecture many things. The men talk as cheerfully as ever; jests are bandied about freely this morning; but to me the cheer is somber and the jests are ghastly.

With some eagerness and some anxiety and some misgiving we enter the canyon below and are carried along by the swift water through walls which rise from its very edge. They have the same structure that we noticed yesterday—tiers of irregular shelves below, and, above these, steep slopes to the foot of marble cliffs. We run six miles in a little more than half an hour and emerge into a more open portion of the canyon, where high hills and ledges of rock intervene between the river and the distant walls. Just at the head of this open place the river runs across a dike; that is, a fissure in the rocks, open to

depths below, was filled with eruptive matter, and
this on cooling was harder than the rocks through
which the crevice was made, and when these were
washed away the harder volcanic matter remained as
a wall, and the river has cut a gateway through it several hundred feet high and as many wide. As it crosses the wall, there is a fall below and a bad rapid, filled
with boulders of trap; so we stop to make a portage.
Then on we go, gliding by hills and ledges, with distant walls in view; sweeping past sharp angles of
rock; stopping at a few points to examine rapids,
which we find can be run, until we have made
another five miles, when we land for dinner.

Then we let down with lines over a long rapid and
start again. Once more the walls close in, and we
find ourselves in a narrow gorge, the water again filling the channel and being very swift. With great
care and constant watchfulness we proceed, making
about four miles this afternoon, and camp in a cave.

August 14.—At daybreak we walk down the bank
of the river, on a little sandy beach, to take a view of
a new feature in the canyon. Heretofore hard rocks
have given us bad river; soft rocks, smooth water; and
a series of rocks harder than any we have experienced
sets in. The river enters the gneiss! We can see but a little way into the granite gorge, but it looks threatening.

After breakfast we enter on the waves. At the very
introduction it inspires awe. The canyon is narrower
than we have ever before seen it: the water is swifter;

there are but few broken rocks in the channel; but the walls are set, on either side, with pinnacles and crags; and sharp, angular buttresses, bristling with wind- and wave-polished spires, extend far out into the river.

Ledges of rock jut into the stream, their tops sometimes just below the surface, sometimes rising a few or many feet above; and island ledges and island pinnacles and island towers break the swift course of the stream into chutes and eddies and whirlpools. We soon reach a place where a creek comes in from the left, and, just below, the channel is choked with boulders, which have washed down this lateral canyon and formed a dam, over which there is a fall of 30 or 40 feet; but on the boulders foothold can be had, and we make a portage. Three more such dams are found. Over one we make a portage; at the other two are chutes through which we can run.

As we proceed the granite rises higher, until nearly a thousand feet of the lower part of the walls are composed of this rock.

About eleven o'clock we hear a great roar ahead, and approach it very cautiously. The sound grows louder and louder as we run, and at last we find ourselves above a long, broken fall, with ledges and pinnacles of rock obstructing the river. There is a descent of perhaps 75 or 80 feet in a third of a mile, and the rushing waters break into great waves on the rocks, and lash themselves into a mad, white foam.

We can land just above, but there is no foothold on either side by which we can make a portage. It is nearly a thousand feet to the top of the granite; so it will be impossible to carry our boats around, though we can climb to the summit up a side gulch and, passing along a mile or two, descend to the river. This we find on examination; but such a portage would be impracticable for us, and we must run the rapid or abandon the river. There is no hesitation. We step into our boats, push off, and away we go, first on smooth but swift water, then we strike a glassy wave and ride to its top, down again into the trough, up again on a higher wave, and down and up on waves higher and still higher until we strike one just as it curls back, and a breaker rolls over our lit-tle boat. Still on we speed, shooting past projecting rocks, till the little boat is caught in a whirlpool and spun round several times. At last we pull out again into the stream. And now the other boats have passed us. The open compartment of the *Emma Dean* is filled with water and every breaker rolls over us. Hurled back from a rock, now on this side, now on that, we are carried into an eddy, in which we struggle for a few minutes, and are then out again, the breakers still rolling over us. Our boat is unman-ageable, but she cannot sink, and we drift down another hundred yards through breakers—how, we scarcely know. We find the other boats have turned into an eddy at the foot of the fall and are waiting to catch us as we come, for the men have seen that our boat is swamped. They push out as we come near and pull us in against the wall. Our boat bailed, on we go again.

The walls now are more than a mile in height—a vertical distance difficult to appreciate. Stand on the south steps of the Treasury building in Washington and look down Pennsylvania Avenue to the Capitol; measure this distance overhead, and imagine cliffs to extend to that altitude, and you will understand what is meant; or stand at Canal Street in New York and look up Broadway to Grace Church, and you have about the distance; or stand at Lake Street bridge in Chicago and look down to the Central Depot, and you have it again.

A thousand feet of this is up through granite crags; then steep slopes and perpendicular cliffs rise one above another to the summit. The gorge is black and narrow below, red and gray and flaring above, with crags and angular projections on the walls, which, cut in many places by side canyons, seem to be a vast wilderness of rocks. Down in these grand, gloomy depths we glide, ever listening, for the mad waters keep up their roar; ever watching, ever peering ahead, for the narrow canyon is winding and the river is closed in so that we can see but a few hundred yards, and what there may be below we know not; so we listen for falls and watch for rocks, stopping now and then in the bay of a recess to admire the gigantic scenery; and ever as we go there is some new pinnacle or tower, some crag or peak, some distant view of the upper plateau, some strangely shaped rock, or some deep, narrow side canyon.

Then we come to another broken fall, which appears more difficult than the one we ran this morning. A small creek comes in on the right, and the first fall of the water is over boulders, which have been carried down by this lateral stream. We land at its mouth and stop for an hour or two to examine the fall. It seems possible to let down with lines, at least a part of the way, from point to point, along the righthand wall. So we make a portage over the first rocks and find footing on some boulders below. Then we let down one of the boats to the end of her line, when she reaches a corner of the projecting rock, to which one of the men clings and steadies her while I examine an eddy below. I think we can pass the other boats down by us and catch them in the eddy. This is soon done, and the men in the boats in the eddy pull us to their side. On the shore of this little eddy there is about two feet of gravel beach above the water. Standing on this beach, some of the men take the line of the little boat and let it drift down against another projecting angle. Here is a little shelf, on which a man from my boat climbs, and a shorter line is passed to him, and he fastens the boat to the side of the cliff; then the second one is let down, bringing the line of the third. When the second boat is tied up, the two men standing on the beach above spring into the last boat, which is pulled up alongside of ours; then we let down the boats for 25 or 30 yards by walking along the shelf, landing them again in the mouth of a side canyon. Just bellow this there is another pile of boulders, over which we make another portage. From the foot of these rocks we can climb to another shelf, 40 or 50 feet above the water.

On this bench we camp for the night. It is raining hard, and we have no shelter, but find a few sticks which have lodged in the rocks, and kindle a fire and have supper. We sit on the rocks all night, wrapped in our *ponchos,* getting what sleep we can.

August 15.—This morning we find we can let down for 300 or 400 yards, and it is managed in this way: we pass along the wall by climbing from projecting point to point, sometimes near the water's edge, at other places 50 or 60 feet above, and hold the boat with a line while two men remain aboard and prevent her from being dashed against the rocks and keep the line from getting caught on the wall. In two hours we have brought them all down, as far as it is possible, in this way. A few yards below, the river strikes with great violence against a projecting rock and our boats are pulled up in a little bay above. The little boat is held by the bow obliquely up the stream. We jump in and pull out only a few strokes, and sweep clear of the dangerous rock. The other boats follow in the same manner and the rapid is passed.

It is not easy to describe the labor of such navigation. We must prevent the waves from dashing the boats against the cliffs. Sometimes, where the river is swift, we must put a bight of rope about a rock, to prevent the boat from being snatched from us by a wave; but where the plunge is too great or the chute too swift, we must let her leap and catch her below or the undertow will drag her under the falling water and sink her. Where we wish to run her out a little way from shore through a channel between rocks, we first throw in little sticks of driftwood and watch their course, to see where we must steer so that she will pass the channel in safety. And so we hold, and let go, and pull, and lift, and ward—among rocks, around rocks, and over rocks.

And now we go on through this solemn, mysterious way. The river is very deep, the canyon very narrow, and still obstructed, so that there is no steady flow of the stream; but the waters reel and roll and boil, and we are scarcely able to determine where we can go. Now the boat is carried to the right, perhaps close to the wall; again, she is shot into the stream, and perhaps is dragged over to the other side, where, caught in a whirlpool; she spins about. We can neither land nor run as we please. The boats are entirely unmanageable; no order in their running can be preserved; now one, now another, is ahead, each crew laboring for its own preservation. In such a place we come to another rapid. Two of the boats run it perforce. One succeeds in landing, but there is no foothold by which to make a portage and she is pushed out again into the stream. The next minute a great reflex wave fills the open compartment; she is water-logged, and drifts unmanageable. Breaker after breaker rolls over her and one capsizes her. The men are thrown out; but they cling to the boat, and she drifts down some distance alongside of us and we are able to catch her. She is soon bailed out and the men are aboard once more; but the oars are lost, and so a pair from the *Emma Dean* is spared. Then for two miles we find smooth water.

Clouds are playing in the canyon today. Sometimes they roll down in great masses, filling the gorge with gloom; sometimes they hang aloft from wall to wall and cover the canyon with a roof of impending storm, and we can peer long distances up and down this canyon corridor, with its cloud-roof overhead, its walls of black granite, and its river bright with the sheen of broken waters. Then a gust of wind sweeps down a side gulch and, making a rift in the clouds, reveals the blue heavens, and a stream of sunlight pours in. Then the clouds drift away into the distance, and hang around crags and peaks and pinnacles and towers and walls, and cover them with a mantle that lifts from time to time and sets them all in sharp relief. Then baby clouds creep out of side canyons, glide around points, and creep back again into more distant gorges. Then clouds arrange in strata across the canyon, with intervening vista views to cliffs and rocks beyond. The clouds are children of the heavens, and when they play among the rocks they lift them to the region above.

It rains! Rapidly little rills are formed above, and these soon grow into brooks, and the brooks grow into creeks and tumble over the walls in innumerable cascades, adding their wild music to the roar of the river. When the rain ceases the rills, brooks, and creeks run dry. The waters that fall during a rain on these steep rocks are gathered at once into the river; they could scarcely be poured in more suddenly if some vast spout ran from the clouds to the stream itself. When a storm bursts over the canyon a side gulch is dangerous, for a sudden flood may come, and the inpouring waters will raise the river so as to hide the rocks.

Early in the afternoon we discover a stream entering from the north—a clear, beautiful creek, coming down through a gorgeous red canyon. We land and camp on a sand beach above its mouth, under a great, overspreading tree with willow-shaped leaves.

August 16.—We must dry our rations again to-day and make oars.

The Colorado is never a clear stream, but for the past three or four days it has been raining much of the time, and the floods poured over the walls have brought down great quantities of mud, making it exceedingly turbid now. The little affluent which we have discovered here is a clear, beautiful creek, or river, as it would be termed in this western country, where streams are not abundant. We have named one stream, away above, in honor of the great chief of the "Bad Angels," and as this is in beautiful contrast to that, we conclude to name it "Bright Angel."

Early in the morning the whole party starts up to explore the Bright Angel River, with the special purpose of seeking timber from which to make oars. A couple of miles above we find a large pine log, which has been floated down from the plateau, probably from an altitude of more than 6,000 feet, but not many miles back. On its way it must have passed over many cataracts and falls, for it bears scars in evidence of the rough usage which it has received. The men roll it on skids, and the work of sawing oars is commenced.

This stream heads away back under a line of abrupt cliffs that terminates the plateau, and tumbles down more than 4,000 feet in the first mile or two of its course; then runs through a deep, narrow canyon until it reaches the river.

Late in the afternoon I return and go up a little gulch just above this creek, about 200 yards from camp, and discover the ruins of two or three old houses, which were originally of stone laid in mortar. Only the foundations are left, but irregular blocks, of which the houses were constructed, lie scattered about. In one room I find an old mealing-stone, deeply worn, as if it had been much used. A great deal of pottery is strewn around, and old trails, which in some places are deeply worn into the rocks, are seen.

It is ever a source of wonder to us why these ancient people sought such inaccessible places for their homes. They were, doubtless, an agricultural race, but there are no lands here of any considerable extent that they could have cultivated. To the west of Oraibi, one of the towns in the Province of Tusayan, in northern Arizona, the inhabitants have actually built little terraces along the face of the cliff where a spring gushes out, and thus made their sites for gardens. It is possible that the ancient inhabitants of this place made their agricultural lands in the same way. But why should they seek such spots? Surely the country was not so crowded with peoples to demand the utilization of so barren a region. The only solution suggested of the problem is this: We know that for a century or two after the settlement of Mexico many expeditions were sent into the country now comprising Arizona and New Mexico, for the purpose of bringing the town-building people under the dominion of the Spanish government. Many of their villages were destroyed, and the inhabitants fled to regions at that time unknown; and there are traditions among the people who inhabit the pueblos that still remain that the canyons were these unknown lands. It may be these buildings were erected at that time; sure it is that they have a much more modern appearance than the ruins scattered over Nevada, Utah, Colorado, Arizona, and New Mexico. Those old Spanish conquerors had a monstrous greed for gold and a wonderful lust for saving souls. Treasures they must have, if not on earth, why, then, in heaven; and when they failed to find heathen temples bedecked with silver, they propitiated Heaven by seizing the heathen themselves. There is yet extant a copy of a record made by a heathen artist to express his conception of the demands of the conquerors. In one part of the picture we have a lake, and near by stands a priest pouring water on the head of a native. On the other side, a poor Indian has a cord about his throat. Lines run from these two groups to a central figure, a man with beard and full Spanish panoply. The interpretation of the picture-writing is this: "Be baptized as this saved heathen, or be hanged as that damned heathen." Doubtless, some of these people preferred another alternative, and rather than be baptized or hanged they chose to imprison themselves within these canyon walls.

August 17.—Our rations are still spoiling; the bacon is so badly injured that we are compelled to throw it away. By an accident, this morning, the saleratus was lost overboard. We have now only musty flour sufficient for ten days and a few dried apples, but plenty of coffee. We must make all haste possible. If we meet with difficulties such as we have encountered in the canyon above, we may be compelled to give up the expedition and try to reach the Mormon settlements to the north. Our hopes are that the worst places are passed, but our barometers are all so much injured as to be useless, and so we have lost our reckoning in altitude, and know not how much descent the river has yet to make.

The stream is still wild and rapid and rolls through a narrow channel. We make but slow progress, often landing against a wall and climbing around some point to see the river below. Although very anxious to advance, we are determined to run with great caution, lest by another accident we lose our remaining supplies. How precious that little flour has become! We divide it among the boats and carefully store it away, so that it can be lost only by the loss of the boat itself.

We make ten miles and a half, and camp among the rocks on the right. We have had rain from time to time all day, and have been thoroughly drenched and chilled; but between showers the sun shines with great power and the mercury in our thermometers stands at 115°, so that we have rapid changes from great extremes, which are very disagreeable. It is especially cold in the rain to-night. The little canvas we have is rotten and useless; the rubber *ponchos* with which we started from Green River City have all been lost; more than half the party are without hats, not one of us has an entire suit of clothes, and we have not a blanket apiece. So we gather driftwood and build a fire; but after supper the rain, coming down in torrents, extinguished it, and we sit up all night on the rocks, shivering, and are more exhausted by the night's discomfort than by the day's toil.

August 18.—The day is employed in making portages and we advance but two miles on our journey. Still it rains.

While the men are at work making portages I climb up the granite to its summit and go away back over the rust-colored sandstones and greenish-yellow shales to the foot of the marble wall. I climb so high that the men and boats are lost in the black depths below and the dashing river is a rippling brook, and still there is more canyon above than below. All about me are interesting geologic records. The book is open and I can read as I run. All about me are grand views, too, for the clouds are playing again in the gorges. But somehow I think of the nine days' rations and the bad river, and the lesson of the rocks and the glory of the scene are but half conceived.

I push on to an angle, where I hope to get a view of the country beyond, to see if possible what the prospect may be of our soon running through this plateau, or at least of meeting with some geologic change that will let us out of the granite; but, arriving at the point, I can see below only a labyrinth of black gorges.

August 19.—Rain again this morning. We are in our granite prison still, and the time until noon is occupied in making a long, bad portage.

After dinner, in running a rapid the pioneer boat is upset by a wave. We are some distance in advance of the larger boats. The river is rough and swift and we are unable to land, but cling to the boat and are carried down stream over another rapid. The men in the boats above see our trouble, but they are caught in whirlpools and are spinning about in eddies, and it seems a long time before they come to our relief. At last they do come; our boat is turned right side up and bailed out; the oars, which fortunately have floated along in company with us, are gathered up, and on we go, without even landing. The clouds break away and we have sunshine again.

Soon we find a little beach with just room enough to land. Here we camp, but there is no wood. Across the river and a little way above, we see some driftwood lodged in the rocks. So we bring two boat loads over, build a huge fire, and spread everything to dry. It is the first cheerful night we have had for a week—a warm, drying fire in the midst of the camp, and a few bright stars in our patch of heavens overhead.

August 20.—The characteristics of the canyon change this morning. The river is broader, the walls more sloping, and composed of black slates that stand on edge. These nearly vertical slates are washed out in places—that is, the softer beds are washed out between the harder, which are left standing. In this way curious little alcoves are formed, in which are quiet bays of water, but on a much smaller scale than the great bays and buttresses of Marble Canyon.

The river is still rapid and we stop to let down with lines several times, but make greater progress, as we run ten miles. We camp on the right bank. Here, on a terrace of trap, we discover another group of ruins. There was evidently quite a village on this rock. Again we find mealing-stones and much broken pottery, and up on a little natural shelf in the rock back of the ruins we find a globular basket that would hold perhaps a third of a bushel. It is badly broken, and as I attempt to take it up it falls to pieces. There are many beautiful flint chips, also, as if this had been the home of an old arrow-maker.

August 21.—We start early this morning, cheered by the prospect of a fine day and encouraged also by the good run made yesterday. A quarter of a mile below camp the river turns abruptly to the left, and between camp and that point is very swift, running down in a long, broken chute and piling up against the foot of the cliff, where it turns to the left. We try to pull across, so as to go down on the other side, but the waters are swift and it seems impossible for us to escape the rock below; but, in pulling across, the bow of the boat is turned to the farther shore, so that we are swept broadside down and are prevented by the rebounding waters from striking against the wall. We toss about for a few seconds in these billows and are then carried past the danger. Below, the river turns again to the right, the canyon is very narrow, and we see in advance but a short distance. The water, too, is very swift, and there is no landing-place. From around this curve there comes a mad roar, and down we are carried with a dizzying velocity to the head of another rapid. On either side high over our heads there are overhanging granite walls, and the sharp bends cut off our view, so that a few minutes will carry us into unknown waters. Away we go on one long, winding chute. I stand on deck, supporting myself with a strap fastened on either side of the gunwale. The boat glides rapidly where the water is smooth, then, striking a wave, she leaps and bounds like a thing of life, and we have a wild, exhilarating ride of ten miles, which we make in less than an hour. The excitement is so great that we forget the danger until we hear the roar of a great fall below; then we back on our oars and are carried slowly toward its head and succeed in landing just above and find that we have to make another portage. At this we are engaged until some time after dinner.

Just here we run out of the granite. Ten miles in less than half a day, and limestone walls below. Good cheer returns; we forget the storms and the gloom and the cloud-covered canyons and the black granite and the raging river, and push our boats from shore in great glee.

Though we are out of the granite, the river is still swift, and we wheel about a point again to the right, and turn, so as to head back in the direction from which we came; this brings the granite in sight again, with its narrow gorge and black crags; but we meet with no more great falls or rapids. Still, we run cautiously and stop from time to time to examine some places which look bad. Yet we make ten miles this afternoon; twenty miles in all to-day.

August 22.—We come to rapids again this morning and are occupied several hours in passing them, letting the boats down from rock to rock with lines for nearly half a mile, and then have to make a long portage. While the men are engaged in this I climb the wall on the northeast to a height of about 2,500 feet, where I can obtain a good view of a long stretch of canyon below. Its course is to the southwest. The walls seem to rise very abruptly for 2,500 or 3,000 feet, and then there is a gently sloping terrace on each side for two or three miles, when we again find cliffs, 1,500 or 2,000 feet high. From the brink of these the plateau stretches back to the north and south for a long distance. Away down the canyon on the right wall I can see a group of mountains, some of which appear to stand on the brink of the canyon. The effect of the terrace is to give the appearance of a narrow winding valley with high walls on either side and a deep, dark, meandering gorge down its middle. It is impossible from this point of view to determine whether or not we have granite at the bottom; but from geologic considerations, I conclude that we shall have marble walls below.

After my return to the boats we run another mile and camp for the night. We have made but little over seven miles to-day, and a part of our flour has been soaked in the river again.

August 23.—Our way to-day is again through marble walls. Now and then we pass for a short distance through patches of granite, like hills thrust up into the limestone. At one of these places we have to make another portage, and, taking advantage of the delay, I go up a little stream to the north, wading it all the way, sometimes having to plunge in to my neck, in other places being compelled to swim across little basins that have been excavated at the foot of the falls. Along its course are many cascades and springs, gushing out from the rocks on either side. Sometimes a cottonwood tree grows over the water. I come to one beautiful fall, of more than 150 feet, and climb around it to the right on the broken rocks. Still going up, the canyon is found to narrow very much, being but 15 or 20 feet wide; yet the walls rise on either side many hundreds of feet, perhaps thousands; I can hardly tell.

In some places the stream has not excavated its channel down vertically through the rocks, but has cut obliquely, so that one wall overhangs the other. In other places it is cut vertically above and obliquely below, or obliquely above and vertically below, so that it is impossible to see out overhead. But I can go no farther; the time which I estimated it would take to make the portage has almost expired, and I start back on a round trot, wading in the creek where I must and plunging through basins. The men are waiting for me, and away we go on the river.

Just after dinner we pass a stream on the right, which leaps into the Colorado by a direct fall of more than 100 feet, forming a beautiful cascade. There is a bed of very hard rock above, 30 or 40 feet in thickness, and there are much softer beds below. The hard beds above project many yards beyond the softer, which are washed out, forming a deep cave behind the fall, and the stream pours through a narrow crevice above into a deep pool below. Around on the rocks in the cavelike chamber are set beautiful ferns, with delicate fronds and enameled stalks. The frondlets have their points turned down to form spore cases. It has very much the appearance of the maidenhair fern, but is much larger. This delicate foliage covers the rocks all about the fountain, and gives the chamber great beauty. But we have little time to spend in admiration; so on we go.

We make fine progress this afternoon, carried along by a swift river, shooting over the rapids and finding no serious obstructions. The canyon walls for 2,500 or 3,000 feet are very regular, rising almost perpendicularly, but here and there set with narrow steps, and occasionally we can see away above the broad terrace to distant cliffs.

We camp to-night in a marble cave, and find on looking at our reckoning that we have run 22 miles.

August 24.—The canyon is wider to-day. The walls rise to a vertical height of nearly 3,000 feet. In many places the river runs under a cliff in great curves, forming amphitheaters half-dome shaped.

Though the river is rapid, we meet with no serious obstructions and run 20 miles. How anxious we are to make up our reckoning every time we stop, now that our diet is confined to plenty of coffee, a very little spoiled flour, and very few dried apples! It has come to be a race for a dinner. Still, we make such fine progress that all hands are in good cheer, but not a moment of daylight is lost.

August 25.—We make 12 miles this morning, when we come to monuments of lava standing in the river,—low rocks mostly, but some of them shafts more than a hundred feet high. Going on down three or four miles, we find them increasing in number. Great quantities of cooled lava and many cinder cones are seen on either side; and then we come to an abrupt cataract. Just over the fall on the right wall a cinder cone, or extinct volcano, with a well-defined crater, stands on the very brink of the canyon. This, doubt-less, is the one we saw two or three days ago. From this volcano vast floods of lava have been poured down into the river, and a stream of molten rock has run up the canyon three or four miles and down we know not how far. Just where it poured over the canyon wall is the fall. The whole north side as far as we can see is lined with the black basalt, and high up on the oppo-site wall are patches of the same material, resting on the benches and filling old alcoves and caves, giving the wall a spotted appearance.

The rocks are broken in two along a line which here crosses the river, and the beds we have seen while com-ing down the canyon for the last 30 miles have dropped 800 feet on the lower side of the line, form-ing what geologists call a "fault." The volcanic cone stands directly over the fissure thus formed. On the left side of the river, opposite, mammoth springs burst out of this crevice, 100 or 200 feet above the river, pouring in a stream quite equal in volume to the Colorado Chiquito.

This stream seems to be loaded with carbonate of lime, and the water, evaporating, leaves an incrustation on the rocks; and this process has been continued for a long time, for extensive deposits are noticed in which are basins with bubbling springs. The water is salty.

We have to make a portage here, which is complet-ed in about three hours; then on we go.

We have no difficulty as we float along, and I am able to observe the wonderful phenomena connected with this flood of lava. The canyon was doubtless filled to a height of 1,200 or 1,500 feet, perhaps by more than one flood. This would dam the water back; and in cutting through this great lava bed, a new channel has been formed, sometimes on one side, sometimes on the other. The cooled lava, being of firmer texture than the rocks of which the walls are composed, remains in some places; in others a narrow channel has been cut, leaving a line of basalt on either side. It is possible that the lava cooled faster on the sides against the walls and that the center ran out; but of this we can only conjecture. There are other places where almost the whole of the lava is gone, only patches of it being seen where it has caught on the walls. As we float down we can see that it ran out into side canyons. In some places this basalt has a fine, columnar structure, often in concentric prisms, and masses of these concentric columns have coalesced. In some places, when the flow occurred the canyon was probably about the same depth that it is now, for we can see where the basalt has rolled out on the sands, and—what seems curious to me—the sands are not melted or metamorphosed to any appreciable extent. In places the bed of the river is of sandstone or limestone, in other places of lava, showing that it has all been cut out again where the sandstones and limestones appear; but there is a little yet left where the bed is of lava.

What a conflict of water and fire there must have been here! Just imagine a river of molten rock running down into a river of melted snow. What a seething and boiling of the waters; what clouds of steam rolled into the heavens!

Thirty-five miles to-day. Hurrah!

August 26.—The canyon walls are steadily becoming higher as we advance. They are still bold and nearly vertical up to the terrace. We still see evidence of the eruption discovered yesterday, but the thickness of the basalt is decreasing as we go down stream; yet it has been reinforced at points by streams that have come down from volcanoes standing on the terrace above, but which we cannot see from the river below.

Since we left the Colorado Chiquito we have seen no evidences that the tribe of Indians inhabiting the plateaus on either side ever come down to the river; but about eleven o'clock to-day we discover an Indian garden at the foot of the wall on the right, just where a little stream with a narrow flood plain comes down through a side canyon. Along the valley the Indians have planted corn, using for irrigation the water which bursts out in springs at the foot of the cliff. The corn is looking quite well, but it is not sufficiently advanced to give us roasting ears; but there are some nice green squashes. We carry ten or a dozen of these on board our boats and hurriedly leave, not willing to be caught in the robbery, yet excusing ourselves by pleading our great want. We run down a short distance to where we feel certain no Indian can follow, and what a kettle of squash sauce we make! True, we have no salt with which to season it, but it makes a fine addition to our unleavened bread and coffee. Never was fruit so sweet as these stolen squashes.

After dinner we push on again and make fine time, finding many rapids, but none so bad that we cannot run them with safety; and when we stop, just at dusk, and foot up our reckoning, we find we have run 35 miles again. A few days like this, and we are out of prison.

We have a royal supper—unleavened bread, green squash sauce, and strong coffee. We have been for a few days on half rations, but now have no stint of roast squash.

August 27.—This morning the river takes a more southerly direction. The dip of the rocks is to the north and we are running rapidly into lower formations. Unless our course changes we shall very soon run again into the granite. This gives some anxiety. Now and then the river turns to the west and excites hopes that are soon destroyed by another turn to the south. About nine o'clock we come to the dreaded rock. It is with no little misgiving that we see the river enter these black, hard walls. At its very entrance we have to make a portage; then let down with lines past some ugly rocks. We run a mile or two farther, and then the rapids below can be seen.

About eleven o'clock we come to a place in the river which seems much worse than any we have yet met in all its course. A little creek comes down from the left. We land first on the right and clamber up over the granite pinnacles for a mile or two, but can see no way by which to let down, and to run it would be sure destruction. After dinner we cross to examine on the left. High above the river we can walk along on the top of the granite, which is broken off at the edge and set with crags and pinnacles, so that it is very difficult to get a view of the river at all. In my eagerness to reach a point where I can see the roaring fall below, I go too far on the wall, and can neither advance nor retreat. I stand with one foot on a little projecting rock and cling with my hand fixed in a little crevice. Finding I am caught here, suspended 400 feet above the river, into which I must fall if my footing fails, I call for help. The men come and pass me a line, but I cannot let go of the rock long enough to take hold of it. Then they bring two or three of the largest oars. All this takes time which seems very precious to me; but at last they arrive. The blade of one of the oars is pushed into a little crevice in the rock beyond me in such a manner that they can hold me pressed against the wall. Then another is fixed in such a way that I can step on it; and thus I am extricated.

Still another hour is spent in examining the river from this side, but no good view of it is obtained; so now we return to the side that was first examined, and the afternoon is spent in clambering among the crags and pinnacles and carefully scanning the river again. We find that the lateral streams have washed boulders into the river, so as to form a dam, over which the water makes a broken fall of 18 or 20 feet; then there is a rapid, beset with rocks, for 200 or 300 yards, while on the other side, points of the wall project into the river. Below, there is a second fall; how great, we cannot tell. Then there is a rapid, filled with huge rocks, for 100 or 200 yards. At the bottom of it, from the right wall, a great rock projects quite halfway across the river. It has a sloping surface extending up stream, and the water, coming down with all the momentum gained in the falls and rapids above, rolls up this inclined plane many feet, and tumbles over to the left. I decide that it is possible to let down over the first fall, then run near the right cliff to a point just above the second, where we can pull out into a little chute, and, having run over that in safety, if we pull with all our power across the stream, we may avoid the great rock below. On my return to the boat I announce to the men that we are to run it in the morning. Then we cross the river and go into camp for the night on some rocks in the mouth of the little side canyon.

After supper Captain Howland asks to have a talk with me. We walk up the little creek a short distance, and I soon find that his object is to remonstrate against my determination to proceed. He thinks that we had better abandon the river here. Talking with him, I learn that he, his brother, and William Dunn have determined to go no farther in the boats. So we return to camp. Nothing is said to the other men.

For the last two days our course has not been plotted. I sit down and do this now, for the purpose of finding where we are by dead reckoning. It is a clear night, and I take out the sextant to make observation for latitude, and I find that the astronomic determination agrees very nearly with that of the plot—quite as closely as might be expected from a meridian observation on a planet. In a direct line, we must be about 45 miles from the mouth of the Rio Virgen. If we can reach that point, we know that there are settlements up that river about 20 miles. This 45 miles in a direct line will probably be 80 or 90 by the meandering line of the river. But then we know that there is comparatively open country for many miles above the mouth of the Virgen, which is our point of destination.

As soon as I determine all this, I spread my plot on the sand and wake Howland, who is sleeping down by the river, and show him where I suppose we are, and where several Mormon settlements are situated.

We have another short talk about the morrow, and he lies down again; but for me there is no sleep. All night long I pace up and down a little path, on a few yards of sand beach, along by the river. Is it wise to go on? I go to the boats again to look at our rations.

I feel satisfied that we can get over the danger immediately before us; what there may be below I know not. From our outlook yesterday on the cliffs, the canyon seemed to make another great bend to the south, and this, from our experience heretofore, means more and higher granite walls. I am not sure that we can climb out of the canyon here, and, if at the top of the wall, I know enough of the country to be certain that it is a desert of rock and sand between this and the nearest Mormon town, which, on the most direct line, must be 75 miles away. True, the late rains have been favorable to us, should we go out, for the probabilities are that we shall find water still standing in holes; and at one time I almost conclude to leave the river. But for years I have been contemplating this trip. To leave the exploration unfinished, to say that there is a part of the canyon which I cannot explore, having already nearly accomplished it, is more than I am willing to acknowledge, and I determine to go on.

I wake my brother and tell him of Howland's determination, and he promises to stay with me; then I call up Hawkins, the cook, and he makes a like promise; then Sumner and Bradley and Hall, and they all agree to go on.

August 28.—At last daylight comes and we have breakfast without a word being said about the future. The meal is as solemn as a funeral. After breakfast I ask the three men if they still think it best to leave us. The elder Howland thinks it is, and Dunn agrees with him. The younger Howland tries to persuade them to go on with the party; failing in which, he decides to go with his brother.

Then we cross the river. The small boat is very much disabled and unseaworthy. With the loss of hands, consequent on the departure of the three men, we shall not be able to run all of the boats; so I decide to leave my *Emma Dean*.

Two rifles and a shotgun are given to the men who are going out. I ask them to help themselves to the rations and take what they think to be a fair share. This they refuse to do, saying they have no fear but that they can get something to eat; but Billy, the cook, has a pan of biscuits prepared for dinner, and these he leaves on a rock.

Before starting, we take from the boat our barometers, fossils, and minerals, and some ammunition and leave them on the rocks. We are going over this place as light as possible. The three men help us lift our boats over a rock 25 or 30 feet high and let them down again over the first fall, and now we are all ready to start. The last thing before leaving, I write a letter to my wife and I give it to Howland. Sumner gives him his watch, directing that it be sent to his sister should he not be heard from again. The records of the expedition have been kept in duplicate. One set of these is given to Howland; and now we are ready. For the last time they entreat us not to go on, and tell us that it is madness to set out in this place; that we can never get safety through it; and, further, that the river turns again to the south into the granite, and a few miles of such rapids and falls will exhaust our entire stock of rations, and then it will be too late to climb out. Some tears are shed; it is rather a solemn parting; each party thinks the other is taking the dangerous course.

My old boat left, I go on board of the *Maid of the Canyon*. The three men climb a crag that overhangs the river to watch us off. The *Maid of the Canyon* pushes out. We glide rapidly along the foot of the wall, just grazing one great rock, then pull out a little into the chute of the second fall and plunge over it. The open compartment is filled when we strike the first wave below, but we cut through it, and then the men pull with all their power toward the left wall and swing clear of the dangerous rock below all right. We are scarcely a minute in running it, and find that, although it looked bad from above, we have passed many places that were worse.

The other boat follows without more difficulty. We land at the first practicable point below, and fire our guns, as a signal to the men above that we have come over in safety. Here we remain a couple of hours, hoping that they will take the smaller boat and follow us. We are behind a curve in the canyon and cannot see up to where we left them, and so we wait until their coming seems hopeless, and then push on.

And now we have a succession of rapids and falls until noon, all of which we run in safety. Just after dinner we come to another bad place. A little stream comes in from the left, and below there is a fall, and still below another fall. Above, the river tumbles down, over and among the rocks, in whirlpools and great waves, and the waters are lashed into mad, white foam. We run along the left, above this, and soon see that we cannot get down on this side, but it seems possible to let down on the other. We pull up stream again for 200 or 300 yards and cross. Now there is a bed of basalt on this northern side of the canyon, with a bold escarpment that seems to be a hundred feet high. We can climb it and walk along its summit to a point where we are just at the head of the fall. Here the basalt is broken down again, so it seems to us, and I direct the men to take a line to the top of the cliff and let the boats down along the wall. One man remains in the boat to keep her clear of the rocks and prevent her line from being caught on the projecting angles. I climb the cliff and pass along to a point just over the fall and descend by broken rocks, and find that the break of the fall is above the break of the wall, so that we cannot land, and that still below the river is very bad, and that there is no possibility of a portage. Without waiting further to examine and determine what shall be done, I hasten back to the top of the cliff to stop the boats from coming down. When I arrive I find the men have let one of them down to the head of the fall. She is in swift water and they are not able to pull her back; nor are they able to go on with the line, as it is not long enough to reach the higher part of the cliff which is just before them; so they take a bight around a crag. I send two men back for the other line. The boat is in very swift water, and Bradley is standing in the open compartment, holding out his oar to prevent her from striking against the foot of the cliff. Now she shoots out into the stream and up as far as the line will permit, and then, wheeling, drives headlong against the rock, and then out and back again, now straining on the line, now striking against the rock. As soon as the second line is brought, we pass it down to him; but his attention is all taken up with his own situation, and he does not see that we are passing him the line. I stand on a projecting rock, waving my hat to gain his attention, for my voice is drowned by the roaring of the falls. Just at this moment I see him take his knife from its sheath and step forward to cut the line. He has evidently decided that it is better to go over with the boat as it is than to wait for her to be broken to pieces. As he leans over, the boat sheers again into the stream, the stem-post breaks away and she is loose. With perfect composure Bradley seizes the great scull oar, places it in the stern rowlock, and pulls with all his power (and he is an athlete) to turn the bow of the boat down stream, for he wishes to go bow down, rather than to drift broadside on. One, two strokes he makes, and a third just as she goes over, and the boat is fairly turned, and she goes down almost beyond our sight, though we are more than a hundred feet above the river. Then she comes up again on a great wave, and down and up, then around behind some great rocks, and is lost in the mad, white foam below. We stand frozen with fear, for we see no boat. Bradley is gone! so it seems. But now, away below, we see something coming out of the waves. It is evidently a boat. A moment more, and we see Bradley standing on deck, swinging his hat to show that he is all right. But he is in a whirlpool. We have the stem-post of his boat attached to the line. How badly she may be disabled we know not. I direct Sumner and Powell to pass along the cliff and see if they can reach him from below. Hawkins, Hall, and myself run to the other boat, jump aboard, push out, and away we go over the falls. A wave rolls over us and our boat is unmanageable. Another great wave strikes us, and the boat rolls over, and tumbles and tosses, I know not how. All I know is that Bradley is picking us up. We soon have all right again, and row to the cliff and wait until Sumner and Powell can come. After a difficult climb they reach us. We run two or three miles farther and turn again to the northwest, continuing until night, when we have run out of the granite once more.

August 29.—We start very early this morning. The river still continues swift, but we have no serious difficulty, and at twelve o'clock emerge from the Grand Canyon of the Colorado. We are in a valley now, and low mountains are seen in the distance, coming to the river below. We recognize this as the Grand Wash.

A few years ago a party of Mormons set out from St. George, Utah, taking with them a boat, and came down to the Grand Wash, where they divided, a portion of the party crossing the river to explore the San Francisco Mountains. Three men—Hamblin, Miller, and Crosby—taking the boat, went on down the river to Callville, landing a few miles below the mouth of the Rio Virgen. We have their manuscript journal with us, and so the stream is comparatively well known.

To-night we camp on the left bank, in a mesquite thicket.

The relief from danger and the joy of success are great. When he who has been chained by wounds to a hospital cot until his canvas tent seems like a dungeon cell, until the groans of those who lie about tortured with probe and knife are piled up, a weight of horror on his ears that he cannot throw off, cannot forget, and until the stench of festering wounds and anaesthetic drugs has filled the air with its loathsome burthen,—when he at last goes out into the open field, what a world he sees! How beautiful the sky, how bright the sunshine, what "floods of delirious music" pour from the throats of birds, how sweet the fragrance of earth and tree and blossom! The first hour of convalescent freedom seems rich recompense for all pain and gloom and terror.

Something like these are the feelings we experience to-night. Ever before us has been an unknown danger, heavier than immediate peril. Every waking hour passed in the Grand Canyon has been one of toil. We have watched with deep solicitude the steady disappearance of our scant supply of rations, and from time to time have seen the river snatch a portion of the little left, while we were a-hungered. And danger and toil were endured in those gloomy depths, where oft-times clouds hid the sky by day and but a narrow zone of stars could be seen at night. Only during the few hours of deep sleep, consequent on hard labor, has the roar of the waters been hushed. Now the danger is over, now the toil has ceased, now the gloom has disappeared, now the firmament is bounded only by the horizon, and what a vast expanse of constellations can be seen!

The river rolls by us in silent majesty; the quiet of the camp is sweet; our joy is almost ecstasy. We sit till long after midnight talking of the Grand Canyon, talking of home, but talking chiefly of the three men who left us. Are they wandering in those depths, unable to find a way out? Are they searching over the desert lands above for water? Or are they nearing the settlements?

The Battle of the Marten and the Porcupine

MAYNE REID

It was in the middle of the winter. A light snow had fallen upon the ground—just enough to enable us to follow the trail of any animal we might light upon. Of course, the snow filled us with the idea of hunting; and Harry and I started out upon the tracks of a brace of Elk that had passed through our opening during the night. The tracks were very fresh-looking; and it was evident that the animals had passed in the morning, just before we were up. We concluded, therefore, that they had not gone far off; and we hoped soon to come up with them.

The trail led us along the side of the lake, and then up the left bank of the stream. Castor and Pollux were with us; but in our hunting excursions we usually led them on a leash, so that they might not frighten the game by running ahead of us.

When about half a mile from the house, we found that the Elk had crossed to the right bank of the stream. We were about to follow, when all at once our eyes fell upon a most singular track or tracks that led off into the woods. They were *the tracks of human feet—the feet of children!*

So thought we, at first sight of them; and you may fancy the surprise into which we were suddenly thrown. They were about five inches in length, and exactly such as would have been made by a bare-footed urchin of six years old. There appeared to be two sets of them, as if two children had passed, following one another, on the same trail. What could it mean? After all, were there human beings in the valley besides ourselves? Could these be the footprints of two young Indians?

All at once, I thought of the Diggers—the *Yamparicos*—the root eaters—who are found in almost every hole and corner of the American Desert. Could it be possible that a family of these wretched creatures existed in the valley? "Quite possible," thought I, when I reflected upon their habits. Living upon roots, insects, and reptiles, burrowing in holes and caves like the wild animals around them, a family or more might have been living all this time in some unexplored corner of the valley, without our having encountered any traces of them. Was this really so? and were the tracks before us the footmarks of a brace of young Diggers who had been passing from point to point?

Of course, our Elk hunt was given up until this mystery should be solved; and we turned off from the trail of the latter to follow that of the children.

In coming out to an open place, where the snow lay smoothly, and the foot-prints appeared well defined, I stooped down to examine them more minutely, in order to be satisfied that they were the tracks of human feet. Sure enough, there were the heels, the regular widening of the foot near the toes, and the toes themselves, all plainly stamped upon the snow. Here, however, arose another mystery. On counting the toes, I found that in some of the tracks there were five,—as there should have been,—while in others there were only four! This led me to examine the print of the toes more carefully; and I now saw that each of them was armed with a claw, which on account of some hairy covering, had made but a very indefinite impression in the snow. The tracks, then, were *not* the footmarks of children, but those of some animal with claws.

Notwithstanding that we had come to this conclusion, we still continued to follow the trail. We were curious to see what sort of a creature had made it. Perhaps it might be some animal unknown to naturalists—some new species; and we might one day have the merit of being the first to describe it. We had not far to go: a hundred yards or so brought us in sight of a grove of young cottonwoods; and these we saw at a glance were "barked" by a Porcupine. The whole mystery was cleared up—we had been following in the trail of this animal.

I now remembered that the Porcupine was one of the *plantigrade* family, with five toes on his hind feet, and only four on the fore ones. The tracks were undoubtedly his.

My companion and I were somewhat chagrined at being thus drawn away from our hunt by such an insignificant object; and we vowed to take vengeance upon the Porcupine, as soon as we should set our eyes upon him. We were not long in doing this; for, as we stole quietly forward, we caught sight of a shaggy animal moving among the branches of a tree about fifty yards ahead of us. It was he, of course. At the same moment, however, another animal "hove in sight," in appearance as different from the Porcupine as a Bull from a bluebottle.

This creature—tail and all—was not less than a yard and a quarter in length, and yet its body was not thicker than the upper part of a man's arm. Its head was broad and somewhat flattened, with short erect ears and pointed nose. It was bearded like a Cat, although the face had more of the Dog in its expression. Its legs were short and strong; and both legs and body denoted the possession of agility and strength. It was of a reddish brown color, with a white mark on the breast, and darker along the back and on the legs, feet, nose, and tail. Its whole appearance reminded one of a gigantic Weasel,—which in fact it was,—the great Marten of America, generally though improperly, called the "Fisher." When we first saw it, it was crouching along a high log that ran directly towards the tree, upon which was the Porcupine. Its eyes were fixed intently upon the latter; and it was evidently meditating an attack. We stopped to watch it.

The Porcupine had not yet perceived his enemy, as he was busily engaged in splitting the bark from the cottonwood. The Marten, after reconnoitring him for some moments, sprang off from the log, and came running towards the tree. The other now saw him, and at the same instant uttered a sort of shrill, querulous cry, and appeared to be greatly affrighted. To our astonishment, however, instead of remaining where it was, it suddenly dropped to the ground, almost at the very nose of its adversary! I could not, at first, understand the policy of this strange tactic on the part of the Porcupine; but a moment's reflection convinced me it was sound policy. The Marten would have been as much at home on the tree as himself; and had he remained among the branches—which were slender ones,—his throat and the under part of his body— both of which are soft, and without quills—would have been exposed to the teeth of his adversary. This, then, was why he had let himself down so unexpectedly; and we noticed that the instant he touched the ground, he rolled himself into a round clew, presenting on all sides the formidable *chevaux-de-frise* of his quills.

The Marten now ran around him, doubling his long, vermiform body with great activity—at intervals showing his teeth, erecting his back, and snarling like a Cat. We expected every moment to see him spring forward upon his victim; but he did not do so. He evidently understood the peril of such an act; and appeared for a moment puzzled as to how he should proceed. All this while, the Porcupine lay quiet—except the tail. This was, in fact, the only "feature" of the animal that could be seen, as the head and feet were completely hidden under the body. The tail, however, was kept constantly in motion—jerked from side to side, and flirted occasionally upwards.

What would the Marten do? There was not an inch of the other's body that was not defended by the sharp and barbed quills—not a spot where he could insert the tip of his nose. Would he abandon the contest? So thought we, for a while; but we were soon convinced of our error.

After running around several times, as we have described, he at length posted himself near the hind quarters of the Porcupine, and with his nose a few inches from the tail of the latter. In this position, he stood for some moments, apparently watching the tail, which still continued to oscillate rapidly. He stood in perfect silence, and without making a movement.

The Porcupine, not being able to see him, and perhaps thinking that he was gone, now waved his tail more slowly, and then suffered it to drop motionless.

This was what the other was waiting for; and, the next moment, he had seized the tail in his teeth. We saw that he held it by the tip, where it is destitute of the thorny spines.

What would he do next? Was he going to bite off the end of the Porcupine's tail? No such thing. He had a different game from that to play as we soon witnessed.

The moment he caught the tail, the Porcupine uttered its querulous cries; but the Marten, heeding not these, commenced walking backward, dragging the other after him. Where was he dragging it to? We soon saw. He was pulling it to a tree close by, with low branches, that forked out near the ground. "But for what purpose?" thought we. We wondered as we watched.

The Porcupine could offer no resistance. Its feet gave way, and slipped along the snowy ground; for the Marten was evidently the much stronger animal.

In a short time, the latter had reached the tree, dragging the other after him to its foot. He now commenced ascending, still holding the Porcupine's tail in his teeth, and taking precious care not to brush too closely to the quills. "Surely," thought we, "he cannot climb up, carrying a body almost as big as himself, in that manner!" It was not his intention to climb up,—only to one of the lowermost branches,—and the next moment, he had reached it, stretching his long body out on the limb, and clutching it firmly with his Cat-like claws. He still held fast hold of the Porcupine's tail, which animal was now lifted into such a position that only its fore quarters rested on the ground, and it appeared to stand upon its head, all the while uttering its pitiful cries.

For the life of us, we could not guess what the Marten meant by all this manoeuvring. *He* knew well enough, as he gave proof the moment after. When he had got the other, as it were, on a balance, he suddenly sprang back to the ground, in such a direction that the impetus of his leap jerked the Porcupine upon its back. Before the clumsy creature was able to turn over and "clew" itself, the active Weasel had pounced upon its belly, and buried his claws in the soft flesh, while, at the same time, his teeth were made fast in the throat!

In vain the Porcupine struggled. The other rode him with such agility, that he was unable to get right side up again; and in a few moments the struggle would have ended by the Porcupine's throat being cut; but we saw that it was time for us to interfere; and, slipping Castor and Pollux from the leash, we ran forward.

The Dogs soon drove the Marten from his victim, but he did not run from them. On the contrary, he turned round upon them, keeping them at bay with his sharp teeth and fierce snarling. In truth, they would have had a very tough job of it, had we not been near; but, on seeing us approach, the animal took to a tree, running up it like a Squirrel. A rifle bullet soon brought him down again; and his long body lay stretched out on the earth, emitting a strong odor of musk, that was quite disagreeable.

On returning to the Porcupine, which our Dogs took care not to meddle with—we found the animal already better than half dead. The blood was running from its throat, which the Marten had torn open. Of course, we put the creature out of pain, by killing it outright; and taking the Marten along with us for the purpose of skinning it, we returned homeward, leaving the Elk hunt for another day.

Robinson Crusoe

DANIEL DEFOE

An excerpt from the granddaddy of all survival fiction, mellow now but still great reading. You ought to treat yourself to the entire book, if you have never done so. In this selection from the text, the narrator is the sole survivor of a shipwreck in September, 1659, and now is coping with life alone on a mysterious island somewhere in the South Atlantic.

I mentioned before that I had a great mind to see the whole island and that I had traveled up the brook and so on to where I built my bower and where I had an opening quite to the sea, on the other side of the island; I now resolved to travel quite cross to the seashore on that side; so taking my gun, a hatchet, and my dog, and a larger quantity of powder and shot than usual, with two biscuit cakes and a great bunch of raisins in my pouch for my store, I began my journey. When I had passed the vale where my bower stood, as above, I came within view of the sea to the west, and it being a very clear day, I fairly descried land, whether an island or a continent I could not tell; but it lay very high, extending from the west to the west-southwest, at a very great distance; by my guess it could not be less than fifteen or twenty leagues off.

I could not tell what part of the world this might be, otherwise than that I knew it must be part of America and, as I concluded by all my observations, must be near the Spanish dominions and perhaps was all inhabited by savages, where if I should have landed, I had been in a worse condition than I was now; and therefore I acquiesced in the dispositions of Providence, which, I began now to own and to believe, ordered everything for the best; I say, I quieted my mind with this, and left afflicting myself with fruitless wishes of being there.

Besides, after some pause upon this affair, I considered that if this land was the Spanish coast, I should certainly, one time or other, see some vessel pass or repass one way or other; but if not, then it was the savage coast between the Spanish country and Brazils, which are indeed the worst of savages; for they are cannibals, or men-eaters, and fail not to murder and devour all the human bodies that fall into their hands.

With these considerations I walked very leisurely forward. I found that side of the island, where I now was, much pleasanter than mine, the open or savanna fields sweet, adorned with flowers and grass and full of very fine woods. I saw abundance of parrots, and fain I would have caught one, if possible, to have kept it to be tame and taught it to speak to me. I did, after some painstaking, catch a young parrot, for I knocked it down with a stick, and having recovered it, I brought it home; but it was some years before I could make him speak. However, at last I taught him to call me by my name very familiarly. But the accident that followed, though it be a trifle, will be very diverting in its place.

I was exceedingly diverted with this journey. I found in the low grounds hares, as I thought them to be, and foxes, but they differed greatly from all the other kinds I had met with; nor could I satisfy myself to eat them, though I killed several. But I had no need to be venturous; for I had no want of food, and of that which was very good too; especially these three sorts, viz., goats, pigeons, and turtle or tortoise; which, added to my grapes, Leadenhall Market could not have furnished a table better than I, in proportion to the company; and though my case was deplorable enough, yet I had great cause for thankfulness; and that I was not driven to any extremities for food; but rather plenty, even to dainties.

I never traveled in this journey above two miles outright in a day, or thereabouts; but I took so many turns and returns, to see what discoveries I could make, that I came weary enough to the place where I resolved to sit down for all night; and then I either reposed myself in a tree, or surrounded myself with a row of stakes set upright in the ground, either from one tree to another, or so as no wild creature could come at me without waking me.

As soon as I came to the seashore, I was surprised to see that I had taken up my lot on the worst side of the island; for here indeed the shore was covered with innumerable turtles, whereas on the other side I had found but three in a year and a half. Here was also an infinite number of fowls of many kinds, some which I had seen, and some which I had not seen of before, and many of them very good meat; but such as I knew not the names of, except those called pigeons.

I could have shot as many as I pleased, but was very sparing of my powder and shot; and therefore had more mind to kill a she-goat, if I could, which I could better feed on; and though there were many goats here, more than on my side the island, yet it was with much more difficulty that I could come near them, the country being flat and even, and they saw me much sooner than when I was on the hill.

I confess this side of the country was much pleasanter than mine, but yet I had not the least inclination to remove; for as I was fixed in my habitation, it became natural to me, and I seemed all the while I was here to be, as it were, upon a journey and from home. However, I traveled along the shore of the sea towards the east, I suppose about twelve miles;

and then setting up a great pole upon the shore for a mark, I concluded I would go home again; and that the next journey I took should be on the other side of the island, east from my dwelling, and so round till I came to my post again. Of which in its place.

I took another way to come back than that I went, thinking I could easily keep all the island so much in my view that I could not miss finding my first dwelling by viewing the country. But I found myself mistaken; for being come about two or three miles, I found myself descended into a very large valley, but so surrounded with hills, and those hills covered with wood, that I could not see which was my way by any direction but that of the sun, nor even then, unless I knew very well the position of the sun at that time of the day.

It happened to my farther misfortune that the weather proved hazy for three or four days while I was in this valley; and not being able to see the sun, I wandered about very uncomfortably and at last was obliged to find out the seaside, look for my post, and come back the same way I went; and then by easy journeys I turned homeward, the weather being exceeding hot and my gun, ammunition, hatchet, and other things very heavy.

In this journey my dog surprised a young kid, and seized upon it, and I, running in to take hold of it, caught it and saved it alive from the dog. I had a great mind to bring it home if I could; for I had often been musing whether it might not be possible to get a kid or two and so raise a breed of tame goats, which might supply me when my powder and shot should be all spent.

I made a collar to this little creature, and with a string which I made of some rope-yarn, which I always carried about me, I led him along, though with some difficulty, till I came to my bower, and there I enclosed him and left him; for I was very impatient to be at home from whence I had been absent above a month.

I cannot express what a satisfaction it was to me to come into my old hutch and lie down in my hammock-bed. This little wandering journey, without settled place of abode, had been so unpleasant to me that my own house, as I called it to myself, was a perfect settlement to me compared to that; and it rendered everything about me so comfortable that I resolved I would never go a great way from it again while it should be my lot to stay on the island.

I reposed myself here a week, to rest and regale myself after my long journey; during which most of the time was taken up in the weighty affair of making a cage for my Poll, who began now to be a mere domestic and to be mighty well acquainted with me. Then I began to think of the poor kid, which I had penned in within my little circle, and resolved to go and fetch it home, or give it some food; accordingly

I went, and found it where I left it; for indeed it could not get out, but almost starved for want of food. I went and cut boughs of trees, and branches of such shrubs as I could find and threw it over, and having fed it, I tied it as I did before to lead it away; but it was so tame with being hungry that I had no need to have tied it, for it followed me like a dog; and as I continually fed it, the creature became so loving, so gentle, and so fond, that it became from that time one of my domestics also, and would never leave me afterwards.

The rainy season of the autumnal equinox was now come, and I kept the 30th of September in the same solemn manner as before, being the anniversary of my landing on the island, having now been there two years, and no more prospect of being delivered than the first day I came there. I spent the whole day in humble and thankful acknowledgments of the many wonderful mercies which my solitary condition was attended with and without which it might have been infinitely more miserable. I gave humble and hearty thanks that God had been pleased to   discover to me even that it was possible I might be more happy in this solitary condition than I should have been in a liberty of society and in all the pleasures of the world; that He could fully make up to me the deficiencies of my solitary state and the want of human society by His presence and the communications of His grace to my soul, supporting, comforting, and encouraging me to depend upon His Providence here and hope for His eternal presence hereafter.

It was now that I began sensibly to feel how much more happy this life I now led was, with all its miserable circumstances, than the wicked, cursed, abominable life I led all the past part of my days; and now I changed both my sorrows and my joys; my very desires altered, my affections changed their gusts and my delights were perfectly new, from what they were at my first coming, or indeed for the two years past.

Before, as I walked about, either on my hunting or for viewing the country, the anguish of my soul at my condition would break out upon me on a sudden, and my very heart would die within me to think of the woods, the mountains, the deserts I was in; and how I was a prisoner locked up with the eternal bars and bolts of the ocean in an uninhabited wilderness, without redemption. In the midst of the greatest composures of my mind, this would break out upon me like a storm and make me wring my hands and weep like a child. Sometimes it would take me in the middle of my work, and I would immediately sit down and sigh and look upon the ground for an hour or two together; and this was still worse to me, for if I could burst out into tears or vent myself by words, it would go off, and the grief having exhausted itself would abate.

But now I began to exercise myself with new thoughts; I daily read the Word of God and applied all the comforts of it to my present state. One morning, being very sad, I opened the Bible upon these words: "I will never, never leave thee, nor forsake thee"; immediately it occurred that these words were to me; why else should they be directed in such a manner, just at the moment when I was mourning over my condition, as one forsaken of God and man? "Well then," said I, "if God does not forsake me, of what ill consequence can it be or what matters it though the world should all forsake me, seeing on the other hand, if I had all the world and should lose the favor and blessing of God, there would be no comparison in the loss?"

From this moment I began to conclude in my mind that it was possible for me to be more happy in this forsaken solitary condition than it was probable I should ever have been in any other particular state in the world; and with this thought I was going to give thanks to God for bringing me to this place.

I know not what it was but something shocked my mind at that thought and I durst not speak the words. "How canst thou be such a hypocrite," said I, even audibly, "to pretend to be thankful for a condition which however thou may'st endeavor to be contented with, thou would'st rather pray heartily to be delivered from?" So I stopped there. But though I could not say I thanked God for being there, yet I sincerely gave thanks to God for opening my eyes, by whatever afflicting providences, to see the former condition of my life and to mourn for my wickedness and repent. I never opened the Bible or shut it, but my very soul within me blessed God for directing my friend in England, without any order of mine, to pack it up among my goods and for assisting me afterwards to save it out of the wreck of the ship.

Thus, and in this disposition of mind, I began my third year; and though I have not given the reader the trouble of so particular account of my works this year as the first, yet in general it may be observed that I was very seldom idle; but having regularly divided my time, according to the several daily employments that were before me, such as, first, my duty to God and the reading of the Scriptures, which I constantly set apart some time for thrice every day; secondly, the going abroad with my gun for food, which generally took me up three hours in every morning, when it did not rain; thirdly, the ordering, curing, preserving, and cooking what I had killed or catched for my supply; these took up great part of the day; also it is to be considered that the middle of the day when the sun was in the zenith, the violence of the heat was too great to stir out; so that about four hours in the evening was all the time I could be supposed to work in; with this exception, that sometimes I changed my hours of hunting and working and went to work in the morning and abroad with my gun in the afternoon.

To this short time allowed for labor, I desire may be added the exceeding laboriousness of my work; the many hours which for want of tools, want of help, and want of skill everything I did took up out of my time. For example, I was full two and forty days making me a board for a long shelf, which I wanted in my cave; whereas two sawyers with their tools and a saw-pit would have cut six of them out of the same tree in half a day.

My case was this: it was to be a large tree which was to be cut down, because my board was to be a broad one. This tree I was three days a-cutting down, and two more cutting off the boughs, and reducing it to a log, or piece of timber. With inexpressible hacking and hewing, I reduced both the sides of it into chips till it began to be light enough to move; then I turned it and made one side of it smooth and flat as a board from end to end; then turning that side downward, cut the other side, till I brought the plank to be about three inches thick and smooth on both sides. Anyone may judge the labor of my hands in such a piece of work; but labor and patience carried me through that and many other things. I only observe this in particular, to show the reason why so much of my time went away with so little work, viz., that what might be a little to be done with help and tools was a vast labor and required a prodigious time to do alone and by hand.

But notwithstanding this, with patience and labor I went through many things; and indeed everything that my circumstances made necessary to me to do, as will appear by what follows.

I was now, in the months of November and December, expecting my crop of barley and rice. The ground I had manured or dug up for them was not great; for as I observed, my seed of each was not above the quantity of half a peck; for I had lost one whole crop by sowing in the dry season; but now my crop promised very well, when on a sudden I found I was in danger of losing it all again by enemies of several sorts, which it was scarce possible to keep from it; at first, the goats, and wild creatures which I called hares, who, tasting the sweetness of the blade, lay in it night and day, as soon as it came up, and eat it so close that it could get no time to shoot up into stalk.

This I saw no remedy for, but by making an enclosure about it with a hedge, which I did with a great deal of toil; and the more, because it required speed. However, as my arable land was but small, suited to my crop, I got it totally well fenced in about three weeks' time; and shooting some of the creatures in the daytime, I set my dog to guard it in the night, tying him up to a stake at the gate, where he would stand and bark all night long; so in a little time the enemies forsook the place, and the corn grew very strong and well, and began to ripen apace.

But as the beasts ruined me before, while my corn was in the blade, so the birds were as likely to ruin me now, when it was in the ear; for going alone by the place to see how it throve, I saw my little crop surrounded with fowls of I know not how many sorts, who stood, as it were, watching till I should be gone. I immediately let fly among them (for I always had my gun with me). I had no sooner shot, but there rose up a little cloud of fowls, which I had not seen at all, from among the corn itself.

This touched me sensibly, for I foresaw that in a few days they would devour all my hopes, that I should be starved and never be able to raise a crop at all, and what to do I could not tell. However, I resolved not to lose my corn, if possible, though I should watch it night and day. In the first place, I went among it to see what damage was already done and found they had spoiled a good deal of it, but that as it was yet too green for them, the loss was not so great, but that the remainder was like to be a good crop if it could be saved.

I stayed by it to load my gun, and then coming away I could easily see the thieves sitting upon all the trees about me, as if they only waited till I was gone away, and the event proved it to be so; for as I walked off as if I was gone, I was no sooner out of their sight but they dropped down one by one into the corn again. I was so provoked that I could not have patience to stay till more came on, knowing that every grain that they eat now was, as it might be said, a peck-loaf to me in the consequence; but coming up to the hedge, I fired again, and killed three of them. This was what I wished for; so I took them up and served them as we serve notorious thieves in England, viz., hanged them in chains for a terror to others; it is impossible to imagine, almost, that this should have such an effect as it had; for the fowls would not only not come at the corn but, in short, they forsook all that part of the island and I could never see a bird near the place as long as my scarecrows hung there.

This I was very glad of, you may be sure, and about the latter end of December, which was our second harvest of the year, I reaped my crop.

I was sadly put to it for a scythe or a sickle to cut it down, and all I could do was to make one as well as I could out of one of the broadswords, or cutlasses, which I saved among the arms out of the ship. However, as my first crop was but small, I had no great difficulty to cut it down; in short, I reaped it my way, for I cut nothing off but the ears, and carried it away in a great basket which I had made, and so rubbed it out with my hands; and at the end of all my harvesting, I found that out of my half peck of seed I had near two bushels of rice and above two bushels and a half of barley, this is to say, by my guess, for I had no measure at that time.

However, this was a great encouragement to me, and I foresaw that in time it would please God to supply me with bread. And yet here I was perplexed again, for I neither knew how to grind or make meal of my corn, or indeed how to clean it and part it; nor if made into meal, how to make bread of it; and if how to make it, yet I knew not how to bake it; these things being added to my desire of having a good quantity for store, and to secure a constant supply, I resolved not to taste any of this crop, but to preserve it all for seed against the next season, and in the meantime to employ all my study and hours of working to accomplish this great work of providing myself with corn and bread.

It might be truly said that now I worked for my bread; 'tis a little wonderful, and what I believe few people have thought much upon, viz., the strange multitude of little things necessary in the providing, producing, curing, dressing, making, and finishing this one article of bread.

I, that was reduced to a mere state of nature, found this to my daily discouragement and was made more and more sensible of it every hour, even after I had got the first handful of seed corn, which, as I have said, came up unexpectedly and indeed to a surprise.

First, I had no plough to turn up the earth, no spade or shovel to dig it. Well, this I conquered by making a wooden spade, as I observed before; but this did my work in but a wooden manner, and though it cost me a great many days to make it, yet for want of iron it not only wore out the sooner, but made my work the harder and made it be performed much worse.

However, this I bore with, and was content to work it out with patience and bear with the badness of the performance. When the corn was sowed, I had no harrow but was forced to go over it myself and drag a great heavy bough of a tree over it, to scratch it, as it may be called, rather than rake or harrow it.

When it was growing and grown, I have observed already how many things I wanted, to fence it, secure it, mow or reap it, cure and carry it home, thrash, part it from the chaff and save it. Then I wanted a mill to grind it, sieves to dress it, yeast and salt to make it into bread and an oven to bake it; and yet all these things I did without, as shall be observed; and yet the corn was an inestimable comfort and advantage to me too. All this, as I said, made everything laborious and tedious to me, but that there was no help for; neither was my time so much loss to me, because, as I had divided it, a certain part of it was every day appointed to these works; and as I resolved to use none of the corn for bread till I had a greater quantity by me, I had the next six months to apply myself wholly by labor and invention to furnish myself with utensils proper for the performing all the operations necessary for the making the corn (when I had it) fit for my use.

But first I was to prepare more land, for I had now seed enough to sow above an acre of ground. Before I did this, I had a week's work at least to make me a spade, which when it was done was but a sorry one indeed, and very heavy, and required double labor to work with it; however, I went through that and sowed my seed in two large flat pieces of ground, as near my house as I could find them to my mind, and fenced them in with a good hedge, the stakes of which were all cut of that wood which I had set before, and knew it would grow; so that in one year's time I knew I should have a quick or living hedge that would want but little repair. This work was not so little as to take me up less than three months, because great part of that time was of the wet season, when I could not go abroad.

Within doors, that is, when it rained, and I could not go out, I found employment on the following occasions; always observing, that all the while I was at work I diverted myself with talking to my parrot and teaching him to speak, and I quickly learned him to know his own name and at last to speak it out pretty loud, "Poll," which was the first word I ever heard spoken in the island by any mouth but my own. This therefore was not my work, but an assistant to my work, for now, as I said, I had a great employment upon my hand, as follows, viz., I had long studied, by some means or other, to make myself some earthen vessels, which indeed I wanted sorely, but knew not where to come at them. However, considering the heat of the climate, I did not doubt but if I could find out any such clay, I might botch up some such pot, as might, being dried in the sun, be hard enough and strong enough to bear handling, and to hold anything that was dry, and required to be kept so; and as this was necessary in the preparing corn, meal, etc., which was the thing I was upon, I resolved to make some as large as I could and fit only to stand like jars, to hold what should be put into them.

It would make the reader pity me, or rather laugh at me, to tell how many awkward ways I took to raise this paste; what odd, misshapen, ugly things I made; how many of them fell in, and how many fell out, the clay not being stiff enough to bear its own weight; how many cracked by the over-violent heat of the sun, being set out too hastily; and how many fell in pieces with only removing, as well before as after they were dried; and in a word, how after having labored hard to find the clay, to dig it, to temper it, to bring it home and work it, I could not make above two large earthen ugly things, I cannot call them jars, in about two months' labor.

However, as the sun baked these two very dry and hard, I lifted them very gently up, and set them down again in two great wicker baskets, which I had made on purpose for them, that they might not break, and as between the pot and the basket there was a little room to spare, I stuffed it full of the rice and barley straw, and these two pots being to stand always dry, I thought would hold my dry corn and perhaps the meal, when the corn was bruised.

Though I miscarried so much in my design for large pots, yet I made several smaller things with better success; such as little round pots, flat dishes, pitchers, and pipkins, and any things my hand turned to; and the heat of the sun baked them strangely hard.

But all this would not answer my end, which was to get an earthen pot to hold what was liquid and bear the fire, which none of these could do. It happened after some time, making a pretty large fire for cooking my meat, when I went to put it out after I had done with it, I found a broken piece of one of my earthenware vessels in the fire, burnt as hard as a stone, and red as a tile. I was agreeably surprised to see it and said to myself that certainly they might be made to burn whole, if they would burn broken.

This set me to studying how to order my fire, so as to make it burn me some pots. I had no notion of a kiln such as the potters burn in or of glazing them with lead, though I had some lead to do it with; but I placed three large pipkins and two or three pots in a pile one upon another and placed my firewood all round it with a great heap of embers under them; I plied the fire with fresh fuel round the outside and upon the top, till I saw the pots in the inside red hot quite through, and observed that they did not crack at all; when I saw them clear red, I let them stand in that heat about five or six hours, till I found one of them, though it did not crack, did melt or run, for the sand which was mixed with the clay melted by the violence of the heat, and would have run into glass if I had gone on; so I slacked my fire gradually till the pots began to abate of the red color; and watching them all night that I might not let the fire abate too fast, in the morning I had three very good, I will not say handsome, pipkins and two other earthen pots, as hard burnt as could be desired; and one of them perfectly glazed with the running of the sand.

After this experiment, I need not say that I wanted no sort of earthenware for my use; but I must needs say, as to the shapes of them, they were very indifferent, as anyone may suppose, when I had no way of making them but as the children make dirt pies or as a woman would make pies that never learned to raise paste.

No joy at a thing of so mean a nature was ever equal to mine, when I found I had made an earthen pot that would bear the fire; and I had hardly patience to stay till they were cold, before I set one upon the fire again, with some water in it, to boil me some meat, which it did admirably well; and with a piece of a kid I made some very good broth, though I wanted oatmeal and several other ingredients requisite to make it so good as I would have had it been.

My next concern was to get me a stone mortar to stamp or beat some corn in; for as to the mill, there was no thought at arriving to that perfection of art with one pair of hands. To supply this want I was at a great loss; for of all trades in the world I was as perfectly unqualified for a stone-cutter as for any whatever; neither had I any tools to go about it with. I spent many a day to find out a great stone big enough to cut hollow and make fit for a mortar, and could find none at all, except what was in the solid rock, and which I had no way to dig or cut out; nor indeed were the rocks in the island of hardness sufficient, but were all of a sandy crumbling stone, which neither would bear the weight of a heavy pestle or would break the corn without filling it with sand; so after a great deal of time lost in searching for a stone, I gave it over, and resolved to look out for a great block of hard wood, which I found indeed much easier; and getting one as big as I had strength to stir, I rounded it, and formed it in the outside with my axe and hatchet, and then with the help of fire, and infinite labor, made a hollow place in it, as the Indians in Brazil make their canoes. After this, I made a great heavy pestle, or beater, of the wood called the iron-wood, and this I prepared and laid by against I had my next crop of corn, when I proposed to myself to grind, or rather pound, my corn into meal, to make my bread.

My next difficulty was to make a sieve, or searce, to dress my meal and to part it from the bran and the husk, without which I did not see it possible I could have any bread. This was a most difficult thing, so much as but to think on; for to be sure, I had nothing like the necessary thing to make it; I mean fine thin canvas or stuff, to searce the meal through. And here I was at a full stop for many months, nor did I really know what to do; linen I had none left, but what was mere rags; I had goats' hair, but neither knew I how to weave it or spin it; and had I known how, here was no tools to work it with; all the remedy that I found for this was that at last I did remember I had among the seamen's clothes which were saved out of the ship, some neckcloths of calico or muslin; and with some pieces of these, I made three small sieves, but proper enough for the work; and thus I made shift for some years. How I did afterwards, I shall show in its place.

The baking part was the next thing to be considered and how I should make bread when I came to have corn; for, first, I had no yeast; as to that part, as there was no supplying the want, so I did not concern myself much about it; but for an oven I was indeed in great pain; at length I found out an experiment for that also, which was this; I made some earthen vessels very broad, but not deep; that is to say, about two feet diameter, and not above nine inches deep; these I burnt in the fire, as I had done the other, and laid them by; and when I wanted to bake, I made a great fire upon my hearth, which I had paved with some square tiles of my own making and burning also; but I should not call them square.

When the firewood was burnt pretty much into embers, or live coals, I drew them forward upon this hearth, so as to cover it all over, and there I let them lie, till the hearth was very hot; then sweeping away all the embers, I set down my loaf, or loaves, and whelming down the earthen pot upon them, drew the embers all round the outside of the pot, to keep in and add to the heat; and thus, as well as in the best oven in the world, I baked my barley loaves, and became in little time a mere pastry-cook into the bargain; for I made myself several cakes of the rice and puddings; indeed I made no pies, neither had I anything to put into them, supposing I had, except the flesh either of fowls or goats.

It need not be wondered at, if all these things took me up most part of the third year of my abode here; for it is to be observed that in the intervals of these things I had my new harvest and husbandry to manage; for I reaped my corn in its season and carried it home as well as I could and laid it up in the ear, in my large baskets, till I had time to rub it out; for I had no floor to thrash it on or instrument to thrash it with.

And now indeed my stock of corn increasing, I really wanted to build my barns bigger. I wanted a place to lay it up in; for the increase of the corn now yielded me so much that I had of the barley about twenty bushels and of the rice as much or more; insomuch that now I resolved to begin to use it freely, for my bread had been quite gone a great while; also I resolved to see what quantity would be sufficient for me a whole year, and to sow but once a year.

Upon the whole, I found that the forty bushels of barley and rice was much more than I could consume in a year; so I resolved to sow just the same quantity every year that I sowed the last, in hopes that such a quantity would fully provide me with bread, etc.

All the while these things were doing, you may be sure my thoughts run many times upon the prospect of land which I had seen from the other side of the island, and I was not without secret wishes that I were on shore there, fancying that seeing the mainland and an inhabited country, I might find some way or other to convey myself farther, and perhaps at last find some means of escape.

But all this while I made no allowance for the dangers of such a condition, and how I might fall into the hands of savages, and perhaps such as I might have reason to think far worse than the lions and tigers of Africa. That if I once came into their power, I should run a hazard more than a thousand to one of being killed and perhaps of being eaten; for I had heard that the people of the Caribbean coasts were cannibals, or man-eaters, and I knew by the latitude that I could not be far off from that shore. That suppose they were not cannibals, yet that they might kill me, as many Europeans who had fallen into their hands had been served, even when they had been ten or twenty together; much more I, that was but one, and could make little or no defense. All these things, I say, which I ought to have considered well of and did cast up in my thoughts afterwards yet took up none of my apprehensions at first; but my head run mightily upon the thought of getting over to the shore.

Now I wished for my boy Xury and the longboat with the shoulder-of-mutton sail with which I sailed above a thousand miles on the coast of Africa; but this was in vain. Then I thought I would go and look at our ship's boat, which, as I have said, was blown up upon the shore a great way in the storm, when we were first cast away. She lay almost where she did at first, but not quite; and was turned by the force of the waves and the winds almost bottom upward against a high ridge of beachy rough sand; but no water about her as before.

If I had had hands to have refitted her and to have launched her into the water, the boat would have done well enough, and I might have gone back into the Brazils with her easily enough; but I might have foreseen that I could no more turn her and set her upright upon her bottom than I could remove the island. However, I went to the woods and cut levers and rollers and brought them to the boat, resolved to try what I could do, suggesting to myself that if I could but turn her down, I might easily repair the damage she had received, and she would be a very good boat, and I might go to sea in her very easily.

I spared no pains, indeed, in this piece of fruitless toil and spent, I think, three or four weeks about it; at last finding it impossible to heave it up with my little strength, I fell to digging away the sand, to undermine it and so to make it fall down, setting pieces of wood to thrust and guide it right in the fall.

But when I had done this, I was unable to stir it up again, or to get under it, much less to move it forward towards the water; so I was forced to give it over; and yet, though I gave over the hopes of the boat, my desire to venture over for the main increased, rather than decreased, as the means for it seemed impossible.

This at length put me upon thinking whether it was not possible to make myself a canoe, or *periagua,* such as the natives of those climates make, even without tools, or, as I might say, without hands, viz., of the trunk of a great tree. This I not only thought possible but easy, and pleased myself extremely with the thoughts of making it and with my having much more convenience for it than any of the Negroes or

Indians; but not at all considering the particular inconveniences which I lay under, more than the Indians did, viz., want of hands to move it, when it was made, into the water, a difficulty much harder for me to surmount than all the consequences of want of tools could be to them; for what was it to me, that when I had chosen a vast tree in the woods, I might with much trouble cut it down, if after I might be able with my tools to hew and dub the outside into the proper shape of a boat, and burn or cut out the inside to make it hollow, so to make a boat of it—if after all this, I must leave it just there where I found it, and was not able to launch it into the water?

One would have thought I could not have had the least reflection upon my mind of my circumstance, while I was making this boat; but I should have immediately thought how I should get it into the sea; but my thoughts were so intent upon my voyage over the sea in it that I never once considered how I should get it off of the land; and was really in its own nature more easy for me to guide it over forty-five miles of sea than about forty-five fathoms of land, where it lay, to set it afloat in the water.

I went to work upon this boat the most like a fool that ever man did, who had any of his senses awake. I pleased myself with the design, without determining whether I was ever able to undertake it; not but that the difficulty of launching my boat came often into my head; but I put a stop to my own inquiries into it, by this foolish answer which I gave myself, "Let's first make it; I'll warrant I'll find some way or other to get it along, when 'tis done."

This was a most preposterous method; but the eagerness of my fancy prevailed, and to work I went. I felled a cedar tree. I question much whether Solomon ever had such a one for the building of the Temple at Jerusalem. It was five foot ten inches diameter at the lower part next the stump and four foot eleven inches diameter at the end of twenty-two foot, after which it lessened for a while, and then parted into branches. It was not without infinite labor that I felled this tree. I was twenty days hacking and hewing at it at the bottom. I was fourteen more getting the branches and limbs, and the vast spreading head of it cut off, which I hacked and hewed through with axe and hatchet and inexpressible labor. After this, it cost me a month to shape it and dub it to a proportion, and to something like the bottom of a boat, that it might swim upright as it ought to do. It cost me near three months more to clear the inside, and work it so as to make an exact boat of it. This I did indeed without fire, by mere mallet and chisel, and by the dint of hard labor, till I had brought it to be a very handsome *periagua* and big enough to have carried six and twenty men, and consequently big enough to have carried me and all my cargo.

When I had gone through this work, I was extremely delighted with it. The boat was really much bigger than I ever saw a canoe, or *periagua,* that was made of one tree, in my life. Many a weary stroke it had cost, you may be sure; and there remained nothing but to get it into the water; and had I gotten it into the water, I make no question but I should have begun the maddest voyage and the most unlikely to be performed that ever was undertaken.

But all my devices to get it into the water failed me; though they cost me infinite labor, too. It lay about one hundred yards from the water, and not more. But the first inconvenience was, it was uphill towards the creek; well, to take away this discouragement, I resolved to dig into the surface of the earth, and so make a declivity. This I begun, and it cost me a prodigious deal of pains; but who grudges pains, that have their deliverance in view? But when this was worked through, and this difficulty managed, it was still much at one; for I could no more stir the canoe than I could the other boat.

Then I measured the distance of ground, and resolved to cut a dock, or canal, to bring the water up to the canoe, seeing I could not bring the canoe down to the water. Well, I began this work; and when I began to enter into it and calculate how deep it was to be dug, how broad, how the stuff to be thrown out, I found that by the number of hands I had, being none but my own, it must have been ten or twelve years before I should have gone through with it; for the shore lay high, so that at the upper end it must have been at least twenty foot deep: so at length, though with great reluctancy, I gave this attempt over also.

This grieved me heartily, and now I saw, though too late, the folly of beginning a work before we count the cost and before we judge rightly of our own strength to go through with it.

In the middle of this work I finished my fourth year in this place, and kept my anniversary with the same devotion and with as much comfort as ever before; for by a constant study, and serious application of the Word of God, and by the assistance of His grace, I gained a different knowledge from what I had before. I entertained different notions of things. I looked now upon the world as a thing remote, which I had nothing to do with, no expectation from, and, indeed, no desires about. In a word, I had nothing indeed to do with it, nor was ever like to have; so, I thought, it looked as we may perhaps look upon it hereafter, viz., as a place I had lived in but was come out of it; and well might I say, as Father Abraham to Dives, "Between me and thee is a great gulf fixed."

In the first place, I was removed from all the wickedness of the world here. I had neither the lust of the flesh, the lust of the eye or the pride of life. I had nothing to covet; for I had all that I was now capable of enjoying. I was lord of the whole manor; or if I pleased, I might call myself king, or emperor over the whole country which I had possession of. There were no rivals. I had no competitor, none to dispute sovereignty or command with me. I might have raised shiploadings of corn; but I had no use for it; so I let as little grow as I thought enough for my occasion. I had tortoise or turtles enough; but now and then one was as much as I could put to any use. I had timber enough to have built a fleet of ships. I had grapes enough to have made wine, or to have cured into raisins, to have loaded that fleet, when they had been built.

But all I could make use of was all that was valuable. I had enough to eat, and to supply my wants, and what was all the rest to me? If I killed more flesh than I could eat, the dog must eat it, or the vermin. If I sowed more corn than I could eat, it must be spoiled. The trees that I cut down were lying to rot on the ground. I could make no more use of them than for fuel; and that I had no occasion for but to dress my food.

In a word, the nature and experience of things dictated to me upon just reflection that all the good things of this world are no farther good to us than they are for our use; and that whatever we may heap up indeed to give others, we enjoy just as much as

we can use, and no more. The most covetous grip-
ing miser in the world would have been cured of the
vice of covetousness, if he had been in my case; for
I possessed infinitely more than I knew what to do
with. I had not room for desire, except it was of
things which I had not, and they were but trifles,
though indeed of great use to me. I had, as I hinted
before, a parcel of money, as well gold as silver, about
thirty-six pounds sterling. Alas! There the nasty,
sorry, useless stuff lay; I had no manner of business
for it; and I often thought with myself that I would
have given a handful of it for a gross of tobacco-
pipes or for a hand-mill to grind my corn; nay, I
would have given it all for sixpenny-worth of turnip
and carrot seed out of England or for a handful of
peas and beans and a bottle of ink. As it was, I had
not the least advantage by it or benefit from it; but
there it lay in a drawer and grew moldy with the
damp of the cave in the wet season; and if I had had
the drawer full of diamonds, it had been the same
case; and they had been of no manner of value to me
because of no use.

I had now brought my state of life to be much easier in itself than it was at first and much easier to my
mind, as well as to my body. I frequently sat down to
my meat with thankfulness and admired the hand of
God's providence, which had thus spread my table in
the wilderness. I learned to look more upon the
bright side of my condition and less upon the dark

side and to consider what I enjoyed rather than what I wanted; and this gave me sometimes such secret comforts that I cannot express them; and which I take notice of here, to put those discontented people in mind of it who cannot enjoy comfortable what God had given them because they see and covet something that He has not given them. All our discontents about what we want appeared to me to spring from the want of thankfulness for what we have.

Another reflection was of great use to me and doubtless would be so to anyone that should fall into such distress as mine was; and this was to compare my present condition with what I at first expected it should be; nay, with what it would certainly have been, if the good providence of God had not wonderfully ordered the ship to be cast up nearer to the shore, where I not only could come at her but could bring what I got out of her to the shore for my relief and comfort; without which, I had wanted for tools to work, weapons for defense, or gunpowder and shot for getting my food.

I spent whole hours, I may say whole days, in representing to myself, in the most lively colors, how I must have acted if I had got nothing out of the ship. How I could not have so much as got any food, except fish and turtles; and that, as it was long before I found any of them, I must have perished first. That I should have lived, if I had not perished, like a mere savage. That if I had killed a goat, or a fowl, by any contrivance, I had no way to flay or open them, or part the flesh from the skin and the bowels, or to cut it up; but must gnaw it with my teeth and pull it with my claws like a beast.

These reflections made me very sensible of the goodness of Providence to me and very thankful for my present condition, with all its hardships and misfortunes. And this part also I cannot but recommend to the reflection of those who are apt in their misery to say, "Is any affliction like mine?" Let them consider how much worse the cases of some people are and their case might have been, if Providence had thought fit.

I had another reflection which assisted me also to comfort my mind with hopes; and this was comparing my present condition with what I had deserved and had therefore reason to expect from the hand of Providence. I had lived a dreadful life, perfectly destitute of the knowledge and fear of God. I had been well instructed by father and mother; neither had they been wanting to me in their early endeavors to infuse a religious awe of God into my mind, a sense of my duty and of what the nature and end of my being required of me. But alas! falling early into the seafaring life, which of all the lives is the most destitute of the fear of God, though His terrors are always before them; I say, falling early into the seafaring life and into seafaring company, all that little sense of religion which I had entertained was laughed out of me by my messmates; by a hardened despising of dangers and the views of death, which grew habitual to me; by my long absence from all manner of opportunities to converse with anything but what was like myself or to hear anything that was good or tended towards it.

So void was I of everything that was good, or of the least sense of what I was or was to be, that in the greatest deliverances I enjoyed, such as my escape from Sallee, my being taken up by the Portuguese master of the ship, my being planted so well in the Brazils, my receiving the cargo from England and the like, I never had once the words, "Thank God," as much as on my mind or in my mouth; nor in the greatest distress had I so much a thought to pray to Him or so much as to say, "Lord, have mercy upon me"; no, nor to mention the name of God, unless it was to swear by and blaspheme it.

I had terrible reflections upon my mind for many months, as I have already observed, on the account of my wicked and hardened life past; and when I looked about me and considered what particular providences had attended me since my coming into this place, and how God had dealt bountifully with me; had not only punished me less than my iniquity had deserved, but had so plentifully provided for me; this gave me great hopes that my repentance was accepted, and that God had yet mercy in store for me.

With these reflections I worked my mind up not only to resignation to the will of God in the present disposition of my circumstances but even to a sincere thankfulness for my condition; and that I, who was yet a living man, ought not to complain, seeing I had not the due punishment of my sins; that I enjoyed so many mercies which I had no reason to have expected in that place; that I ought never more to repine at my condition but to rejoice and to give daily thanks for that daily bread, which nothing but a crowd of wonders could have brought. That I ought to consider I had been fed even by miracle, even as great as that of feeding Elijah by ravens; nay, by a long series of miracles; and that I could hardly have named a place in the unhabitable part of the world where I could have been cast more to my advantage. A place, where as I had no society, which was my affliction on one hand, so I found no ravenous beast, no furious wolves or tigers to threaten my life, no venomous creatures or poisonous which I might feed on to my hurt, no savages to murder and devour me.

In a word, as my life was a life of sorrow one way, so it was a life of mercy another; and I wanted nothing to make it a life of comfort but to be able to make my sense of God's goodness to me, and care over me in this condition, be my daily consolation; and after I did make a just improvement of these things, I went away and was no more sad.

I had now been here so long that many things which I brought on shore for my help were either quite gone, or very much wasted and near spent.

My ink, as I observed, had been gone for some time, all but a very little, which I eked out with water, a little and a little, till it was so pale it scarce left any appearance of black upon the paper. As long as it lasted, I made use of it to minute down the days of the month on which any remarkable thing happened to me; and first, by casting up times past, I remember that there was a strange concurrence of days in the various providences which befell me and which, if I had been superstitiously inclined to observe days as fatal or fortunate, I might have had reason to have looked upon with a great deal of curiosity.

First, I had observed that the same day that I broke away from my father and my friends and ran away to Hull in order to go to sea, the same day afterwards I was taken by the Sallee man-of-war and made a slave.

The same day of the year that I escaped out of the wreck of that ship in Yarmouth Roads, that same day-year afterwards I made my escape from Sallee in the boat.

The same day of the year I was born on, viz., the 30th of September, that same day I had my life so miraculously saved twenty-six years after, when I was cast on shore in this island; so that my wicked life and my solitary life begun both on a day.

The next thing to my ink's being wasted was that of my bread, I mean the biscuit which I brought out of the ship. This I had husbanded to the last degree, allowing myself but one cake of bread a day for above a year, and yet I was quite without bread for near a year before I got any corn of my own, and great reason I had to be thankful that I had any at all, the getting it being, as has been already observed, next to miraculous.

My clothes began to decay, too, mightily. As to linen, I had none a good while, except some checkered shirts which I found in the chests of the other seamen, and which I carefully preserved, because many times I could bear no other clothes on but a shirt; and it was a very great help to me that I had among all the men's clothes of the ship almost three dozen of shirts. There were also several thick watch coats of the seamen's, which were left indeed, but they were too hot to wear; and though it is true that the weather was so violent hot that there was no need of clothes, yet I could not go quite naked; no, though I had been inclined to it, which I was not, nor could abide the thoughts of it, though I was all alone.

The reason why I could not go quite naked was, I could not bear the heat of the sun so well when quite naked, as with some clothes on; nay, the very heat frequently blistered my skin; whereas with a shirt on, the air itself made some motion and, whistling under that shirt, was twofold cooler than

without it. No more could I ever bring myself to go
out in the heat of the sun without a cap or a hat; the
heat of the sun, beating with such violence as it does
in that place, would give me the headache presently,
by darting so directly on my head, without a cap or
hat on, so that I could not bear it; whereas, if I put
on my hat, it would presently go away.

Upon those views I began to consider about putting the few rags I had, which I called clothes, into
some order; I had worn out all the waistcoats I had,
and my business was now to try if I could not make
jackets out of the great watch coats which I had by
me, and with such other materials as I had; so I set
to work a-tailoring, or rather indeed a-botching, for
I made most piteous work of it. However, I made
shift to make two or three new waistcoats, which I
hoped would serve me a great while; as for breeches
or drawers, I made but a very sorry shift indeed till
afterward.

I have mentioned that I saved the skins of all the
creatures that I killed, I mean four-footed ones, and
I had hung them up stretched out with sticks in the
sun, by which means some of them were so dry and
hard that they were fit for little, but others it seems
were very useful. The first thing I made of these was
a great cap for my head, with the hair on the outside,
to shoot off the rain; and this I performed so well,
that after this I made me a suit of clothes wholly of
these skins, that is to say, a waistcoat, and breeches

open at knees, and both loose, for they were rather wanting to keep me cool than to keep me warm. I must not omit to acknowledge that they were wretchedly made; for if I was a bad carpenter, I was a worse tailor. However, they were such as I made very good shift with; and when I was abroad, if it happened to rain, the hair of my waistcoat and cap being outermost, I was kept very dry.

After this I spent a great deal of time and pains to make me an umbrella; I was indeed in great want of one, and had a great mind to make one; I had seen them made in the Brazils, where they are very useful in the great heats which are there. And I felt the heats every jot as great here, and greater too, being nearer the equinox; besides as I was obliged to be much abroad, it was a most useful thing to me, as well for the rains as the heats. I took a world of pains at it, and was a great while before I could make anything likely to hold; nay, after I thought I had hit the way, I spoiled two or three before I made one to my mind; but at last I made one that answered indifferently well. The main difficulty I found was to make it to let down. I could make it to spread, but if it did not let down too and draw in, it was not portable for me any way but just over my head, which would not do. However, at last, as I said, I made one to answer and covered it with skins, the hair upwards, so that it cast off the rains like a penthouse and kept off the sun so effectually, that I could walk out in the hottest

of the weather with greater advantage than I could
before in the coolest, and when I had no need of it,
could close it and carry it under my arm.

Thus I lived mighty comfortably, my mind being
entirely composed by resigning to the will of God
and throwing myself wholly upon the disposal of
His Providence. This made my life better than sociable, for when I began to regret the want of conversation, I would ask myself whether thus conversing
mutually with my own thoughts and, as I hope I may
say, with even God Himself, by ejaculations, was not
better than the utmost enjoyment of human society
in the world.

I cannot say that after this, for five years, any extraordinary thing happened to me, but I lived on in the
same course, in the same posture and place, just as
before; the chief thing I was employed in, besides my
yearly labor of planting my barley and rice and curing my raisins, of both which I always kept up just
enough to have sufficient stock of one year's provisions beforehand; I say, besides this yearly labor and
my daily labor of going out with my gun, I had one
labor, to make me a canoe, which at last I finished.
So that by digging a canal to it of six foot wide, and
four foot deep, I brought it into the creek, almost

half a mile. As for the first, which was so vastly big, as I made it without considering beforehand, as I ought to do, how I should be able to launch it; so, never being able to bring it to the water, or bring the water to it, I was obliged to let it lie where it was, as a memorandum to teach me to be wiser next time. Indeed, the next time, though I could not get a tree proper for it, and in a place where I could not get the water to it at any less distance than, as I have said, near half a mile, yet as I saw it was practicable at last, I never gave it over; and though I was near two years about it, yet I never grudged my labor, in hopes of having a boat to go off to sea at last.

However, though my little *periagua* was finished, yet the size of it was not at all answerable to the design which I had in view, when I made the first; I mean, of venturing over to the *terra firma,* where it was above forty miles broad; accordingly, the smallness of my boat assisted to put an end to that design, and now I thought no more of it. But as I had a boat, my next design was to make a tour round the island; for as I had been on the other side in one place, crossing, as I have already described it, over the land, so the discoveries I made in that little journey made me very eager to see other parts of the coast; and now I had a boat, I thought of nothing but sailing round the island.

For this purpose, that I might do everything with discretion and consideration, I fitted up a little mast

to my boat, and made a sail to it out of some of the
pieces of the ship's sail, which lay in store, and of
which I had a great stock by me.

Having fitted my mast and sail and tried the boat,
I found she would sail very well. Then I made little
lockers, or boxes, at either end of my boat, to put
provisions, necessaries and ammunition, etc., into, to
be kept dry, either from rain or the spray of the sea;
and a little long hollow place I cut in the inside of
the boat, where I could lay my gun, making a flap
to hang down over it to keep it dry.

I fixed my umbrella also in a step at the stern, like
a mast, to stand over my head, and keep the heat of
the sun off of me like an awning; and thus I every
now and then took a little voyage upon the sea but
never went far out, nor far from the little creek; but
at last being eager to view the circumference of my
little kingdom, I resolved upon my tour and accordingly I victualed my ship for the voyage, putting in
two dozen of my loaves (cakes I should rather call
them) of barley bread, an earthen pot full of
parched rice, a food I eat a great deal of, a little bottle of rum, half a goat and powder and shot for
killing more, and two large watch coats, of those
which, as I mentioned before, I had saved out of the
seamen's chests; these I took, one to lie upon, and
the other to cover me in the night.

It was the 6th of November, in the sixth year of
my reign, or my captivity, which you please, that I set

out on this voyage, and I found it much longer than I expected; for though the island itself was not very large, yet when I came to the east side of it, I found a great ledge of rocks lie out above two leagues into the sea, some above water, some under it, and beyond that, a shoal of sand lying dry half a league more; so that I was obliged to go a great way out to sea to double the point.

When first I discovered them, I was going to give over my enterprise, and come back again, not knowing how far it might oblige me to go out to sea; and above all, doubting how I should get back again; so I came to an anchor; for I had made me a kind of an anchor with a piece of a broken grappling, which I got out of the ship.

Having secured my boat, I took my gun and went on shore, climbing up upon a hill, which seemed to overlook that point, where I saw the full extent of it, and resolved to venture.

In my viewing the sea from that hill where I stood, I perceived a strong, and indeed a most furious current, which run to the east, and even came close to the point; and I took the more notice of it, because I saw there might be some danger that when I came into it, I might be carried out to sea by the strength of it and not be able to make the island again; and indeed, had I not gotten first up upon this hill, I believe it would have been so; for there was the same current on the other side the island, only that it set off at a farther distance; and I saw there was a strong eddy under the shore; so I had nothing to do but to get in out of the first current, and I should presently be in an eddy.

I lay there, however, two days; because the wind blowing pretty fresh at east-southeast, and that being just contrary to the said current, made a great breach of the sea upon the point; so that it was not safe for me to keep too close to the shore for the breach, nor to go too far off because of the stream.

The third day in the morning, the wind having abated overnight, the sea was calm, and I ventured; but I am a warning piece again to all rash and ignorant pilots; for no sooner was I come to the point, when even I was not my boat's length from the shore, but I found myself in a great depth of water, and a current like the sluice of a mill. It carried my boat along with it with such violence that all I could do could not keep her so much as on the edge of it; but I found it hurried me farther and farther out from the eddy, which was on my left hand. There was no wind stirring to help me, and all I could do with my paddles signified nothing; and now I began to give myself over for lost; for as the current was on both sides of the island, I knew in a few leagues' distance they must join again, and then I was irrecoverably gone; nor did I see any possibility of avoiding it; so that I had no prospect before me but of perishing; not by the sea, for that was calm enough, but of starving for hunger. I had indeed found a tortoise on the shore, as big almost as I could lift, and had tossed it into the boat; and I had a great jar of fresh water, that is to say, one of my earthen pots; but what was all this to being driven into the vast ocean, where, to be sure, there was no shore, no mainland or island, for a thousand leagues at least?

And now I saw how easy it was for the Providence of God to make the most miserable condition mankind could be in worse. Now I looked back upon my desolate solitary island as the most pleasant place in the world, and all the happiness my heart could wish for was to be but there again. I stretched out my hands to it, with eager wishes. "O happy desert!" said I, "I shall never see thee more. O miserable creature," said I, "whither am I going?" Then I reproached myself with my unthankful temper and how I had repined at my solitary condition; and now what would I give to be on shore there again! Thus we never see the true state of our condition till it is illustrated to us by its contraries; nor know how to value what we enjoy, but by the want of it. It is scarce possible to imagine the consternation I was now in, being driven from my beloved island (for so it appeared to me now to be) into the wide ocean almost two leagues, and in the utmost despair of ever recovering it again. However, I worked hard, till indeed my strength was almost exhausted, and kept my boat as much to the northward, that is, towards the side of the current which the eddy lay on, as possibly I could; when about noon, as the sun passed the meridian, I thought I felt a little breeze of wind in my face, springing up from the south-southeast. This cheered my heart a little and especially when, in about half an hour more, it blew a pretty small gentle gale. By this time I was gotten at a frightful distance from the island, and had the least cloud or hazy weather intervened, I had been undone another way too; for I had no compass on board, and should never have known how to have steered towards the island, if I had but once lost sight of it; but the weather continuing clear, I applied myself to get up my mast again and spread my sail, standing away to the north as much as possible, to get out of the current.

Just as I had set my mast and sail, and the boat began to stretch away, I saw even by the clearness of the water some alteration of the current was near; for where the current was so strong, the water was foul; but perceiving the water clear, I found the current abate, and presently I found to the east, at about half a mile, a breach of the sea upon some rocks; these rocks I found caused the current to part again, and as the main stress of it ran away more southerly, leaving the rocks to the northeast, so the other returned by the repulse of the rocks and made a strong eddy, which run back again to the northwest, with a very sharp stream.

They who know what it is to have a reprieve brought to them upon the ladder or to be rescued from thieves just a-going to murder them, or who have been in such like extremities, may guess what my present surprise of joy was and how gladly I put my boat into the stream of this eddy, and the wind also freshening, how gladly I spread my sail to it, running cheerfully before the wind and with a strong tide or eddy under foot.

This eddy carried me about a league in my way back again, directly towards the island, but about two leagues more to the northward than the current which carried me away at first; so that when I came near the island, I found myself open to the northern shore of it, that is to say, the other end of the island, opposite to that which I went out from.

When I had made something more than a league of way by the help of this current or eddy, I found it was spent and served me no farther. However, I found that being between the two great currents, viz., that on the south side, which had hurried me away, and that on the north, which lay about a league on the other side: I say, between these two, in the wake of the island, I found the water at least still and running no way, and having still a breeze of wind fair for me, I kept on steering directly for the island, though not making such fresh way as I did before.

About four o'clock in the evening, being then within about a league of the island, I found the point of the rocks which occasioned this disaster stretching out, as is described before, to the southward, and casting off the current more southwardly, had of course made another eddy to the north, and this I found very strong, but not directly setting the way my course lay, which was due west, but almost full north. However, having a fresh gale, I stretched across this eddy, slanting northwest, and in about an hour came within about a mile of the shore, where, it being smooth water, I soon got to land.

When I was on shore, I fell on my knees, and gave God thanks for my deliverance, resolving to lay aside all thoughts of my deliverance by my boat; and refreshing myself with such things as I had, I brought my boat close to the shore in a little cove that I had spied under some trees and laid me down to sleep, being quite spent with the labor and fatigue of the voyage.

I was now at a great loss which way to get home with my boat. I had run so much hazard, and knew too much the case, to think of attempting it by the way I went out, and what might be at the other side (I mean the west side) I knew not, nor had I any mind to run any more ventures; so I only resolved in the morning to make my way westward along the shore and to see if there was no creek where I might lay up my frigate in safety, so as to have her again if I wanted her; in about three miles, or there about, coasting the shore, I came to a very good inlet or bay about a mile over, which narrowed till it came to a very little rivulet or brook, where I found a very convenient harbor for my boat and where she lay as if she had been in a little dock made on purpose for her. Here I put in, and having stowed my boat very safe, I went on shore to look about me and see where I was.

I soon found I had but a little passed by the place where I had been before, when I traveled on foot to that shore; so taking nothing out of my boat but my gun and my umbrella, for it was exceedingly hot, I began my march. The way was comfortable enough after such a voyage as I had been upon, and I reached my old bower in the evening, where I found   everything standing as I left it; for I always kept it in good order, being, as I said before, my country house.

I got over the fence and laid me down in the shade to rest my limbs, for I was very weary, and fell asleep. But judge you, if you can, that read my story, what a surprise I must be in, when I was waked out of my sleep by a voice calling me by my name several times, "Robin, Robin, Robin Crusoe, poor Robin Crusoe! Where are you, Robin Crusoe? Where are you? Where have you been?"

I was so dead asleep at first, being fatigued with rowing, or paddling, as it is called, the first part of the day and with walking the latter part that I did not wake thoroughly, but dozing between sleeping and waking, thought I dreamed that somebody spoke to me. But as the voice continued to repeat "Robin Crusoe, Robin Crusoe," at last I began to wake more perfectly and was at first dreadfully frighted and started up in the utmost consternation. But no sooner were my eyes open, but I saw my Poll sitting on the top of the hedge; and immediately knew that it was he that spoke to me; for just in such bemoaning language I had used to talk to him, and teach him; and he had learned it so perfectly that he would sit upon my finger and lay his bill close to my face, and cry, "Poor Robin Crusoe! Where are you? Where have you been? How come you here?" and such things as I had taught him.

However, even though I knew it was the parrot, and that indeed it could be nobody else, it was a good while before I could compose myself. First, I was amazed how the creature got thither and then, how he should just keep about the place and nowhere else. But as I was well satisfied it could be nobody but honest Poll, I got it over; and holding out my hand, and calling him by his name, "Poll," the sociable creature came to me, and sat upon my thumb, as he used to do, and continued talking to me, "Poor Robin Crusoe!" and how did I come here? and where had I been? just as if he had been overjoyed to see me again; and so I carried him home along with me.

I had now had enough of rambling to sea for some time and had enough to do for many days to sit still and reflect upon the danger I had been in. I would have been very glad to have had my boat again on my side of the island; but I knew not how it was practicable to get it about. As to the east side of the island, which I had gone round, I knew well enough there was no venturing that way; my very heart would shrink and my very blood run chill but to think of it. And as to the other side of the island, I did not know how it might be there; but supposing the current ran with the same force against the shore at the east as it passed by it on the other, I might run the same risk of being driven down the stream, and carried by the island, as I had been before of being carried away from it; so, with these thoughts, I contented myself to be without any boat, though it had been the product of so many months' labor to make it, and of so many more to get it unto the sea.

In this government of my temper I remained near a year, lived a very sedate, retired life, as you may well suppose; and my thoughts being very much composed as to my condition and fully comforted in resigning myself to the dispositions of Providence, I thought I lived really very happily in all things, except that of society.

I improved myself in this time in all the mechanic exercises which my necessities put me upon applying myself to and I believe could, upon occasion, make a very good carpenter, especially considering how few tools I had.

Besides this, I arrived at an unexpected perfection in my earthenware, and contrived well enough to make them with a wheel, which I found infinitely easier and better; because I made things round and shapable which before were filthy things indeed to look on. But I think I was never more vain of my own performance, or more joyful for anything I found out, than for my being able to make a tobacco-pipe. And though it was a very ugly, clumsy thing when it was done, and only burnt red, like other earthenware, yet as it was hard and firm, and would draw the smoke, I was exceedingly comforted with it, for I had been always used to smoke and there were pipes in the ship, but I forgot them at first, not knowing that there was tobacco in the island; and afterwards, when I searched the ship again, I could not come at any pipes at all.

In my wickerware also I improved much and made abundance of necessary baskets, as well as my invention showed me; though not very handsome, yet they were such as were very handy and convenient for my laying things up in, or fetching things home in. For example, if I killed a goat abroad, I could hang it up in a tree, flay it and dress it and cut it in pieces and bring it home in a basket; and the like by a turtle, I could cut it up, take out the eggs, and a piece or two of the flesh, which was enough for me, and bring them home in a basket, and leave the rest behind me. Also large deep baskets were my receivers for my corn, which I always rubbed out as soon as it was dry and cured and kept it in great baskets.

I began now to perceive my powder abated considerably, and this was a want which it was impossible for me to supply; and I began seriously to consider what I must do when I should have no more powder; that is to say, how I should do to kill any goat. I had, as is observed in the third year of my being here, kept a young kid, and bred her up tame, and I was in hope of getting a he-goat; but I could not by any means bring it to pass, till my kid grew an old goat; and I could never find in my heart to kill her, till she died at last of mere age.

But being now in the eleventh year of my residence, and, as I have said, my ammunition growing low, I set myself to study some art to trap and snare the goats, to see whether I could not catch some of them alive, and particularly, I wanted a she-goat great with young.

To this purpose I made snares to hamper them, and I do believe they were more than once taken in them, but my tackle was not good, for I had no wire, and I always found them broken and my bait devoured.

At length I resolved to try a pitfall, so I dug several large pits in the earth, in places where I had observed the goats used to feed, and over these pits I placed hurdles, of my own making too, with a great weight upon them; and several times I put ears of barley and dry rice, without setting the trap, and I could easily perceive that the goats had gone in and eaten up the corn, for I could see the mark of their feet. At length I set three traps in one night, and going the next morning, I found them all standing, and yet the bait eaten and gone. This was very discouraging. However, I altered my trap, and, not to trouble you with particulars, going one morning to see my trap, I found in one of them a large old he-goat, and in one of the other, three kids, a male and two females.

As to the old one, I knew not what to do with him, he was so fierce I durst not go into the pit to him; that is to say, to go about to bring him away alive, which was what I wanted. I could have killed him, but that was not my business, nor would it answer my end. So I e'en let him out, and he ran away, as if he had been frighted out of his wits. But I had forgot then what I learned afterwards, that hunger will tame a lion. If I had let him stay there three or four days without food and then have carried him some water to drink, and then a little corn, he would have been as tame as one of the kids, for they are mighty sagacious, tractable creatures where they are well used.

However, for the present I let him go, knowing no better at that time; then I went to the three kids, and taking them one by one, I tied them with strings together and with some difficulty brought them all home.

It was a good while before they would feed, but throwing them some sweet corn, it tempted them and they began to be tame; and now I found that if I expected to supply myself with goat-flesh when I had no powder or shot left, breeding some up tame was my only way, when perhaps I might have them about my house like a flock of sheep.

But then it presently occurred to me that I must keep the tame from the wild, or else they would always run wild when they grew up, and the only way for this was to have some enclosed piece of ground, well fenced either with hedge or pale, to keep them in so effectually that those within might not break out, or those without break in.

This was a great undertaking for one pair of hands, yet as I saw there was an absolute necessity of doing it, my first piece of work was to find a proper piece of ground, viz., where there was likely to be herbage for them to eat, water for them to drink, and cover to keep them from the sun.

Those who understand such enclosures will think I had very little contrivance, when I pitched upon a place very proper for all these, being a plain open piece of meadow land, or savanna (as our people call it in the western colonies), which had two or three little drills of fresh water in it and at one end was very woody. I say, they will smile at my forecast, when I shall tell them I began my enclosing of this piece of ground in such a manner that my hedge or pale must have been at least two mile about. Nor was the madness of it so great as to the compass, for

if it was ten mile about, I was like to have time
enough to do it in. But I did not consider that my
goats would be as wild in so much compass as if they
had had the whole island, and I should have so much
room to chase them in that I should never catch
them.

My hedge was begun and carried on, I believe,
about fifty yards, when this thought occurred to me,
so I presently stopped short and for the first beginning
I resolved to enclose a piece of about 150 yards in
length, and 100 yards in breadth, which, as it would
maintain as many as I should have in any reasonable
time, so, as my flock increased, I could add more
ground to my enclosure.

This was acting with some prudence, and I went to
work with courage. I was about three months hedg-
ing in the first piece, and till I had done it I tethered
the three kids in the best part of it and used them to
feed as near me as possible to make them familiar; and
very often I would go and carry them some ears of
barley or a handful of rice and feed them out of my
hand; so that after my enclosure was finished and I let
them loose, they would follow me up and down,
bleating after me for a handful of corn.

This answered my end, and in about a year and a
half I had a flock of about twelve goats, kids and all;
and in two years more I had three and forty, besides
several that I took and killed for my food. And after
that I enclosed five several pieces of ground to feed

them in, with little pens to drive them into, to take them as I wanted, and gates out of one piece of ground into another.

But this was not all, for now I not only had goat's flesh to feed on when I pleased, but milk too, a thing which indeed in my beginning I did not so much as think of, and which, when it came into my thoughts, was really an agreeable surprise. For now I set up my dairy and had sometimes a gallon or two of milk in a day. And as Nature, who gives supplies of food to every creature, dictates even naturally how to make use of it, so I that had never milked a cow, much less a goat, or seen butter or cheese made, very readily and handily, though after a great many essays and miscarriages, made me both butter and cheese at last and never wanted it afterwards.

How mercifully can our great Creator treat His creatures, even in those conditions in which they seemed to be overwhelmed in destruction! How can He sweeten the bitterest providences and give us cause to praise Him for dungeons and prisons! What a table was here spread for me in a wilderness, where I saw nothing at first but to perish for hunger!

It would have made a stoic smile to have seen me and my little family sit down to dinner; there was my majesty, the prince and lord of the whole island; I had the lives of all my subjects at my absolute command. I could hang, draw, give liberty, and take it away, and no rebels among all my subjects.

Then to see how like a king I dined, too, all alone, attended by my servants; Poll, as if he had been my favorite, was the only person permitted to talk to me. My dog, who was now grown very old and crazy and had found no species to multiply his kind upon, sat always at my right hand, and two cats, one on one side the table and one on the other, expecting now and then a bit from my hand, as a mark of special favor.

But these were not the two cats which I brought on shore at first, for they were both of them dead and had been interred near my habitation by my own hand; but one of them having multiplied by I know not what kind of creature, these were two which I had preserved tame, whereas the rest run wild in the woods and became indeed troublesome to me at last; for they would often come into my house and plunder me too, till at last I was obliged to shoot them, and did kill a great many; at length they left me with this attendance, and in this plentiful manner, I lived; neither could I be said to want anything but society, and of that in some time after this, I was like to have too much.

I was something impatient, as I have observed, to have the use of my boat, though very loath to run any more hazards; and therefore sometimes I sat contriving ways to get her about the island, and at other times I sat myself down contented enough without her. But I had a strange uneasiness in my mind to go

down to the point of the island where, as I have said,
in my last ramble I went up the hill to see how the
shore lay and how the current set that I might see
what I had to do. This inclination increased upon
me every day, and at length I resolved to travel thither by land; following the edge of the shore I did so.
But had anyone in England been to meet such a man
as I was, it must either have frighted them or raised
a great deal of laughter; and as I frequently stood still
to look at myself, I could not but smile at the notion
of my traveling through Yorkshire with such an
equipage and in such a dress. Be pleased to take a
sketch of my figure as follows:

I had a great high shapeless cap, made of a goatskin,
with a flap hanging down behind, as well to keep the
sun from me as to shoot the rain off from running
into my neck; nothing being so hurtful in these climates as the rain upon the flesh under the clothes.

I had a short jacket of goatskin, the skirts coming
down to about the middle of my thighs; and a pair
of open-kneed breeches of the same; the breeches
were made of the skin of an old he-goat, whose hair
hung down such a length on either side that, like
pantaloons, it reached to the middle of my legs;
stockings and shoes I had none, but had made me a
pair of somethings, I scarce know what to call them,
like buckskins, to flap over my legs, and lace on
either side like spatterdashes; but of a most barbarous
shape, as indeed were all the rest of my clothes.

I had on a broad belt of goatskin dried, which I drew together with two thongs of the same, instead of buckles; and in a kind of a frog on either side of this, instead of a sword and a dagger, hung a little saw and a hatchet, one on one side, one on the other. I had another belt, not so broad and fastened in the same manner, which hung over my shoulder; and at the end of it, under my left arm, hung two pouches, both made of goatskin too; in one of which hung my powder, in the other my shot. At my back I carried my basket, on my shoulder my gun, and over my head a great clumsy ugly goatskin umbrella, but which, after all, was the most necessary thing I had about me, next to my gun. As for my face, the color of it was really not so Mulatto like as one might expect from a man not at all careful of it and living within nineteen degrees of the equinox. My beard I had once suffered to grow till it was about a quarter of a yard long; but as I had both scissors and razors sufficient, I had cut it pretty short, except what grew on my upper lip, which I had trimmed into a large pair of Mahometan whiskers, such as I had seen worn by some Turks who I saw at Sallee; for the Moors did not wear such, though the Turks did; of these mustachios or whiskers, I will not say they were long enough to hang my hat upon them, but they were of a length and shape monstrous enough and such as in England would have passed for frightful.

But all this is by the bye; for as to my figure, I had

so few to observe me that it was of no manner of consequence; so I say no more to that part. In this kind of figure I went my new journey, and was out five or six days. I traveled first along the seashore, directly to the place where I first brought my boat to an anchor, to get up upon the rocks; and having no boat now to take care of, I went over the land a nearer way to the same height that I was upon before, when, looking forward to the point of the rocks which lay out, and which I was obliged to double with my boat, as is said above, I was surprised to see the sea all smooth and quiet, no rippling, no motion, no current, any more there than in other places.

I was at a strange loss to understand this, and resolved to spend some time in the observing it, to see if nothing from the sets of the tide had occasioned it; but I was presently convinced how it was, viz., that the tide of ebb setting from the west and joining with the current of waters from some great river on the shore must be the occasion of this current; and that according as the wind blew more forcibly from the west or from the north, this current came near, or went farther from the shore; for waiting thereabouts till evening, I went up to the rock again, and then the tide of the ebb being made, I plainly saw the current again as before, only that it run farther off, being near half a league from the shore; whereas in my case it set close upon the shore, and hurried me and my canoe along with it, which at another time it would not have done.

This observation convinced me that I had nothing to do but to observe the ebbing and the flowing of the tide, and I might very easily bring my boat about the island again. But when I began to think of putting it in practice, I had such a terror upon my spirits at the remembrance of the danger I had been in that I could not think of it again with any patience; but on the contrary, I took up another resolution, which was more safe, though more laborious; and this was that I would build, or rather make me another *periagua,* or canoe; and so have one for one side of the island and one for the other.

You are to understand that now I had, as I may call it, two plantations in the island; one my little fortification or tent, with the wall about it under the rock, with the cave behind me, which by this time I had enlarged into several apartments, or caves, one within another. One of these, which was the driest and largest, and had a door out beyond my wall or fortification, that is to say, beyond where my wall joined to the rock, was all filled up with the large earthen pots, of which I have given an account, and with fourteen or fifteen great baskets, which would hold five or six bushels each, where I laid up my stores of provision, especially my corn, some in the ear cut off short from the straw, and the other rubbed out with my hand.

As for my wall, made, as before, with long stakes, or piles, those piles grew all like trees and were by this time grown so big and spread so very much that there was not the least appearance to any one's view of any habitation behind them.

Near this dwelling of mine but a little farther within the land and upon lower ground, lay my two pieces of corn ground, which I kept duly cultivated and sowed, and which duly yielded me their harvest in its season; and whenever I had occasion for more corn, I had more land adjoining as fit as that.

Besides this, I had my country seat, and I had now a tolerable plantation there also; for first, I had my little bower, as I called it, which I kept in repair; that is to say, I kept the hedge which circled it in constantly fitted up to its usual height, the ladder standing always in the inside; I kept the trees, which at first were no more than my stakes, but were now grown very firm and tall, I kept them always so cut that they might spread and grow thick and wild, and make the more agreeable shade, which they did effectually to my mind. In the middle of this I had my tent always standing, being a piece of a sail spread over poles set up for that purpose, and which never wanted any repair or renewing; and under this I had made me a squab, or couch, with the skins of the creatures I had killed and with other soft things, and a blanket laid on them such as belong to our seabedding, which I had saved, and a great watch coat to cover me; and here, whenever I had occasion to be absent from my chief seat, I took up my country habitation.

Adjoining to this I had my enclosures for my cat-
tle, that is to say, my goats. And as I had taken an
inconceivable deal of pains to fence and enclose this
ground, so I was so uneasy to see it kept entire, lest
the goats should break through, that I never left off
till with infinite labor I had struck the outside of the
hedge so full of small stakes, and so near to one
another, that it was rather a pale than a hedge, and
there was scarce room to put a hand through between
them; which afterwards, when those stakes grew, as
they all did in the next rainy season, made the enclosure strong like a wall, indeed, stronger than any wall.

This will testify for me that I was not idle and that
I spared no pains to bring to pass whatever appeared
necessary for my comfortable support; for I considered the keeping up a breed of tame creatures thus
at my hand would be a living magazine of flesh,
milk, butter, and cheese for me as long as I lived in
the place, if it were to be forty years; and that keeping them in my reach depended entirely upon my
perfecting my enclosures to such a degree that I
might be sure of keeping them together; which by
this method indeed, I so effectually secured that
when these little stakes began to grow, I had planted
them so very thick I was forced to pull some of
them up again.

In this place also I had my grapes growing, which
I principally depended on for my winter store of
raisins and which I never failed to preserve very

carefully, as the best and most agreeable dainty of my whole diet; and indeed they were not agreeable only, but physical, wholesome, nourishing, and refreshing to the last degree.

As this was also about halfway between my other habitation and the place where I had laid up my boat, I generally stayed and lay here in my way thither; for I used frequently to visit my boat, and I kept all things about or belonging to her in very good order; sometimes I went out in her to divert myself, but no more hazardous voyages would I go nor scarce ever above a stone's cast or two from the shore, I was so apprehensive of being hurried out of my knowledge again by the currents, or winds, or any other accident.

Love of Life

JACK LONDON

"This out of all will remain—
They have lived and have tossed;
So much of the game will be gain,
Though the gold of the dice has been lost."

They limped painfully down the bank, and once the foremost of the two men staggered among the rough-strewn rocks. They were tired and weak, and their faces had the drawn expression of patience which comes of hardship long endured. They were heavily burdened with blanket packs which were strapped to their shoulders. Head-straps, passing across the forehead, helped support these packs. Each man carried a rifle. They walked in a stooped posture, the shoulders well forward, the head still farther forward, the eyes bent upon the ground.

"I wish we had just about two of them cartridges that's layin' in that cache of ourn," said the second man.

His voice was utterly and drearily expressionless. He spoke without enthusiasm; and the first man, limping into the milky stream that foamed over the rocks, vouchsafed no reply.

The other man followed at his heels. They did not remove their footgear, though the water was icy cold—so cold that their ankles ached and their feet went numb. In places the water dashed against their knees, and both men staggered for footing.

The man who followed slipped on a smooth boulder, nearly fell, but recovered himself with a violent effort, at the same time uttering a sharp exclamation of pain. He seemed faint and dizzy and put out his free hand while he reeled, as though seeking support against the air. When he had steadied himself he stepped forward, but reeled again and nearly fell. Then he stood still and looked at the other man, who had never turned his head.

The man stood still for fully a minute, as though debating with himself. Then he called out:

"I say, Bill, I've sprained my ankle."

Bill staggered on through the milky water. He did not look around. The man watched him go, and though his face was expressionless as ever, his eyes were like the eyes of a wounded deer.

The other man limped up the farther bank and continued straight on without looking back. The man in the stream watched him. His lips trembled a little, so that the rough thatch of brown hair which covered them was visibly agitated. His tongue even strayed out to moisten them.

"Bill!" he cried out.

It was the pleading cry of a strong man in distress, but Bill's head did not turn. The man watched him go, limping grotesquely and lurching forward with stammering gait up the slow slope toward the soft sky-line of the low-lying hill. He watched him go till he passed over the crest and disappeared. Then he turned his gaze and slowly took in the circle of the world that remained to him now that Bill was gone.

Near the horizon the sun was smouldering dimly, almost obscured by formless mists and vapors, which gave an impression of mass and density without outline or tangibility. The man pulled out his watch, the while resting his weight on one leg. It was four o'clock, and as the season was near the last of July or first of August,—he did not know the precise date within a week or two,—he knew that the sun roughly marked the northwest. He looked to the south and knew that somewhere beyond those bleak hills lay the Great Bear Lake; also, he knew that in that direction the Arctic Circle cut its forbidding way across the Canadian Barrens. This stream in which he stood was a feeder to the Coppermine

River, which in turn flowed north and emptied into
Coronation Gulf and the Arctic Ocean. He had
never been there, but he had seen it, once, on a
Hudson Bay Company chart.

Again his gaze completed the circle of the world
about him. It was not a heartening spectacle.
Everywhere was soft sky-line. The hills were all
low-lying. There were no trees, no shrubs, no grasses—naught but a tremendous and terrible desolation
that sent fear swiftly dawning into his eyes.

"Bill!" he whispered, once and twice; "Bill!"

He cowered in the midst of the milky water, as
though the vastness were pressing in upon him with
overwhelming force, brutally crushing him with its
complacent awfulness. He began to shake as with an
ague-fit, till the gun fell from his hand with a splash.
This served to rouse him. He fought with his fear
and pulled himself together, groping in the water
and recovering the weapon. He hitched his pack farther over on his left shoulder, so as to take a portion
of its weight from off the injured ankle. Then he
proceeded, slowly and carefully, wincing with pain,
to the bank.

He did not stop. With a desperation that was madness, unmindful of the pain, he hurried up the slope to
the crest of the hill over which his comrade had disappeared—more grotesque and comical by far than
that limping, jerking comrade. But at the crest he saw
a shallow valley, empty of life. He fought with his fear

again, overcame it, hitched the pack still farther over on his left shoulder, and lurched on down the slope.

The bottom of the valley was soggy with water, which the thick moss held, spongelike, close to the surface. This water squirted out from under his feet at every step, and each time he lifted a foot the action culminated in a sucking sound as the wet moss reluctantly released its grip. He picked his way from muskeg to muskeg, and followed the other man's footsteps along and across the rocky ledges which thrust like islets through the sea of moss.

Though alone, he was not lost. Farther on he knew he would come to where dead spruce and fir, very small and weazened, bordered the shore of a little lake, the *titchin-nichilie*, in the tongue of the country, the "land of little sticks." And into that lake flowed a small stream, the water of which was not milky. There was rush-grass on that stream—this he remembered well—but no timber, and he would follow it till its first trickle ceased at a divide. He would cross this divide to the first trickle of another stream, flowing to the west, which he would follow until it emptied into the river Dease, and here he would find a cache under an upturned canoe and piled over with many rocks. And in this cache would be ammunition for his empty gun, fish-hooks and lines, a small net—all the utilities for the killing and snaring of food. Also, he would find flour,—not much,—a piece of bacon, and some beans.

Bill would be waiting for him there, and they would paddle away south down the Dease to the Great Bear Lake. And south across the lake they would go, ever south, till they gained the Mackenzie. And south, still south, they would go, while the winter raced vainly after them, and the ice formed in the eddies, and the days grew chilly and crisp, south to some warm Hudson Bay Company post, where timber grew tall and generous and there was grub without end.

These were the thoughts of the man as he strove onward. But hard as he strove with his body, he strove equally hard with his mind, trying to think that Bill had not deserted him, that Bill would surely wait for him at the cache. He was compelled to think this thought, or else there would not be any use to strive, and he would have lain down and died. And as the dim ball of the sun sank slowly into the northwest he covered every inch—and many times—of his and Bill's flight south before the downcoming winter. And he conned the grub of the cache and the grub of the Hudson Bay Company post over and over again. He had not eaten for two days; for a far longer time he had not had all he wanted to eat. Often he stooped and picked pale muskeg berries, put them into his mouth, and chewed and swallowed them. A muskeg berry is a bit of seed enclosed in a bit of water. In the mouth the water melts away and the seed chews sharp and bitter. The man knew there was no nourishment in the berries, but he chewed them patiently with a hope greater than knowledge and defying experience.

At nine o'clock he stubbed his toe on a rocky ledge, and from sheer weariness and weakness staggered and fell. He lay for some time, without movement, on his side. Then he slipped out of the pack-straps and clumsily dragged himself into a sitting posture. It was not yet dark, and in the lingering twilight he groped about among the rocks for shreds of dry moss. When he had gathered a heap he built a fire,—a smouldering, smudgy fire,—and put a tin pot of water on to boil.

He unwrapped his pack and the first thing he did was to count his matches. There were sixty-seven. He counted them three times to make sure. He divided them into several portions, wrapping them in oil paper, disposing of one bunch in his empty tobacco pouch, of another bunch in the inside band of his battered hat, of a third bunch under his shirt on the chest. This accomplished, a panic came upon him, and he unwrapped them all and counted them again. There were still sixty-seven.

He dried his wet foot-gear by the fire. The moccasins were in soggy shreds. The blanket socks were worn through in places, and his feet were raw and bleeding. His ankle was throbbing, and he gave it an examination. It had swollen to the size of his knee.

He tore a long strip from one of his two blankets and bound the ankle tightly. He tore other strips and bound them about his feet to serve for both moccasins and socks. Then he drank the pot of water, steaming hot, wound his watch, and crawled between his blankets.

He slept like a dead man. The brief darkness around midnight came and went. The sun arose in the northeast—at least the day dawned in that quarter, for the sun was hidden by gray clouds.

At six o'clock he awoke, quietly lying on his back. He gazed straight up into the gray sky and knew that he was hungry. As he rolled over on his elbow he was startled by a loud snort, and saw a bull caribou regarding him with alert curiosity. The animal was not more than fifty feet away, and instantly into the man's mind leaped the vision and the savor of a caribou steak sizzling and frying over a fire. Mechanically he reached for the empty gun, drew a bead, and pulled the trigger. The bull snorted and leaped away, his hoofs rattling and clattering as he fled across the ledges.

The man cursed and flung the empty gun from him. He groaned aloud as he started to drag himself to his feet. It was a slow and arduous task. His joints were like rusty hinges. They worked harshly in their sockets, with much friction, and each bending or unbending was accomplished only through a sheer exertion of will. When he finally gained his feet, another minute or so was consumed in straightening up, so that he could stand erect as a man should stand.

He crawled up a small knoll and surveyed the prospect. There were no trees, no bushes, nothing but a gray sea of moss scarcely diversified by gray rocks, gray lakelets, and gray streamlets. The sky was gray. There was no sun nor hint of sun. He had no idea of north, and he had forgotten the way he had come to this spot the night before. But he was not lost. He knew that. Soon he would come to the land of the little sticks. He felt that it lay off to the left somewhere, not far—possibly just over the next low hill.

He went back to put his pack into shape for traveling. He assured himself of the existence of his three separate parcels of matches, though he did not stop to count them. But he did linger, debating, over a squat moose-hide sack. It was not large. He could hide it under his two hands. He knew that it weighed fifteen pounds,—as much as all the rest of the pack,—and it worried him. He finally set it to one side and proceeded to roll the pack. He paused to gaze at the squat moose-hide sack. He picked it up hastily with a defiant glance about him, as though the desolation were trying to rob him of it; and when he rose to his feet to stagger on into the day, it was included in the pack on his back.

He bore away to the left, stopping now and again to eat muskeg berries. His ankle had stiffened, his limp was more pronounced, but the pain of it was as nothing compared with the pain of his stomach. The hunger pangs were sharp. They gnawed and gnawed until he could not keep his mind steady on the course he must pursue to gain the land of little sticks. The muskeg berries did not allay this gnawing, while they made his tongue and the roof of his mouth sore with their irritating bite.

He came upon a valley where rock ptarmigan rose on whirring wings from the ledges and muskegs. Ker—ker—ker was the cry they made. He threw stones at them, but could not hit them. He placed his pack on the ground and stalked them as a cat stalks a sparrow. The sharp rocks cut through his pants' legs till his knees left a trail of blood; but the hurt was lost in the hurt of his hunger. He squirmed over the wet moss, saturating his clothes and chilling his body; but he was not aware of it, so great was his fever for food. And always the ptarmigan rose, whirring, before him, till their ker—ker—ker became a mock to him, and he cursed them and cried aloud at them with their own cry.

Once he crawled upon one that must have been asleep. He did not see it till it shot up in his face from its rocky nook. He made a clutch as startled as was the rise of the ptarmigan, and there remained in his hand three tail-feathers. As he watched its flight he hated it, as though it had done him some terrible wrong. Then he returned and shouldered his pack.

As the day wore along he came into valleys or swales where game was more plentiful. A band of caribou passed by, twenty and odd animals, tantalizingly within rifle range. He felt a wild desire to run after them, a certitude that he could run them down. A black fox came toward him, carrying a ptarmigan in his mouth. The man shouted. It was a fearful cry, but the fox, leaping away in fright, did not drop the ptarmigan.

Late in the afternoon he followed a stream, milky with lime, which ran through sparse patches of rush-grass. Grasping these rushes firmly near the root, he pulled up what resembled a young onion-sprout no larger than a shingle-nail. It was tender, and his teeth sank into it with a crunch that promised deliciously of food. But its fibers were tough. It was composed of stringy filaments saturated with water, like the berries, and devoid of nourishment. He threw off his pack and went into the rush-grass on hands and knees, crunching and munching, like some bovine creature.

He was very weary and often wished to rest—to lie down and sleep; but he was continually driven on— not so much by his desire to gain the land of little sticks as by his hunger. He searched little ponds for frogs and dug up the earth with his nails for worms, though he knew in spite that neither frogs nor worms existed so far north.

He looked into every pool of water vainly, until, as the long twilight came on, he discovered a solitary fish, the size of a minnow, in such a pool. He plunged his arm in up to the shoulder, but it eluded him. He reached for it with both hands and stirred up the milky mud at the bottom. In his excitement he fell in, wetting himself to the waist. Then the water was too muddy to admit of his seeing the fish, and he was compelled to wait until the sediment had settled.

The pursuit was renewed, till the water was again muddied. But he could not wait. He unstrapped the tin bucket and began to bale the pool. He baled wildly at first, splashing himself and flinging the water so short a distance that it ran back into the pool. He worked more carefully, striving to be cool, though his heart was pounding against his chest and his hands were trembling. At the end of half an hour the pool was nearly dry. Not a cupful of water remained. And there was no fish. He found a hidden crevice among the stones through which it had escaped to the adjoining and larger pool—a pool which he could not empty in a night and a day. Had he known of the crevice, he could have closed it with a rock at the beginning and the fish would have been his.

Thus he thought, and crumpled up and sank down upon the wet earth. At first he cried softly to himself, then he cried loudly to the pitiless desolation that ringed him around; and for a long time after he was shaken by great dry sobs.

He built a fire and warmed himself by drinking quarts of hot water, and made camp on a rocky ledge in the same fashion he had the night before.

The last thing he did was to see that his matches were dry and to wind his watch. The blankets were wet and clammy. His ankle pulsed with pain. But he knew only that he was hungry, and through his restless sleep he dreamed of feasts and banquets and of food served and spread in all imaginable ways.

He awoke chilled and sick. There was no sun. The gray of earth and sky had become deeper, more profound. A raw wind was blowing, and the first flurries of snow were whitening the hilltops. The air about him thickened and grew white while he made a fire and boiled more water. It was wet snow, half rain, and the flakes were large and soggy. At first they melted as soon as they came in contact with the earth, but ever more fell, covering the ground, putting out the fire, spoiling his supply of moss-fuel.

This was a signal for him to strap on his pack and stumble onward, he knew not where. He was not concerned with the land of little sticks, nor with Bill and the cache under the upturned canoe by the river Dease. He was mastered by the verb "to eat." He was hunger-mad. He took no heed of the course he pursued, so long as that course led him through the swale bottoms. He felt his way through the wet snow to the watery muskeg berries, and went by feel as he pulled up the rush-grass by the roots. But it was tasteless stuff and did not satisfy. He found a weed that tasted sour and he ate all he could find of it, which was not much, for it was a creeping growth, easily hidden under the several inches of snow.

He had no fire that night, nor hot water, and crawled under his blanket to sleep the broken hunger-sleep. The snow turned into a cold rain. He awakened many times to feel it falling on his upturned face. Day came—a gray day and no sun. It had ceased raining. The keenness of his hunger had departed. Sensibility, as far as concerned the yearning for food, had been exhausted. There was a dull, heavy ache in his stomach, but it did not bother him so much. He was more rational, and once more he was chiefly interested in the land of little sticks and the cache by the river Dease.

He ripped the remnant of one of his blankets into strips and bound his bleeding feet. Also, he recinched the injured ankle and prepared himself for a day of travel. When he came to his pack, he paused long over the squat moose-hide sack, but in the end it went with him.

The snow had melted under the rain, and only the hilltops showed white. The sun came out, and he succeeded in locating the points of the compass, though he knew now that he was lost. Perhaps, in his previous days' wanderings, he had edged away too far to the left. He now bore off to the right to counteract the possible deviation from his true course.

Though the hunger pangs were no longer so exquisite, he realized that he was weak. He was compelled to pause for frequent rests, when he attacked the muskeg berries and rush-grass patches. His tongue felt dry and large, as though covered with a fine hairy growth, and it tasted bitter in his mouth. His heart gave him a great deal of trouble. When he had travelled a few minutes it would begin a remorseless thump, thump, thump, and then leap up and away in a painful flutter of beats that choked him and made him go faint and dizzy.

In the middle of the day he found two minnows in a large pool. It was impossible to bale it, but he was calmer now and managed to catch them in his tin bucket. They were no longer than his little finger, but he was not particularly hungry. The dull ache in his stomach had been growing duller and fainter. It seemed almost that his stomach was dozing. He ate the fish raw, masticating with painstaking care, for the eating was an act of pure reason. While he had no desire to eat, he knew that he must eat to live.

In the evening he caught three more minnows, eating two and saving the third for breakfast. The sun had dried stray shreds of moss, and he was able to warm himself with hot water. He had not covered more than ten miles that day; and the next day, travelling whenever his heart permitted him, he covered no more than five miles. But his stomach did not give him the slightest uneasiness. It had gone to sleep. He was in a strange country, too, and the caribou were growing more plentiful, also the wolves. Often their yelps drifted across the desolation, and once he saw three of them slinking away before his path.

Another night; and in the morning, being more rational, he untied the leather string that fastened the squat moose-hide sack. From its open mouth poured a yellow stream of coarse gold-dust and nuggets. He roughly divided the gold in halves, caching one half on a prominent ledge, wrapped in a piece of blanket, and returning the other half to the sack. He also began to use strips of the one remaining blanket for his feet. He still clung to his gun, for there were cartridges in that cache by the river Dease.

This was a day of fog, and this day hunger awoke in him again. He was very weak and was afflicted with a giddiness which at times blinded him. It was no uncommon thing now for him to stumble and fall; and stumbling once, he fell squarely into a ptarmigan nest. There were four newly hatched chicks, a day old—little specks of pulsating life no more than a mouthful; and he ate them ravenously, thrusting them alive into his mouth and crunching them like eggshells between his teeth. The mother ptarmigan beat about him with great outcry. He used his gun as a club with which to knock her over, but she dodged out of reach. He threw stones at her and with one chance shot broke a wing. Then she fluttered away, running, trailing the broken wing, with him in pursuit.

The little chicks had no more than whetted his appetite. He hopped and bobbed clumsily along on his injured ankle, throwing stones and screaming hoarsely at times; at other times hopping and bobbing silently along, picking himself up grimly and patiently when he fell, or rubbing his eyes with his hand when the giddiness threatened to overpower him.

The chase led him across swampy ground in the bottom of the valley, and he came upon footprints in the soggy moss. They were not his own—he could see that. They must be Bill's. But he could not stop, for the mother ptarmigan was running on. He would catch her first, then he would return and investigate.

He exhausted the mother ptarmigan; but he exhausted himself. She lay panting on her side. He lay panting on his side, a dozen feet away, unable to crawl to her. And as he recovered she recovered, fluttering out of reach as his hungry hand went out to her. The chase was resumed. Night settled down and she escaped. He stumbled from weakness and pitched head foremost on his face, cutting his cheek, his pack upon his back. He did not move for a long while; then he rolled over on his side, wound his watch, and lay there until morning.

Another day of fog. Half of his last blanket had gone into foot-wrappings. He failed to pick up Bill's trail. It did not matter. His hunger was driving him too compellingly—only—only he wondered if Bill, too, were lost. By midday the irk of his pack became too oppressive. Again he divided the gold, this time merely spilling half of it on the ground. In the afternoon he threw the rest of it away, there remaining to him only the half-blanket, the tin bucket, and the rifle.

An hallucination began to trouble him. He felt confident that one cartridge remained to him. It was in the chamber of the rifle and he had overlooked it. On the other hand, he knew all the time that the chamber was empty. But the hallucination persisted. He fought it off for hours, then threw his rifle open and was confronted with emptiness. The disappointment was as bitter as though he had really expected to find the cartridge.

He plodded on for half an hour, when the hallucination arose again. Again he fought it, and still it persisted, till for very relief he opened his rifle to unconvince himself. At times his mind wandered farther afield, and he plodded on, a mere automaton, strange conceits and whimsicalities gnawing at his brain like worms. But these excursions out of the real were of brief duration, for ever the pangs of the hunger-bite called him back. He was jerked back abruptly once from such an excursion by a sight that caused him nearly to faint. He reeled and swayed, doddering like a drunken man to keep from falling. Before him stood a horse. A horse! He could not believe his eyes. A thick mist was in them, intershot with

sparkling points of light. He rubbed his eyes savagely to clear his vision, and beheld, not a horse,
but a great brown bear. The animal was studying
him with bellicose curiosity.

The man had brought his gun halfway to his
shoulder before he realized. He lowered it and
drew his hunting-knife from its beaded sheath at
his hip. Before him was meat and life. He ran his
thumb along the edge of his knife. It was sharp.
The point was sharp. He would fling himself upon
the bear and kill it. But his heart began its warning thump, thump, thump. Then followed the wild
upward leap and tattoo of flutters, the pressing as
of an iron band about his forehead, the creeping of
the dizziness into his brain.

His desperate courage was evicted by a great
surge of fear. In his weakness, what if the animal
attacked him? He drew himself up to his most
imposing stature, gripping the knife and staring
hard at the bear. The bear advanced clumsily a
couple of steps, reared up, and gave vent to a ten-
tative growl. If the man ran, he would run after
him; but the man did not run. He was animated
now with the courage of fear. He, too, growled,
savagely, terribly, voicing the fear that is to life ger-
mane and that lies twisted about life's deepest roots.

The bear edged away to one side, growling men-
acingly, himself appalled by this mysterious creature that appeared upright and unafraid. But the

man did not move. He stood like a statue till the danger was past, when he yielded to a fit of trembling and sank down into the wet moss.

He pulled himself together and went on, afraid now in a new way. It was not the fear that he should die passively from lack of food, but that he should be destroyed violently before starvation had exhausted the last particle of the endeavor in him that made toward surviving. There were the wolves. Back and forth across the desolation drifted their howls, weaving the very air into a fabric of menace that was so tangible that he found himself, arms in the air, pressing it back from him as it might be the walls of a wind-blown tent.

Now and again the wolves, in packs of two and three, crossed his path. But they steered clear of him. They were not in sufficient numbers, and besides they were hunting the caribou, which did not battle, while this strange creature that walked erect might scratch and bite.

In the late afternoon he came upon scattered bones where the wolves had made a kill. The débris had been a caribou calf an hour before, squawking and running and very much alive. He contemplated the bones, clean-picked and polished, pink with the cell-life in them which had not yet died. Could it possibly be that he might be that ere the day was done! Such was life, eh? A vain and fleeting thing. It was only life that pained.

There was no hurt in death. To die was to sleep. It meant cessation, rest. Then why was he not content to die?

But he did not moralize long. He was squatting in the moss, a bone in his mouth, sucking at the shreds of life that still dyed it faintly pink. The sweet meaty taste, thin and elusive almost as a memory, maddened him. He closed his jaws on the bones and crunched. Sometimes it was the bone that broke, sometimes his teeth. Then he crushed the bones between rocks, pounded them to a pulp, and swallowed them. He pounded his fingers, too, in his haste, and yet found a moment in which to feel surprise at the fact that his fingers did not hurt much when caught under the descending rock.

Came frightful days of snow and rain. He did not know when he made camp, when he broke camp. He travelled in the night as much as in the day. He rested wherever he fell, crawled on whenever the dying life in him flickered up and burned less dimly. He, as a man, no longer strove. It was the life in him, unwilling to die, that drove him on. He did not suffer. His nerves had become blunted, numb, while his mind was filled with weird visions and delicious dreams.

But ever he sucked and chewed on the crushed bones of the caribou calf, the least remnants of which he had gathered up and carried with him. He crossed no more hills or divides, but automatically followed a large stream which flowed through a wide and shallow valley. He did not see this stream nor this valley. He saw nothing save visions. Soul and body walked or crawled side by side, yet apart, so slender was the thread that bound them.

He awoke in his right mind, lying on his back on a rocky ledge. The sun was shining bright and warm. Afar off he heard the squawking of caribou calves. He was aware of vague memories of rain and wind and snow, but whether he had been beaten by the storm for two days or two weeks he did not know.

For some time he lay without movement, the genial sunshine pouring upon him and saturating his miserable body with its warmth. A fine day, he thought. Perhaps he could manage to locate himself. By a painful effort he rolled over on his side. Below him flowed a wide and sluggish river. Its unfamiliarity puzzled him. Slowly he followed it with his eyes, winding in wide sweeps among the bleak, bare hills, bleaker and barer and lower-lying than any hills he had yet encountered. Slowly, deliberately, without excitement or more than the most casual interest, he followed the course of the strange stream toward the sky-line and saw it emptying into a bright and shining sea. He was still unexcited. Most unusual, he thought, a vision or a mirage—more likely a vision, a trick of his disordered mind. He was confirmed in this by sight of a ship lying at anchor in the midst of the shining sea. He closed his eyes for a while, then opened them. Strange how the vision persisted! Yet not strange. He knew there were no seas or ships in the heart of the barren lands, just as he had known there was no cartridge in the empty rifle.

He heard a snuffle behind him—a half-choking gasp or cough. Very slowly, because of his exceeding weakness and stiffness, he rolled over on his other side. He could see nothing near at hand, but he waited patiently. Again came the snuffle and cough, and outlined between two jagged rocks not a score of feet away he made out the gray head of a wolf. The sharp ears were not pricked so sharply as he had seen them on other wolves; the eyes were bleared and bloodshot, the head seemed to droop limply and forlornly. The animal blinked continually in the sunshine. It seemed sick. As he looked it snuffled and coughed again.

This, at least, was real, he thought, and turned on the other side so that he might see the reality of the world which had been veiled from him before by the vision. But the sea still shone in the distance and the ship was plainly discernible. Was it reality, after all? He closed his eyes for a long while and thought, and then it came to him. He had been making north by east, away from the Dease Divide and into the Coppermine Valley. This wide and sluggish river was the Coppermine. That shining sea was the Arctic Ocean. That ship was a whaler, strayed east, far east, from the mouth of the Mackenzie, and it was lying at anchor in Coronation Gulf. He remembered the Hudson Bay Company chart he had seen long ago, and it was all clear and reasonable to him.

He sat up and turned his attention to immediate affairs. He had worn through the blanket-wrappings, and his feet were shapeless lumps of raw meat. His last blanket was gone Rifle and knife were both missing. He had lost his hat somewhere, with the bunch of matches in the band, but the matches against his chest were safe and dry inside the tobacco pouch and oil paper. He looked at his watch. It marked eleven o'clock and was still running. Evidently he had kept it wound.

He was calm and collected. Though extremely weak, he had no sensation of pain. He was not hungry. The thought of food was not even pleasant to him, and whatever he did was done by reason alone. He ripped off his pants' legs to the knees and bound them about his feet. Somehow he had succeeded in retaining the tin bucket. He would have some hot water before he began what he foresaw was to be a terrible journey to the ship.

His movements were slow. He shook as with a palsy. When he started to collect dry moss, he found he could not rise to his feet. He tried again and again, then contented himself with crawling about on hands and knees. Once he crawled near to the sick wolf. The animal dragged itself reluctantly out of his way, licking its chops with a tongue which seemed hardly to have the strength to curl. The man noticed that tongue was not the customary healthy red. It was a yellowish brown and seemed coated with a rough and half-dry mucus.

After he had drunk a quart of hot water the man found he was able to stand, and even to walk as well as a dying man might be supposed to walk. Every minute or so he was compelled to rest. His steps were feeble and uncertain, just as the wolf's that trailed him were feeble and uncertain; and that night, when the shining sea was blotted out by blackness, he knew he was nearer to it by no more than four miles.

Throughout the night he heard the cough of the sick wolf, and now and then the squawking of the caribou calves. There was life all around him, but it was strong life, very much alive and well, and he knew the sick wolf clung to the sick man's trail in the hope that the man would die first. In the morning, on opening his eyes, he beheld it regarding him with a wistful and hungry stare. It stood crouched, with tail between its legs, like a miserable and woe-begone dog. It shivered in the chill morning wind, and grinned dispiritedly when the man spoke to it in a voice that achieved no more than a hoarse whisper.

The sun rose brightly, and all morning the man tottered and fell toward the ship on the shining sea. The weather was perfect. It was the brief Indian Summer of the high latitudes. It might last a week. To-morrow or next day it might be gone.

In the afternoon the man came upon a trail. It was of another man, who did not walk, but who dragged himself on all fours. The man thought it might be Bill, but he thought in a dull, uninterested way. He had no curiosity. In fact, sensation and emotion had left him. He was no longer susceptible to pain. Stomach and nerves had gone to sleep. Yet the life that was in him drove him on. He was very weary, but it refused to die. It was because it refused to die that he still ate muskeg berries and minnows, drank his hot water, and kept a wary eye on the sick wolf.

He followed the trail of the other man who dragged himself along, and soon came to the end of it—a few fresh-picked bones where the soggy moss was marked by the foot-pads of many wolves. He saw a squat moose-hide sack, mate to his own, which had been torn by sharp teeth. He picked it up, though its weight was almost too much for his feeble fingers. Bill had carried it to the last. Ha! ha! He would have the laugh on Bill. He would survive and carry it to the ship in the shining sea. His mirth was hoarse and ghastly, like a raven's croak, and the sick wolf joined him, howling lugubriously. The man ceased suddenly. How could he have the laugh on Bill if that were Bill; if those bones, so pinky-white and clean, were Bill?

He turned away. Well, Bill had deserted him; but he would not take the gold, nor would he suck Bill's bones. Bill would have, though, had it been the other way around, he mused as he staggered on.

He came to a pool of water. Stooping over in quest of minnows, he jerked his head back as though he had been stung. He had caught sight of his reflected face. So horrible was it that sensibility awoke long enough to be shocked. There were three minnows in the pool, which was too large to drain; and after several ineffectual attempts to catch them in the tin bucket he forbore. He was afraid, because of his great weakness, that he might fall in and drown. It was for this reason that he did not trust himself to the river astride one of the many drift-logs which lined its sand-spits.

That day he decreased the distance between him and the ship by three miles; the next day by two—for he was crawling now as Bill had crawled; and the end of the fifth day found the ship still seven miles away and him unable to make even a mile a day. Still the Indian Summer held on, and he continued to crawl and faint, turn and turn about; and ever the sick wolf coughed and wheezed at his heels. His knees had become raw meat like his feet, and though he padded them with the shirt from his back it was a red track he left behind him on the moss and stones. Once, glancing back, he saw the wolf licking hungrily his bleeding trail, and he saw sharply what his own end might be—unless—unless he could get the wolf. Then began as grim a tragedy of existence as was ever played—a sick man that crawled, a sick wolf that limped, two creatures dragging their dying carcasses across the desolation and hunting each other's lives.

Had it been a well wolf, it would not have mattered so much to the man; but the thought of going to feed the maw of that loathsome and all but dead thing was repugnant to him. He was finicky. His mind had begun to wander again, and to be perplexed by hallucinations, while his lucid intervals grew rarer and shorter.

He was awakened once from a faint by a wheeze close in his ear. The wolf leaped lamely back, losing its footing and falling in its weakness. It was ludicrous, but he was not amused. Nor was he even afraid. He was too far gone for that. But his mind was for the moment clear, and he lay and considered. The ship was no more than four miles away. He could see it quite distinctly when he rubbed the mists out of his eyes, and he could see the white sail of a small boat cutting the water of the shining sea. But he could never crawl those four miles. He knew that, and was very calm in the knowledge. He knew that he could not crawl half a mile. And yet he wanted to live. It was unreasonable that he should die after all he had undergone. Fate asked too much of him. And, dying, he declined to die. It was stark madness, perhaps, but in the very grip of Death he defied Death and refused to die.

He closed his eyes and composed himself with infinite precaution. He steeled himself to keep

above the suffocating languor that lapped like a rising tide through all the wells of his being. It was
very like a sea, this deadly languor, that rose and rose
and drowned his consciousness bit by bit. Sometimes
he was all but submerged, swimming through obliv-
ion with a faltering stroke; and again, by some
strange alchemy of soul, he would find another shred
of will and strike out more strongly.

Without movement he lay on his back, and he
could hear, slowly drawing near and nearer, the
wheezing intake and output of the sick wolf's breath.
It drew closer, ever closer, through an infinitude of
time, and he did not move. It was at his ear. The
harsh dry tongue grated like sandpaper against his
cheek. His hands shot out—or at least he willed them
to shoot out. The fingers were curved like talons, but
they closed on empty air. Swiftness and certitude
require strength, and the man had not this strength.

The patience of the wolf was terrible. The man's
patience was no less terrible. For half a day he lay
motionless, fighting off unconsciousness and waiting
for the thing that was to feed upon him and upon
which he wished to feed. Sometimes the languid sea
rose over him and he dreamed long dreams; but ever
through it all, waking and dreaming, he waited for
the wheezing breath and the harsh caress of the
tongue.

He did not hear the breath, and he slipped slowly
from some dream to the feel of the tongue along his

hand. He waited. The fangs pressed softly; the pressure increased; the wolf was exerting its last strength in an effort to sink teeth in the food for which it had waited so long. But the man had waited long, and the lacerated hand closed on the jaw. Slowly, while the wolf struggled feebly and the hand clutched feebly, the other hand crept across to a grip. Five minutes later the whole weight of the man's body was on top of the wolf. The hands had not sufficient strength to choke the wolf, but the face of the man was pressed close to the throat of the wolf and the mouth of the man was full of hair. At the end of half an hour the man was aware of a warm trickle in his throat. It was not pleasant. It was like molten lead being forced into his stomach, and it was forced by his will alone. Later the man rolled over on his back and slept.

There were some members of a scientific expedition on the whale-ship *Bedford*. From the deck they remarked a strange object on the shore. It was moving down the beach toward the water. They were unable to classify it, and, being scientific men, they climbed into the whale-boat alongside and went ashore to see. And they saw something that was alive but which could hardly be called a man. It was blind, unconscious. It squirmed along the ground like some

monstrous worm. Most of its efforts were ineffectual, but it was persistent, and it writhed and twisted
and went ahead perhaps a score of feet an hour.

Three weeks afterward the man lay in a bunk on the
whale-ship *Bedford,* and with tears streaming down
his wasted cheeks told who he was and what he had
undergone. He also babbled incoherently of his
mother, of sunny Southern California, and a home
among the orange groves and flowers.

The days were not many after that when he sat at
table with the scientific men and ship's officers. He
gloated over the spectacle of so much food, watching it anxiously as it went into the mouths of others. With the disappearance of each mouthful an
expression of deep regret came into his eyes. He was
quite sane, yet he hated those men at meal-time. He
was haunted by a fear that the food would not last.
He inquired of the cook, the cabin-boy, the captain,
concerning the food stores. They reassured him
countless times; but he could not believe them, and
pried cunningly about the lazarette to see with his
own eyes.

It was noticed that the man was getting fat. He
grew stouter with each day. The scientific men
shook their heads and theorized. They limited the

man at his meals, but still his girth increased and he swelled prodigiously under his shirt.

The sailors grinned. They knew. And when the scientific men set a watch on the man, they knew too. They saw him slouch for'ard after breakfast, and, like a mendicant, with outstretched palm, accost a sailor. The sailor grinned and passed him a fragment of sea biscuit. He clutched it avariciously, looked at it as a miser looks at gold, and thrust it into his shirt bosom. Similar were the donations from other grinning sailors.

The scientific men were discreet. They let him alone. But they privily examined his bunk. It was lined with hardtack; the mattress was stuffed with hardtack; every nook and cranny was filled with hardtack. Yet he was sane. He was taking precautions against another possible famine—that was all. He would recover from it, the scientific men said, and he did, ere the *Bedford*'s anchor rumbled down in San Francisco Bay.

Shipwreck of the Whaleship Essex

OWEN CHASE

To make this selection more enjoyable to the reader, I am quoting my own introduction to the story from the book I edited called The Greatest Survival Stories Ever Told:

If you've ever been inclined to think that the images of the great white whale Moby-Dick taking out the whaleship Pequod with a slam-dunk move seemed a bit far-fetched, you might owe Mister Herman Melville an apology. As subsequent history has revealed, it seems old Herm got the original germ of the idea for his great novel from real life— a Nantucket whaleship named Essex *that got the deep six in an attack by a sperm whale in the Pacific. Twenty men survived the sinking of the* Essex *by taking to three open lifeboats, but only eight of these shipwreck survivors lived to tell the story of what happened during the sea journey. For three months and three thousand miles the whaling men suffered the worst ordeals of hunger and thirst imaginable in their epic journey for survival. One of the boats was lost at sea, and eventually the other two became separated. Before they reached the haven of rescue, the survivors resorted to cannibalism to sustain life.*

Owen Chase was the first mate of the Essex *and was one of the eight survivors. Twenty years after his narrative of the ordeal was originally published, Herman Melville borrowed a copy from Chase's son and read it while at sea on a whaling vessel in the South Pacific. "The reading of the wondrous story upon the landless sea and very close to the very latitude of the shipwreck had a surprising effect on me," Melville later wrote. He actually started writing* Moby-Dick *eight years after reading Chase's book.*

This excerpt of the Owen Chase narrative is from the edition published by The Lyons Press in 1999, with an introduction by Tim Cahill. Two separate sections are excerpted. The first describes the actual attack of the whale, and the crew taking to the boats on November 20, 1820. As the second part of the excerpt begins, the whalers are struggling to stay alive in Henderson Island deep in the South Pacific, far west of Easter Island and actually not too far from Pitcairn Island, famous as the last stop of the H.M.S. Bounty. *When the men arrived on the island on December 20, they thought their prayers had been answered, but subsequent exploration has shown that the place is virtually barren of food and water. Thoughts of resuming their dreadful ocean voyage are rampant.*

I have not been able to recur to the scenes which are now to become the subject of description, although a considerable time has elapsed, without feeling a mingled emotion of horror and astonishment at the almost incredible destiny that has preserved me and my surviving companions from a terrible death. Frequently, in my reflections on the subject, even after this lapse of time, I find myself shedding tears of gratitude for our deliverance, and blessing God, by whose divine aid and protection we were conducted through a series of unparalleled suffering and distress, and restored to the bosoms of our families and friends. There is no knowing what a stretch of pain and misery the human mind is capable of contemplating, when it is wrought upon by the anxieties of preservation; nor what pangs and weaknesses the body is able to endure, until they are visited upon it; and when at last deliverance comes, when the dream of hope is realized, unspeakable gratitude takes   possession of the soul, and tears of joy choke the utterance. We require to be taught in the school of some signal suffering, privation, and despair, the great lessons of constant dependence upon an almighty forbearance and mercy. In the midst of the wide ocean, at night, when the sight of the heavens was shut out, and the dark tempest came upon us, then it was that we felt ourselves ready to exclaim, "Heaven have mercy upon us, for nought but that can save us now." But I proceed to the recital.—On the 20th of November (cruising in latitude 0°40′S., longitude 119°0′W.), a shoal of whales was discovered off the lee-bow. The weather at this time was extremely fine and clear, and it was about 8 o'clock in the morning that the man at the mast-head gave the usual cry of, "There she blows." The ship was immediately put away, and we ran down in the direction for them. When we had got within half a mile of the place where they were observed, all our boats were lowered down, manned, and we started in pursuit of them. The ship, in the mean-time, was brought to the wind, and the main-top-sail hove aback, to wait for us. I had the harpoon in the second boat; the captain preceded me in the first. When I arrived at the spot where we calculated they were, nothing was at first to be seen. We lay on our oars in anxious expectation of discovering them come up somewhere near us. Presently one rose, and spouted a short distance ahead of my boat; I made all speed towards it, came up with, and struck it; feeling the harpoon in him, he threw himself, in agony, over towards the boat (which at that time was up along-side of him), and, giving a severe blow with his tail, struck the boat near the edge of the water, amid-ships, and stove a hole in her. I immediately took up the boat hatchet, and cut the line, to disengage the boat from the whale, which by this time was run-

ning off with great velocity. I succeeded in getting
clear of him, with the loss of the harpoon and line;
and finding the water to pour fast in the boat, I
hastily stuffed three or four of our jackets in the
hole, ordered one man to keep constantly bailing,
and the rest to pull immediately for the ship; we succeeded in keeping the boat free, and shortly gained
the ship. The captain and the second mate, in the
other two boats, kept up the pursuit, and soon struck
another whale. They being at this time a considerable distance to leeward, I went forward, braced
around the mainyard, and put the ship off in a direction for them; the boat which had been stove was
immediately hoisted in, and after examining the
hole, I found that I could, by nailing a piece of canvas over it, get her ready to join in a fresh pursuit,
sooner than by lowering down the other remaining
boat which belonged to the ship. I accordingly
turned her over upon the quarter, and was in the act
of nailing on the canvas, when I observed a very
large spermaceti whale, as well as I could judge
about eighty-five feet in length; he broke water
about twenty rods off our weather-bow, and was
lying quietly, with his head in a direction for the
ship. He spouted two or three times, and then disappeared. In less than two or three seconds he came up
again, about the length of the ship off, and made
directly for us, at the rate of about three knots. The
ship was then going with about the same velocity.

His appearance and attitude gave us at first no alarm; but while I stood watching his movements, and observing him but a ship's length off, coming down for us with great celerity, I involuntarily ordered the boy at the helm to put it hard up; intending to sheer off and avoid him. The words were scarcely out of my mouth, before he came down upon us with full speed, and struck the ship with his head, just forward of the fore-chains*; he gave us such an appalling and tremendous jar, as nearly threw us all on our faces. The ship brought up as suddenly and violently as if she had struck a rock, and trembled for a few seconds like a leaf. We looked at each other with perfect amazement, deprived almost of the power of speech. Many minutes elapsed before we were able to realize the dreadful accident; during which time he passed under the ship, grazing her keel as he went along, came up alongside of her to leeward, and lay on the top of the water (apparently stunned with the violence of the blow) for the space of a minute; he then suddenly started off, in a direction to leeward. After a few moments reflection, and recovering, in some measure, from the sudden consternation that had seized us, I of course concluded that he had stove a hole in the ship, and that it would be necessary to set the pumps going. Accordingly they were rigged, but had not been in operation more than one

*Between the platform where the foremast shrouds were secured and the bow of the ship.

minute before I perceived the head of the ship to be
gradually settling down in the water; I then ordered
the signal to be set for the other boats, which, scarcely had I dispatched, before I again discovered the
whale, apparently in convulsions, on the top of the
water, about one hundred rods to leeward. He was
enveloped in the foam of the sea, that his continual
and violent thrashing about in the water had created
around him, and I could distinctly see him smite his
jaws together, as if distracted with rage and fury. He
remained a short time in this situation, and then
started off with great velocity, across the bows of the
ship, to windward. By this time the ship had settled
down a considerable distance in the water, and I gave
her up for lost. I, however, ordered the pumps to be
kept constantly going, and endeavoured to collect
my thoughts for the occasion. I turned to the boats,
two of which we then had with the ship, with an
intention of clearing them away, and getting all
things ready to embark in them, if there should be
no other resource left; and while my attention was
thus engaged for a moment, I was aroused with the
cry of a man at the hatchway, "Here he is—he is
making for us again." I turned around, and saw him
about one hundred rods directly ahead of us,
coming down apparently with twice his ordinary
speed, and to me at that moment, it appeared with
tenfold fury and vengeance in his aspect. The surf
flew in all directions about him, and his course

towards us was marked by a white foam of a rod in width, which he made with the continual violent thrashing of his tail; his head was about half out of water, and in that way he came upon, and again struck the ship. I was in hopes when I descried him making for us, that by a dexterous movement of putting the ship away immediately, I should be able to cross the line of his approach, before he could get up to us, and thus avoid what I knew, if he should strike us again, would prove our inevitable destruction. I bawled out to the helmsman, "Hard up!" but she had not fallen off more than a point, before we took the second shock. I should judge the speed of the ship to have been at this time about three knots, and that of the whale about six. He struck her to windward, directly under the cathead,* and completely stove in her bows. He passed under the ship again, went off to leeward, and we saw no more of him. Our situation at this juncture can be more readily imagined than described. The shock to our feelings was such, as I am sure none can have an adequate conception of that were not there: the misfortune befell us at a moment when we least dreamt of any accident; and from the pleasing anticipations we had formed, of realizing the certain profits of our labour, we were dejected by a sudden, most mysterious, and

---

* A projecting timber near the bow, to which the anchor is hoisted.

overwhelming calamity. Not a moment, however, was to be lost in endeavouring to provide for the extremity to which it was now certain we were reduced. We were more than a thousand miles from the nearest land, and with nothing but a light open boat, as the resource of safety for myself and companions. I ordered the men to cease pumping, and every one to provide for himself; seizing a hatchet at the same time, I cut away the lashings of the spare boat, which lay bottom up across two spars directly over the quarter deck, and cried out to those near me to take her as she came down. They did so accordingly, and bore her on their shoulders as far as the waist of the ship. The steward had in the meantime gone down into the cabin twice, and saved two quadrants, two practical navigators,* and the captain's trunk and mine; all which were hastily thrown into the boat, as she lay on the deck, with the two compasses which I snatched from the binnacle.+ He attempted to descend again; but the water by this time had rushed in, and he returned without being able to effect his purpose. By the time we had got the boat to the waist, the ship had filled with water, and was going down on her beam-ends: we shoved our

---

*Probably Nathaniel Bowditch's *New American Practical Navigator;* the fourth edition was issued in 1817.

+A non-magnetic stand for the compass.

boat as quickly as possible from the plank-shear*
into the water, all hands jumping in her at the same
time, and launched off clear of the ship. We were
scarcely two boat lengths distant from her, when she
fell over to windward, and settled down in the water.

Amazement and despair now wholly took possession of us. We contemplated the frightful situation
the ship lay in, and thought with horror upon the
sudden and dreadful calamity that had overtaken us.
We looked upon each other, as if to gather some
consolatory sensation from an interchange of senti-
ments, but every countenance was marked with the
paleness of despair. Not a word was spoken for several minutes by any of us; all appeared to be bound
in a spell of stupid consternation; and from the time
we were first attacked by the whale, to the period of
the fall of the ship, and of our leaving her in the
boat, more than ten minutes could not certainly
have elapsed! God only knows in what way, or by
what means, we were enabled to accomplish in that
short time what we did; the cutting away and trans-
porting the boat from where she was deposited
would of itself, in ordinary circumstances, have consumed as much time as that, if the whole ship's crew
had been employed in it. My companions had not
saved a single article but what they had on their
backs; but to me it was a source of infinite satisfac-

*A timber around a vessel's hull at deck line.

tion, if any such could be gathered from the horrors of our gloomy situation, that we had been fortunate enough to have preserved our compasses, navigators, and quadrants. After the first shock of my feelings was over, I enthusiastically contemplated them as the probable instruments of our salvation; without them all would have been dark and hopeless. Gracious God! what a picture of distress and suffering now presented itself to my imagination. The crew of the ship were saved, consisting of twenty human souls. All that remained to conduct these twenty beings through the stormy terrors of the ocean, perhaps many thousand miles, were three open light boats. The prospect of obtaining any provisions or water from the ship, to subsist upon during the time, was at least now doubtful. How many long and watchful nights, thought I, are to be passed? How many tedious days of partial starvation are to be endured, before the least relief or mitigation of our sufferings can be reasonably anticipated. We lay at this time in our boat, about two ship lengths off from the wreck, in perfect silence, calmly contemplating her situation, and absorbed in our own melancholy reflections, when the other boats were discovered rowing up to us. They had but shortly before discovered that some accident had befallen us, but of the nature of which they were entirely ignorant. The sudden and mysterious disappearance of the ship was first discovered by the boat-steerer in the captain's boat, and with a horror-struck countenance and voice, he suddenly exclaimed, "Oh, my God! where is the ship?" Their operations upon this were instantly suspended, and a general cry of horror and despair burst from the lips of every man, as their looks were directed for her, in vain, over every part of the ocean. They immediately made all haste towards us. The captain's boat was the first that reached us. He stopped about a boat's length off, but had no power to utter a single syllable: he was so completely overpowered with the spectacle before him that he sat down in his boat, pale and speechless. I could scarcely recognise his countenance, he appeared to be so much altered, awed, and overcome with the oppression of his feelings, and the dreadful reality that lay before him. He was in a short time however enabled to address the inquiry to me, "My God, Mr. Chase, what is the matter?" I answered, "We have been stove by a whale." I then briefly told him the story. After a few moment's reflection he observed that we must cut away her masts, and endeavour to get something out of her to eat. Our thoughts were now all accordingly bent on endeavours to save from the wreck whatever we might possibly want, and for this purpose we rowed up and got on to her. Search was made for every means of gaining access to her hold; and for this purpose the lanyards were cut loose, and with our hatchets we commenced to cut away the masts, that she might right up again, and enable us to scuttle her decks. In doing which we were occupied about three quarters of an hour, owing to our having no axes, nor indeed any other instruments, but the small hatchets belonging to the boat. After her masts were gone she came up about two-thirds of the way upon an even keel. While we were employed about the masts the captain took his quadrant, shoved off from the ship, and got an observation. We found ourselves in latitude 0° 40'S., longitude 119°W. We now commenced to cut a hole through the planks, directly above two large casks of bread, which most fortunately were between decks, in the waist of the ship, and which being in the upper side, when she upset, we had strong hopes was not wet. It turned out according to our wishes, and from these casks we obtained six hundred pounds of hard bread. Other parts of the deck were then scuttled, and we got without difficulty as much fresh water as we dared to take in the boats, so that each was supplied with about sixty-five gallons; we got also from one of the lockers a musket, a small canister of powder, a couple of files, two rasps, about two pounds of boat nails, and a few turtles. In the afternoon the wind came on to blow a strong breeze; and having obtained every thing that occurred to us could then be got out, we began to make arrangements for our safety during the night. A boat's line was made fast to the ship, and to the other end of it one of the boats was moored, at about fifty fathoms to leeward; another boat was then attached to the first one, about eight fathoms astern; and the third boat, the like distance astern of her. Night came on just as we had finished our operations; and such a night as it was to us! so full of feverish and distracting inquietude, that we were deprived entirely of rest. The wreck was constantly before my eyes. I could not, by any effort, chase away the horrors of the preceding day from my mind: they haunted me the live-long night. My companions—some of them were like sick women; they had no idea of the extent of their deplorable situation. One or two slept unconcernedly, while others wasted the night in unavailing murmurs. I now had full leisure to examine, with some degree of coolness, the dreadful circumstances of our disaster. The scenes of yesterday passed in such quick succession in my mind that it was not until after many hours of severe reflection that I was able to discard the idea of the catastrophe as a dream. Alas! it was one from which there was no awaking; it was too certainly true, that but yesterday we had existed as it were, and in one short moment had been cut off from all the hopes and prospects of the living! I have no language to paint out the horrors of our situation. To shed tears was indeed altogether unavailing, and withal unmanly; yet I was not able to deny myself the relief they served to afford me. After several hours of idle sorrow and repining I began to reflect upon the accident, and endeavoured to realize by what unaccountable destiny or design (which I could not at first determine) this sudden and most deadly attack had been made upon us: by an animal, too, never before suspected of premeditated violence, and proverbial for its insensibility and inoffensiveness. Every fact seemed to warrant me in concluding that it was anything but chance which directed his operations; he made two several attacks upon the ship, at a short interval between them, both of which, according to their direction, were calculated to do us the most injury, by being made ahead, and thereby combining the speed of the two objects for the shock; to effect which, the exact manoeuvres which he made were necessary. His aspect was most horrible, and such as indicated resentment and fury. He came directly from the shoal which we had just before entered, and in which we had struck three of his companions, as if fired with revenge for their sufferings. But to this it may be observed, that the mode of fighting which they always adopt is either with repeated strokes of their tails, or snapping of their jaws together; and that a case, precisely similar to this one, has never been heard of amongst the oldest and most experienced whalers. To this I would answer, that the structure and strength of the whale's head is admirably designed for this mode of attack; the most prominent part of which is almost as hard and as tough as iron; indeed, I can compare it to nothing else but the inside of a horse's hoof, upon which a lance or harpoon would not make the slightest impression. The eyes and ears are removed nearly one-third the length of the whole fish, from the front part of the head, and are not in the least degree endangered in this mode of attack. At all events, the whole circumstances taken together, all happening before my own eyes, and producing, at the time, impressions in my mind of decided, calculating mischief on the part of the whale (many of which impressions I cannot now recall) induce me to be satisfied that I am correct in my opinion. It is certainly, in all its bearings, a hitherto unheard of circumstance, and constitutes, perhaps, the most extraordinary one in the annals of the fishery.

As this section begins, the survivors of the Essex's *sinking are on Henderson Island, where they landed on Dec. 20, 1820. At this point in the narrative, it is obvious to them that the landfall they thought would be their salvation for food and water is not unlike a desert wasteland. They realize they will have to sail on . . . and keep hoping.*

December 23rd. At 11 o'clock A.M., we again visited our spring: the tide had fallen to about a foot below it, and we were able to procure, before it rose again, about twenty gallons of water. It was at first a little brackish, but soon became fresh, from the constant

supply from the rock and the departure of the sea.
Our observations this morning tended to give us
every confidence in its quantity and quality, and we,
therefore, rested perfectly easy in our minds on the
subject, and commenced to make further discoveries
about the island. Each man sought for his own daily
living, on whatsoever the mountains, the shore, or the
sea, could furnish him with; and every day, during
our stay there, the whole time was employed in
roving about for food. We found, however, on the
twenty-fourth, that we had picked up, on the island,
every thing that could be got at, in the way of sustenance; and, much to our surprise, some of the men
came in at night and complained of not having gotten sufficient during the day to satisfy the cravings of
their stomachs. Every accessible part of the mountain, contiguous to us, or within the reach of our
weak enterprise, was already ransacked, for birds' eggs
and grass, and was rifled of all that they contained: so
that we began to entertain serious apprehensions that
we should not be able to live long here; at any rate,
with the view of being prepared, as well as possible,
should necessity at any time oblige us to quit it, we
commenced, on the twenty-fourth, to repair our
boats, and continued to work upon them all that and
the succeeding day. We were enabled to do this, with
much facility, by drawing them up and turning them
over on the beach, working by spells of two or three
hours at a time, and then leaving off to seek for food.

We procured our water daily, when the tide would leave the shore: but on the evening of the twenty-fifth, found that a fruitless search for nourishment had not repaid us for the labors of a whole day. There was no one thing on the island upon which we could in the least degree rely, except the peppergrass, and of that the supply was precarious, and not much relished without some other food. Our situation here, therefore, now became worse than it would have been in our boats on the ocean; because, in the latter case, we should be still making some progress towards the land, while our provisions lasted, and the chance of falling in with some vessel be considerably increased. It was certain that we ought not to remain here unless upon the strongest assurances in our own minds, of sufficient sustenance, and that, too, in regular supplies, that might be depended upon. After much conversation amongst us on this subject, and again examining our navigators, it was finally concluded to set sail for Easter Island, which we found to be E.S.E. from us in latitude 27° 9'S., longitude 109° 35'W. All we knew of this island was that it existed as laid down in the books; but of its extent, productions, or inhabitants, if any, we were entirely ignorant; at any rate, it was nearer by eight hundred and fifty miles to the coast, and could not be worse in its productions than the one we were about leaving.

The twenty-sixth of December was wholly employed in preparations for our departure; our boats were hauled down to the vicinity of the spring, and our casks, and everything else that would contain it, filled with water.

There had been considerable talk between three of our companions about their remaining on this island, and taking their chance both for a living, and an escape from it; and as the time drew near at which we were to leave, they made up their minds to stay behind. The rest of us could make no objection to their plan, as it lessened the load of our boats, allowed us their share of the provisions, and the probability of their being able to sustain themselves on the island was much stronger than that of our reaching the mainland. Should we, however, ever arrive safely, it would become our duty, and we so assured them, to give information of their situation, and make every effort to procure their removal from thence; which we accordingly afterwards did.

Their names were William Wright of Barnstable, Massachusetts, Thomas Chapple of Plymouth, England, and Seth Weeks of the former place. They had begun, before we came away, to construct a sort of habitation, composed of the branches of trees, and we left with them every little article that could be spared from the boats. It was their intention to build a considerable dwelling, that would protect them from the rains, as soon as time and materials could be provided. The captain wrote letters, to be left on the island, giving information of the fate of the ship, and that of our own; and stating that we had set out to reach Easter Island, with further particulars, intended to give notice (should our fellow sufferers die there, and the place be ever visited by any vessel) of our misfortunes. These letters were put in a tin case, enclosed in a small wooden box, and nailed to a tree, on the west side of the island, near our landing place. We had observed, some days previously, the name of a ship, *The Elizabeth*, cut out in the bark of this tree, which rendered it indubitable that one of that name had once touched here. There was, however, no date to it, or anything else, by which any further particulars could be made out.

December 27th. I went, before we set sail this morning, and procured for each boat a flat stone, and two armfuls of wood, with which to make a fire in our boats, should it become afterwards necessary in the further prosecution of our voyage; as we calculated we might catch a fish, or a bird, and in that case be provided with the means of cooking it; otherwise, from the intense heat of the weather, we knew they could not be preserved from spoiling. At ten o'clock A.M., the tide having risen far enough to allow our boats to float over the rocks, we made all sail, and steered around the island, for the purpose of making a little further observation, which would not detain us any time, and might be productive of some unexpected good fortune. Before we started we missed our three companions, and found they had not come down, either to assist us to get off, nor to take any kind of leave of us. I walked up the beach towards their rude dwelling, and informed them that we were then about to set sail, and should probably never see them more. They seemed to be very much affected, and one of them shed tears. They wished us to write to their relations, should Providence safely direct us again to our homes, and said but little else. They had every confidence in being able to procure a subsistence there as long as they remained: and, finding them ill at heart about taking any leave of us, I hastily bid them "good-bye," hoped they would do well, and came away. They followed me with their eyes until I was out of sight, and I never saw more of them.

On the N.W. side of the island we perceived a fine white beach, on which we imagined we might land, and in a short time ascertain if any further useful discoveries could be effected, or any addition made to our stock of provisions; and having set ashore five or six of the men for this purpose, the rest of us shoved off the boats and commenced fishing. We saw a number of sharks, but all efforts to take them proved ineffectual; and we got but a few small fish, about the size of a mackerel, which we divided amongst us. In this business we were occupied for the remainder of the day, until six o'clock in the afternoon, when the men, having returned to the shore from their search in the mountains, brought a few birds, and we again set sail and steered directly for Easter Island. During that night, after we had got quite clear of the land, we had a fine strong breeze from the N.W.; we kept our fires going, and cooked our fish and birds, and felt our situation as comfortable as could be expected. We continued on our course, consuming our provisions and water as sparingly as possible, without any material incident, until the thirtieth, when the wind hauled out E.S.E. directly ahead, and so continued until the thirty-first, when it again came to the northward, and we resumed our course.

On the third of January we experienced heavy squalls from the W.S.W. accompanied with dreadful thunder and lightning, that threw a gloomy and cheerless aspect over the ocean, and incited a recurrence of some of those heavy and desponding moments that we had before experienced. We commenced from Ducie's Island to keep a regular reckoning, by which, on the fourth of January, we found we had got to the southward of Easter Island, and the wind prevailing E.N.E. we should not be able to get on to the eastward, so as to reach it. Our birds and fish were all now consumed, and we had begun again upon our short allowance of bread. It was necessary, in this state of things, to change our determination of going to Easter Island, and shape our course in some other direction, where the wind would allow of our going. We had but little hesitation in concluding, therefore, to steer for the island of Juan

Fernandez, which lay about E.S.E. from us, distant two thousand five hundred miles. We bent our course accordingly towards it, having for the two succeeding days very light winds, and suffering excessively from the intense heat of the sun. The seventh brought us a change of wind to the northward, and at twelve o'clock we found ourselves in latitude 30° 18'S., longitude 117° 29'W. We continued to make what progress we could to the eastward.

January 10th. Matthew P. Joy, the second mate, had suffered from debility, and the privations we had experienced, much beyond any of the rest of us, and was on the eighth removed to the captain's boat, under the impression that he would be more comfortable there, and more attention and pains be bestowed in nursing and endeavouring to comfort him. This day being calm, he manifested a desire to be taken back again; but at 4 o'clock in the afternoon, after having been, according to his wishes, placed in his own boat, he died very suddenly after his removal. On the eleventh, at six o'clock in the morning, we sewed him up in his clothes, tied a large stone to his feet, and, having brought all the boats to, consigned him in a solemn manner to the ocean. This man did not die of absolute starvation, although his end was no doubt very much hastened by his sufferings. He had a weak and sickly constitution, and complained of being unwell the whole voyage. It was an incident, however, which threw a gloom over our feelings for many days. In consequence of his death, one man from the captain's boat was placed in that from which he died, to supply his place, and we stood away again on our course.

On the 12th of January we had the wind from the N.W. which commenced in the morning, and came on to blow before night a perfect gale. We were obliged to take in all sail and run before the wind. Flashes of lightning were quick and vivid, and the rain came down in cataracts. As, however, the gale blew us fairly on our course, and our speed being great during the day, we derived, I may say, even pleasure from the uncomfortableness and fury of the storm. We were apprehensive that in the darkness of this night we should be separated, and made arrangements, each boat to keep an E.S.E. course all night. About eleven o'clock my boat being ahead a short distance of the others, I turned my head back, as I was in the habit of doing every minute, and neither of the others were to be seen. It was blowing and raining at this time as if the heavens were separating, and I knew not hardly at the moment what to do. I hove my boat to the wind, and lay drifting about an hour, expecting every moment they would come up with me, but not seeing anything of them, I put away again, and stood on the course agreed upon, with strong hopes that daylight would enable me to discover them again. When the morning dawned, in vain did we look over every part of the ocean for our companions; they were gone! and we saw no more of them afterwards. It was folly to repine at the circumstance; it could neither be remedied, nor could sorrow secure their return; but it was impossible to prevent ourselves feeling all the poignancy and bitterness that characterizes the separation of men who have long suffered in each other's company, and whose interests and feelings fate had so closely linked together. By our observation, we separated in latitude 32° 16'S., longitude 112° 20'W. For many days after this accident, our progress was attended with dull and melancholy reflections. We had lost the cheering of each other's faces, that which strange as it is, we so much required in both our mental and bodily distresses. The 14th January proved another very squally and rainy day. We had now been nineteen days from the island, and had only made a distance of about 900 miles: necessity began to whisper us, that still further reduction of our allowance must take place, or we must abandon altogether the hopes of reaching the land, and rely wholly on the chance of being taken up by a vessel. But how to reduce the daily quantity of food, with any regard to life itself, was a question of the utmost consequence. Upon our first leaving the wreck, the demands of the stomach had been circumscribed to the smallest possible compass; and subsequently before reaching the island, a diminution had taken place of nearly one-half; and it was now, from a reasonable calculation, become necessary even to curtail that at least one-half; which must, in a short time, reduce us to mere skeletons again. We had a full allowance of water, but it only served to contribute to our debility; our bodies deriving but the scanty support which an ounce and a half of bread for each man afforded. It required a great effort to bring matters to this dreadful alternative, either to feed our bodies and our hopes a little longer, or in the agonies of hunger to seize upon and devour our provisions, and coolly await the approach of death.

We were as yet, just able to move about in our boats, and slowly perform the necessary labors appertaining to her; but we were fast wasting away with the relaxing effects of the water, and we daily almost perished under the torrid rays of a meridian sun; to escape which, we would lie down in the bottom of the boat, cover ourselves over with the sails, and abandon her to the mercy of the waves. Upon attempting to rise again, the blood would rush into the head, and an intoxicating blindness come over us, almost to occasion our suddenly falling down again. A slight interest was still kept up in our minds by the distant hopes of yet meeting with the other boats, but it was never realized. An accident occurred at night, which gave me a great cause of uneasiness, and led me to an unpleasant rumination upon the probable consequences of a repetition of it. I had laid down in the boat without taking the usual precaution of securing the lid of the provision chest, as I was accustomed to do, when one of the white men awoke me, and informed me that one of the blacks had taken some bread from it. I felt at the moment the highest indignation and resentment at such conduct in any of our crew and immediately took my pistol in my hand, and charged him if he had taken any, to give it up without the least hesitation, or I should instantly shoot him!—He became at once very much alarmed, and trembling, confessed the fact, pleading the hard necessity that urged him to it: he appeared to be very penitent for his crime, and earnestly swore that he would never be guilty of it again. I could not find it in my soul to extend towards him the least severity on this account, however much, according to the strict imposition which we felt upon ourselves, it might demand it. This was the first infraction; and the security of our lives, our hopes of redemption from our sufferings, loudly called for a prompt and signal punishment; but every humane feeling of nature plead in his behalf, and he was permitted to escape, with the solemn injunction that a repetition of the same offence would cost him his life.

I had almost determined upon this occurrence to divide our provisions, and give to each man his share of the whole stock; and should have done so in the height of my resentment had it not been for the reflection that some might, by imprudence, be tempted to go beyond the daily allowance, or consume it all at once, and bring on a premature weakness or starvation: this would of course disable them for the duties of the boat, and reduce our chances of safety and deliverance.

On the 15th of January, at night, a very large shark was observed swimming about us in a most ravenous manner, making attempts every now and then upon different parts of the boat, as if he would devour the very wood with hunger; he came several times and snapped at the steering oar, and even the stern-post. We tried in vain to stab him with a lance, but we were so weak as not to be able to make any impression upon his hard skin; he was so much larger than an ordinary one, and manifested such a fearless malignity, as to make us afraid of him; and our utmost efforts, which were at first directed to kill him for prey, became in the end self-defense. Baffled however in all his hungry attempts upon us, he shortly made off.

On the 16th of January, we were surrounded with porpoises in great numbers, that followed us nearly an hour, and which also defied all manoeuvres to catch them. The 17th and 18th proved to be calm; and the distresses of a cheerless prospect and a burning hot sun were again visited upon our devoted heads.

We began to think that Divine Providence had abandoned us at last; and it was but an unavailing effort to endeavour to prolong a now tedious existence.

Horrible were the feelings that took possession of us!—The contemplation of a death of agony and torment, refined by the most dreadful and distressing reflections, absolutely prostrated both body and soul. There was not a hope now remaining to us but that which was derived from a sense of the mercies of our Creator. The night of the 18th was a despairing era in our sufferings; our minds were wrought up to the highest pitch of dread and apprehension for our fate, and all in them was dark, gloomy, and confused. About 8 o'clock, the terrible noise of whale spouts near us sounded in our ears: we could distinctly hear the furious thrashing of their tails in the water, and our weak minds pictured out their appalling and hideous aspects. One of my companions, the black man, took an immediate fright, and solicited me to take out the oars, and endeavour to get away from them. I consented to his using any means for that purpose; but alas! it was wholly out of our power to raise a single arm in our own defense. Two or three of the whales came down near us, and went swiftly off across our stern, blowing and spouting at a terrible rate; they, however, after an hour or two disappeared, and we saw no more of them. The next day, the 19th of January, we had extremely boisterous weather, with rain, heavy thunder and lightning, which reduced us again to the necessity of taking in all sail and lying to. The wind blew from every point of the compass within the twenty-four hours, and at last towards the next morning settled at E.N.E. a strong breeze.

January 20th. The black man, Richard Peterson, manifested today symptoms of a speedy dissolution; he had been lying between the seats in the boat, utterly dispirited and broken down, without being able to do the least duty, or hardly to place his hand to his head for the last three days, and had this morning made up his mind to die rather than endure further misery: he refused his allowance; said he was sensible of his approaching end, and was perfectly ready to die: in a few minutes he became speechless, the breath appeared to be leaving his body without producing the least pain, and at four o'clock he was gone. I had two days previously conversations with him on the subject of religion on which he reasoned very sensibly, and with much composure; and begged me to let his wife know his fate, if ever I reached home in safety. The next morning we committed him to the sea, in latitude 35° 07'S., longitude 105° 46'W. The wind prevailed to the eastward until the 24th of January, when it again fell calm. We were now in a most wretched and sinking state of debility, hardly able to crawl around the boat, and possessing but strength enough to convey our scanty morsel to our mouths. When I perceived this morning that it was calm, my fortitude almost forsook me. I thought to suffer another scorching day, like the last we had experienced, would close before night the scene of our miseries; and I felt many a despairing moment that day, that had well nigh proved fatal. It required an effort to look calmly forward, and contemplate what was yet in store for us, beyond what I felt I was capable of making; and what is was that buoyed me above all the terrors which surrounded us, God alone knows. Our ounce and a half of bread, which was to serve us all day, was in some cases greedily devoured, as if life was to continue but another moment; and at other times, it was hoarded up and eaten crumb by crumb, at regular intervals during the day, as if it was to last us for ever. To add to our calamities, biles* began to break out upon us, and our imaginations shortly became as diseased as our bodies. I laid down at night to catch a few moments of oblivious sleep, and immediately my starving fancy was at work. I dreamt of being placed near a splendid and rich repast, where there was every thing that the most dainty appetite could desire; and of contemplating the moment in which we were to commence to eat with enraptured feelings of delight; and just as I was about to partake of it, I suddenly awoke to the cold realities of my miserable situation. Nothing could have oppressed me so much. It set such a longing frenzy for victuals in my mind, that I felt as if I could have

*Boils

wished the dream to continue for ever, that I never might have awoke from it. I cast a sort of vacant stare about the boat, until my eyes rested upon a bit of tough cowhide, which was fastened to one of the oars; I eagerly seized and commenced to chew it, but there was no substance in it, and it only served to fatigue my weak jaws, and add to my bodily pains. My fellow sufferers murmured very much the whole time, and continued to press me continually with questions upon the probability of our reaching land again. I kept constantly rallying my spirits to enable me to afford them comfort. I encouraged them to bear up against all evils, and if we must perish, to die in our own cause, and not weakly distrust the providence of the Almighty by giving ourselves up to despair. I reasoned with them, and told them that we would not die sooner by keeping up our hopes; that the dreadful sacrifices and privations we endured were to preserve us from death, and were not to be put in competition with the price which we set upon our lives, and their value to our families: it was, besides, unmanly to repine at what neither admitted of alleviation nor cure; and withal, that it was our solemn duty to recognise in our calamities an over-ruling divinity, by whose mercy we might be suddenly snatched from peril, and to rely upon him alone, "Who tempers the wind to the shorn lamb."

The three following days, the 25th, 26th, and 27th, were not distinguished by any particular circumstances. The wind still prevailed to the eastward, and by its obduracy, almost tore the very hopes of our hearts away: it was impossible to silence the rebellious repinings of our nature, at witnessing such a succession of hard fortune against us. It was our cruel lot not to have had one bright anticipation realized—not one wish of our thirsting souls gratified. We had, at the end of these three days, been urged to the southward as far as latitude 36° into a chilly region, where rains and squalls prevailed; and we now calculated to tack and stand back to the northward: after much labor, we got our boat about; and so great was the fatigue attending this small exertion of our bodies, that we all gave up for a moment and abandoned her to her own course.—Not one of us had now strength sufficient to steer, or indeed to make one single effort towards getting the sails properly trimmed, to enable us to make any headway. After an hour or two of relaxation, during which the horrors of our situation came upon us with a despairing force and effect, we made a sudden effort and got our sails into such a disposition as that the boat would steer herself; and we then threw ourselves down, awaiting the issue of time to bring us relief, or to take us from the scene of our troubles. We could now do nothing more; strength and spirits were totally gone; and what indeed could have been the narrow hopes, that in our situation, then bound us to life?

January 28th. Our spirits this morning were hardly sufficient to allow of our enjoying a change of the wind, which took place to the westward.—It had nearly become indifferent to us from what quarter it blew: nothing but the slight chance of meeting a vessel remained to us now: it was this narrow comfort alone that prevented me from lying down at once to die. But fourteen days stinted allowance of provisions remained, and it was absolutely necessary to increase the quantity to enable us to live five days longer: we therefore partook of it, as pinching necessity demanded, and gave ourselves wholly up to the guidance and disposal of our Creator.

The 29th and 30th of January, the wind continued west, and we made considerable progress until the 31st, when it again came ahead, and prostrated all our hopes. On the 1st of February, it changed again to the westward, and on the 2nd and 3rd blew to the eastward; and we had it light and variable until the 8th of February. Our sufferings were now drawing to a close; a terrible death appeared shortly to await us; hunger became violent and outrageous, and we prepared for a speedy release from our troubles; our speech and reason were both considerably impaired, and we were reduced to be at this time certainly the most helpless and wretched of the whole human race. Isaac Cole, one of our crew, had the day before this, in a fit of despair, thrown himself down in the boat, and was determined there calmly to wait for death. It was obvious that he had no chance; all was dark he said in his mind, not a single ray of hope was left for him to dwell upon; and it was folly and madness to be struggling against what appeared so palpably to be our fixed and settled destiny. I remonstrated with him as effectually as the weakness both of my body and understanding would allow of; and what I said appeared for a moment to have a considerable effect: he made a powerful and sudden effort, half rose up, crawled forward and hoisted the jib, and firmly and loudly cried that he would not give up; that he would live as long as the rest of us—but alas! this effort was but the hectic fever of the moment, and he shortly again relapsed into a state of melancholy and despair. This day his reason was attacked, and he became about 9 o'clock in the morning a most miserable spectacle of madness: he spoke incoherently about everything, calling loudly for a napkin and water, and then, lying stupidly and senselessly down in the boat again, would close his hollow eyes, as if in death. About 10 o'clock, we suddenly perceived that he became speechless; we got him as well as we were able upon a board, placed on one of the seats of the boat, and covering him up with some old clothes, left him to his fate. He lay in the greatest pain and apparent misery, groaning piteously until four o'clock, when he died, in the most horrid and frightful convulsions I ever witnessed. We kept his corpse all night, and in the morning my two companions began as a course to make preparations to dispose of it in the sea; when after reflecting on the subject all night, I addressed them on the painful subject of keeping the body for food!! Our provisions could not possibly last us beyond three days, within which time, it was not in any degree probable that we should find relief from our present sufferings, and that hunger would at last drive us to the necessity of casting lots. It was without any objection agreed to, and we set to work as fast as we were able to prepare it so as to prevent its spoiling. We separated his limbs from his body, and cut all the flesh from the bones; after which, we opened the body, took out the heart, and then closed it again—sewed it up as decently as we could, and committed it to the sea. We now first commenced to satisfy the immediate cravings of nature from the heart, which we eagerly devoured, and then ate sparingly of a few pieces of the flesh; after which we hung up the remainder, cut in thin strips about the boat, to dry in the sun: we made a fire and roasted some of it, to serve us during the next day. In this manner did we dispose of our fellow sufferer; the painful recollection of which brings to mind at this moment, some of the most disagreeable and revolting ideas that it is capable of conceiving. We knew not then to whose lot it would fall next, either to die or be shot, and eaten like the poor wretch we had just dispatched. Humanity must shudder at the dreadful recital. I have no language to paint the anguish of our souls in this dreadful dilemma. The next morning, the 10th of February, we found that the flesh had become tainted, and had turned of a greenish color upon which we concluded to make a fire and cook it at once, to prevent its becoming so putrid as not to be eaten at all: we accordingly did so, and by that means preserved it for six or seven days longer; our bread during the time remained untouched; as that would not be liable to spoil, we placed it carefully aside for the last moments of our trial. About three o'clock this afternoon a strong breeze set in from the N.W. and we made very good progress, considering that we were compelled to steer the boat by management of the sails alone: this wind continued until the thirteenth, when it changed again ahead. We contrived to keep soul and body together by sparingly partaking of our flesh, cut up in small pieces and eaten with salt water. By the fourteenth, our bodies became so far recruited, as to enable us to make a few attempts at guiding our boat again with the oar; by each taking his turn, we managed to effect it, and to make a tolerable good course. On the fifteenth, our flesh was all consumed, and we were driven to the last morsel of bread, consisting of two cakes; our limbs had for the last two days swelled very much, and now began to pain us most excessively. We were still, as near as we could judge, three hundred miles from the land, and but three days of our allowance on hand. The hope of a continuation of the wind, which came out at west this morning, was the only comfort and solace that remained to us: so strong had our desires at last reached in this respect,

that a high fever had set in, in our veins, and a longing that nothing but its continuation could satisfy.
Matters were now with us at their height; all hope was
cast upon the breeze; and we tremblingly and fearful-
ly awaited its progress, and the dreadful development
of our destiny. On the sixteenth, at night, full of the
horrible reflections of our situation, and panting with
weakness, I laid down to sleep, almost indifferent
whether I should ever see the light again. I had not
lain long, before I dreamt I saw a ship at some distance
off from us, and strained every nerve to get to her, but
could not. I awoke almost overpowered with the
frenzy I had caught in my slumbers, and stung with
the cruelties of a diseased and disappointed imagination. On the seventeenth, in the afternoon, a heavy
cloud appeared to be settling down in an E. by N.
direction from us, which in my view, indicated the
vicinity of some land, which I took for the island of
Mas Afuera. I concluded it could be no other; and
immediately upon this reflection, the life blood began
to flow again briskly in my veins. I told my companions that I was well convinced it was land, and if so,
in all probability we should reach it before two days
more. My words appeared to comfort them much;
and by repeated assurances of the favourable appearance of things, their spirits acquired even a degree
of elasticity that was truly astonishing. The dark features of our distress began now to diminish a little,
and the countenance, even amid the gloomy bodings

of our hard lot, to assume a much fresher hue. We
directed our course for the cloud, and our progress
that night was extremely good. The next morning,
before daylight, Thomas Nicholson, a boy about seventeen years of age, one of my two companions
who had thus far survived with me, after having
bailed the boat, laid down, drew a piece of canvas
over him, and cried out that he then wished to die
immediately. I saw that he had given up, and I
attempted to speak a few words of comfort and
encouragement to him, and endeavoured to persuade him that it was a great weakness and even
wickedness to abandon a reliance upon the
Almighty, while the least hope, and a breath of life
remained; but he felt unwilling to listen to any of
the consolatory suggestions which I made to him;
and, notwithstanding the extreme probability which
I stated there was of our gaining the land before the
end of two days more, he insisted upon lying down
and giving himself up to despair. A fixed look of settled and forsaken despondency came over his face: he
lay for some time silent, sullen, and sorrowful—and
I felt at once satisfied that the coldness of death was
fast gathering upon him: there was a sudden and
unaccountable earnestness in his manner that alarmed
me, and made me fear that I myself might unexpectedly be overtaken by a like weakness, or dizziness of
nature, that would bereave me at once of both reason
and life; but Providence willed it otherwise.

At about seven o'clock this morning, while I was lying asleep, my companion who was steering, suddenly and loudly called out *"There's a Sail!"* I know not what was the first movement I made upon hearing such an unexpected cry: the earliest of my recollections are that immediately I stood up, gazing in a state of abstraction and ecstasy upon the blessed vision of a vessel about seven miles off from us; she was standing in the same direction with us, and the only sensation I felt at the moment was, that of a violent and unaccountable impulse to fly directly towards her. I do not believe it is possible to form a just conception of the pure, strong feelings, and the unmingled emotions of joy and gratitude, that took possession of my mind on this occasion: the boy, too, took a sudden and animated start from his despondency, and stood up to witness the probable instrument of his salvation. Our only fear was now that she would not discover us, or that we might not be able to intercept her course: we, however, put our boat immediately, as well as we were able, in a direction to cut her off; and found, to our great joy, that we sailed faster than she did. Upon observing us, she shortened sail, and allowed us to come up to her. The captain hailed us, and asked who we were. I told him we were from a wreck, and he cried out immediately for us to come alongside the ship. I made an effort to assist myself along to the side, for the purpose of getting up, but strength failed me altogether, and I found it impossible to move a step further without help. We must have formed at that moment, in the eyes of the captain and his crew, a most deplorable and affecting picture of suffering and misery. Our cadaverous countenances, sunken eyes, and bones just starting through the skin, with the ragged remnants of clothes stuck about our sun burnt bodies, must have produced an appearance to him affecting and revolting in the highest degree. The sailors commenced to remove us from our boat, and we were taken to the cabin, and comfortably provided for in every respect. In a few minutes we were permitted to taste of a little thin food, made from tapioca, and in a few days, with prudent management, we were considerably recruited. This vessel proved to be the brig *Indian,* Captain William Crozier, of London; to whom we are indebted for every polite, friendly, and attentive disposition towards us, that can possibly characterize a man of humanity and feeling. We were taken up in latitude 33° 45'S., longitude 81° 03'W. At twelve o'clock this day we saw the island of Mas Afuera, and on the 25th of February, we arrived at Valparaiso in utter distress and poverty. Our wants were promptly relieved there.

An Adventure With a Dog and a Glacier

JOHN MUIR

In the summer of 1880 I set out from Fort
Wrangel in a canoe, with the Rev. S. H. Young,
my former companion, and a crew of Indians, to
continue the exploration of the icy region of south-
eastern Alaska, begun in the fall of 1879. After the
necessary provisions, blankets, etc., had been collected and stowed away, and the Indians were in their
places ready to dip their paddles, while a crowd of
their friends were looking down from the wharf to
bid them good-by and good luck, Mr. Young, for
whom we were waiting, at length came aboard, followed by a little black dog that immediately made
himself at home by curling up in a hollow among
the baggage. I like dogs, but this one seemed so
small, dull, and worthless that I objected to his
going, and asked the missionary why he was taking
him. "Such a helpless wisp of hair will only be in

the way," I said; "you had better pass him up to one of the Indian boys on the wharf, to be taken home to play with the children. This trip is not likely to be a good one for toy dogs. He will be rained on and snowed on for weeks, and will require care like a baby." But the missionary assured me that he would be no trouble at all; that he was a perfect wonder of a dog—could endure cold and hunger like a polar bear, could swim like a seal, and was wondrous wise, etc., making out a list of virtues likely to make him the most interesting of the company.

Nobody could hope to unravel the lines of his ancestry. He was short-legged, bunchy-bodied, and almost featureless—something like a muskrat. Though smooth, his hair was long and silky, so that when the wind was at his back it ruffled, making him look shaggy. At first sight his only noticeable feature was his showy tail, which was about as shady and airy as a squirrel's, and was carried curling forward nearly to his ears. On closer inspection you might see his thin, sensitive ears and his keen dark eye with cunning tan spots. Mr. Young told me that when the dog was about the size of a wood-rat he was presented to his wife by an Irish prospector at Sitka, and that when he arrived at Fort Wrangel he was adopted by the Stickeen Indians as a sort of new good-luck totem, and named "Stickeen" for the tribe, with whom he became a favorite. On our trip he soon proved himself a queer character—odd, concealed, independent, keeping invincibly quiet, and doing many inexplicable things that piqued my curiosity. Sailing week after week through the long, intricate channels and inlets among the innumerable islands and mountains of the coast, he spent the dull days in sluggish ease, motionless, and apparently as unobserving as a hibernating marmot. But I discovered that somehow he always knew what was going forward. When the Indians were about to shoot at ducks or seals, or when anything interesting was to be seen along the shore, he would rest his chin on the edge of the canoe and calmly look out. When he heard us talking about making a landing, he roused himself to see what sort of place we were coming to, and made ready to jump overboard and swim ashore as soon as the canoe neared the beach. Then, with a vigorous shake to get rid of the brine in his hair, he went into the woods to hunt small game. But though always the first out of the canoe, he was always the last to get into it. When we were ready to start he could never be found, and refused to come to our call. We soon found out, however, that though we could not see him at such times, he saw us, and from the cover of the briers and huckleberry-bushes in the fringe of the woods was watching the canoe with wary eye. For as soon as we were fairly off, he came trotting down the beach, plunged into the surf, and swam after us, knowing well that we would cease rowing and take him in. When the contrary little vagabond came alongside, he was lifted by the neck, held at arm's length a moment to drip, and dropped aboard. We tried to cure him of this trick by compelling him to swim farther before stopping for him; but this did no good: the longer the swim, the better he seemed to like it.

Though capable of most spacious idleness, he was always ready for excursions or adventures of any sort. When the Indians went into the woods for a deer, Stickeen was sure to be at their heels, provided I had not yet left camp. For though I never carried a gun, he always followed me, forsaking the hunting Indians, and even his master, to share my wanderings. The days that were too stormy for sailing I spent in the woods, or on the mountains or glaciers, wherever I chanced to be; and Stickeen always insisted on following me, gliding through the dripping huckleberry-bushes and prickly *Panax* and *Rubus* tangles like a fox, scarce stirring their close-set branches, wading and wallowing through snow, swimming ice-cold streams, jumping logs and rocks and the crusty hummocks and crevasses of glaciers with the patience and endurance of a determined mountaineer, never tiring or getting discouraged. Once he followed me over a glacier the surface of which was so rough that it cut his feet until every step was marked with blood; but he trotted on with Indian fortitude until I noticed his pain and, taking pity on him, made him a set of moccasins out of a handkerchief. But he never asked help or made any complaint, as if, like a philosopher, he had learned that without hard work and suffering there could be no pleasure worth having.

Yet nobody knew what Stickeen was good for. He seemed to meet danger and hardships without reason, insisted on having his own way, never obeyed an order, and the hunters could never set him on anything against his will, or make him fetch anything that was shot. I tried hard to make his acquaintance, guessing there must be something in him; but he was as cold as a glacier, and about as invulnerable to fun, though his master assured me that he played at home, and in some measure conformed to the usages of civilization. His equanimity was so immovable it seemed due to unfeeling ignorance. Let the weather blow and roar, he was as tranquil as a stone; and no matter what advances you made, scarce a glance or a tail-wag would you get for your pains. No superannuated mastiff or bulldog grown old in office surpassed this soft midget in stoic dignity. He sometimes reminded me of those plump, squat, unshakable cacti of the Arizona deserts that give no sign of feeling. A true child of the wilderness, holding the even tenor of his hidden life with the silence and serenity of nature, he never displayed a trace of the elfish vivacity and fun of the terriers and collies that we all know, nor of their touching affection and devotion. Like children, most small dogs beg to be loved and allowed to love, but Stickeen seemed a very Diogenes, asking only to be let alone. He seemed neither old nor young. His strength lay in his eyes. They looked as old as the hills, and as young and as wild. I never tired looking into them. It was like looking into a landscape; but they were small and rather deep-set, and had no explaining puckers around them to give out particulars. I was accustomed to look into the faces of plants and animals, and I watched the little sphinx more and more keenly as an interesting study. But there is no estimating the wit and wisdom concealed and latent in our lower fellow-mortals until made manifest by profound experiences; for it is by suffering that dogs as well as saints are developed and made perfect.

After we had explored the glaciers of the Sumdum and Tahkoo inlets, we sailed through Stephen's Passage into Lynn Canal, and thence through Icy Strait into Cross Sound, looking for unexplored inlets leading toward the ice-fountains of the Fairweather Range. While the tide was in our favor in Cross Sound we were accompanied by a fleet of icebergs drifting out to the ocean from Glacier Bay. Slowly we crawled around Vancouver's Point, Wimbleton, our frail canoe tossed like a feather on the massive swells coming in past Cape Spenser. For miles the Sound is bounded by precipitous cliffs which looked terribly stern in gloomy weather. Had our canoe been crushed or upset, we could have gained no landing here; for the cliffs, as high as those of Yosemite, sink perfectly sheer into deep water. Eagerly we scanned the immense wall on the north side for the first sign of an opening, all of us anxious except Stickeen, who dozed in peace or gazed dreamily at the tremendous precipices when he heard us talking about them. At length we discovered the entrance of what is now called Taylor Bay, and about five o'clock reached the head of it, and encamped near the front of a large glacier which extends as an abrupt barrier all the way across from wall to wall of the inlet, a distance of three or four miles.

On first observation the glacier presented some unusual features, and that night I planned a grand excursion for the morrow. I awoke early, called not only by the glacier, but also by a storm. Rain, mixed with trailing films of scud and the ragged, drawn-out nether surfaces of gray clouds, filled the inlet, and was sweeping forward in a thick, passionate, horizontal flood, as if it were all passing over the country instead of falling on it. Everything was streaming with life and motion—woods, rocks, waters, and the sky. The main perennial streams were booming, and hundreds of new ones, born of the rain, were descending in gray and white cascades on each side of the inlet, fairly streaking their rocky slopes, and roaring like the sea. I had intended making a cup of coffee before starting, but when I heard the storm I made haste to join it; for in storms nature has always something extra fine to show us, and if we have wit to keep in right relations with them the danger is no more than in home-keeping, and we can go with them rejoicing, sharing their enthusiasm, and chanting with the old Norsemen, "The blast of the tempest aids our oars; the hurricane is our servant, and drives us whither we wish to go." So I took my ice-ax, buttoned my coat, put a piece of bread in my pocket, and set out. Mr. Young and the Indians were asleep, and so, I hoped, was Stickeen; but I had not gone a dozen rods before he left his warm bed in the tent, and came boring through the blast after me. That a man should welcome storms for their exhilarating music and motion, and go forth to see God making landscapes, is reasonable enough; but what fascination could there be in dismal weather for this poor, feeble wisp of a dog, so pathetically small? Anyhow, on he came, breakfastless, through the choking blast. I stopped, turned my back to the wind, and gave him a good, dissuasive talk. "Now don't," I said, shouting to make myself heard in the storm—"now don't, Stickeen. What has got into your queer noddle now? You must be daft. This wild day has nothing for you. Go back to camp and keep warm. There is no game abroad— nothing but weather. Not a foot or wing is stirring. Wait and get a good breakfast with your master, and be sensible for once. I can't feed you or carry you, and this storm will kill you." But nature, it seems, was at the bottom of the affair; and she gains her ends with dogs as well as with men, making us do as she likes, driving us on her ways, however rough. So after ordering him back again and again to ease my conscience, I saw that he was not to be shaken off; as well might the earth try to shake off the moon. I had once led his master into trouble, when he fell on one of the topmost jags of a mountain, and dislocated his arms. Now the turn of his humble companion was coming. The dog just stood there in the wind, drenched and blinking, saying doggedly, "Where thou goest I will go." So I told him to come on, if he must, and gave him a piece of the bread I had put in my pocket for breakfast. Then we pushed on in company, and thus began the most memorable of all my wild days.

The level flood, driving straight in our faces, thrashed and washed us wildly until we got into the shelter of the trees and ice-cliffs on the east side of the glacier, where we rested and listened and looked on in comfort. The exploration of the glacier was my main object, but the wind was too high to allow excursions over its open surface, where one might be dangerously shoved while balancing for a jump on the brink of a crevasse. In the meantime the storm was a fine study. Here the end of the glacier, descending over an abrupt swell of resisting rock about five hundred feet high, leans forward and falls in majestic ice-cascades. And as the storm came down the glacier from the north, Stickeen and I were beneath the main current of the blast, while favorably located to see and hear it. A broad torrent, draining the side of the glacier, now swollen by scores of new streams from the mountains, was rolling boulders along its rocky channel between the glacier and the woods with thudding, bumping, muffled sounds, rushing toward the bay with tremendous energy, as if in haste to get out of the mountains, the waters above and beneath calling to each other, and all to the ocean, their home. Looking southward from our shelter, we had this great torrent on our left, with mossy woods on the mountain slope above it, the glacier on our right, the wild, cascading portion of it forming a multitude of towers, spires, and flat-topped battlements seen through the trees, and smooth gray gloom ahead. I tried to draw the marvelous scene in my note-book, but the rain fell on my page in spite of all that I could do to shelter it, and the sketch seemed miserably defective.

When the wind began to abate I traced the east side of the glacier. All the trees standing on the edge of the woods were barked and bruised, showing high ice-mark in a very telling way, while tens of thousands of those that had stood for centuries on the bank of the glacier farther out lay crushed and being crushed. In many places I could see, down fifty feet or so beneath, the margin of the glacier mill, where trunks from one to two feet in diameter were being ground to pulp against outstanding rock-ribs and bosses of the bank. About three miles above the front of the glacier, I climbed to the surface of it by means of ax-steps, made easy for Stickeen; and as far as the eye could reach, the level, or nearly level, glacier stretched away indefinitely beneath the gray sky, a seemingly boundless prairie of ice. The rain continued, which I did not mind; but a tendency to fogginess in the drooping clouds made me hesitate about venturing far from land. No trace of the west shore was visible, and in case the misty clouds should settle, or the wind again become violent, I feared getting caught in a tangle of crevasses. Lingering undecided, watching the weather, I sauntered about on the crystal sea. For a mile or two out I found the ice remarkably safe. The marginal crevasses were mostly narrow, while the few wider ones were easily avoided by passing around them, and the clouds began to open here and there. Thus encouraged, I at last pushed out for the other side; for nature can make us do anything she likes, luring us along appointed ways for the fulfillment of her plans. At first we made rapid progress, and the sky was not very threatening, while I took bearings occasionally with a pocket-compass, to enable me to retrace my way more surely in case the storm should become blinding; but the structure-lines of the ice were my main guide. Toward the west side we came to a closely crevassed section, in which we had to make long, narrow tacks and doublings, tracing the edges of tremendous longitudinal crevasses, many of which were from twenty to thirty feet wide, and perhaps a thousand feet deep, beautiful and awful. In working a way through them I was severely cautious, but Stickeen came on as unhesitatingly as the flying clouds. Any crevasse that I could jump he would leap without so much as halting to examine it. The weather was bright and dark, with quick flashes of summer and winter close together. When the clouds opened and the sun shone, the glacier was seen from shore to shore, with a bright array of encompassing mountains partly revealed, wearing the clouds as garments, black in the middle, burning on the edges, and the whole icy prairie seemed to burst into a bloom of iris colors from myriads of crystals. Then suddenly all the glorious show would be again smothered in gloom. But Stickeen seemed to care for none of these things, bright or dark, nor for the beautiful wells filled to the brim with water so pure that it was nearly invisible, the rumbling, grinding moulins, or the quick-flashing, glinting, swirling streams in frictionless channels of living ice. Nothing seemed novel to him. He showed neither caution nor curiosity. His courage was so unwavering that it seemed due to dullness of perception, as if he were only blindly bold; and I warned him that he might slip or fall short. His bunchy body seemed all one skipping muscle, and his peg legs appeared to be jointed only at the top.

We gained the west shore in about three hours, the width of the glacier here being about seven miles. Then I pushed northward, in order to see as far back as possible into the fountains of the Fairweather Mountains, in case the clouds should rise. The walking was easy along the margin of the forest, which, of course, like that on the other side, had been invaded and crushed by the swollen glacier. In an hour we rounded a massive headland and came suddenly on another outlet of the glacier, which, in the form of a wild ice-cascade, was pouring over the rim of the main basin toward the ocean with the volume of a thousand Niagaras. The surface was broken into a multitude of sharp blades and pinnacles leaning forward, something like the updashing waves of a flood of water descending a rugged channel. But these ice-waves were many times higher than those of river cataracts, and to all appearance motionless. It was a dazzling white torrent two miles wide, flowing between high banks black with trees. Tracing its left bank three or four miles, I found that it discharged into a fresh-water lake, filling it with icebergs.

I would gladly have followed the outlet, but the day was waning, and we had to make haste on the return trip to get off the ice before dark. When we were about two miles from the west shore the clouds dropped misty fringes, and snow soon began to fly. Then I began to feel anxiety as to finding a way in the storm through the intricate net-work of crevasses which we had entered. Stickeen showed no fear. He was still the same silent, sufficient, uncomplaining Indian philosopher. When the storm-darkness fell he kept close behind me. The snow warned us to make haste, but at the same time hid our way. At rare intervals the clouds thinned, and mountains, looming in the gloom, frowned and quickly vanished. I pushed on as best I could, jumping innumerable crevasses, and for every hundred rods or so of direct advance traveling a mile in doubling up and down in the turmoil of chasms and dislocated masses of ice. After an hour or two of this work we came to a series of longitudinal crevasses of appalling width, like immense furrows. These I traced with firm nerve, excited and strengthened by the danger, making wide jumps, poising cautiously on the dizzy edges after cutting hollows for my feet before making the spring, to avoid slipping or any uncertainty on the farther sides, where only one trial is granted—exercise at once frightful and inspiring. Stickeen flirted across every gap I jumped, seemingly without effort. Many a mile we thus traveled, mostly up and down, making but little real headway in crossing, most of the time running instead of walking, as the danger of spending the night on the glacier became threatening. No doubt we could have weathered the storm for one night, and I faced the chance of being compelled to do so; but we were hungry and wet,

and the north wind was thick with snow and bit-
terly cold, and of course that night would have
seemed a long one. Stickeen gave me no concern.
He was still the wonderful, inscrutable philosopher,
ready for anything. I could not see far enough to
judge in which direction the best route lay, and had
simply to grope my way in the snow-choked air and
ice. Again and again I was put to my mettle, but
Stickeen followed easily, his nerves growing more
unflinching as the dangers thickened; so it always is
with mountaineers.

At length our way was barred by a very wide and
straight crevasse, which I traced rapidly northward a
mile or so without finding a crossing or hope of one,
then southward down the glacier about as far, to
where it united with another crevasse. In all this distance of perhaps two miles there was only one place
where I could possibly jump it; but the width of this
jump was nearly the utmost I dared attempt, while the
danger of slipping on the farther side was so great that
I was loath to try it. Furthermore, the side I was on
was about a foot higher than the other, and even with
this advantage it seemed dangerously wide. One is
liable to underestimate the width of crevasses where
the magnitudes in general are great. I therefore measured this one again and again, until satisfied that I
could jump it if necessary, but that in case I should be
compelled to jump back to the higher side, I might
fail. Now a cautious mountaineer seldom takes a step

on unknown ground which seems at all dangerous, that he cannot retrace in case he should be stopped by unseen obstacles ahead. This is the rule of mountaineers who live long; and though in haste, I compelled myself to sit down and deliberate before I broke it. Retracing my devious path in imagination, as if it were drawn on a chart, I saw that I was recrossing the glacier a mile or two farther up-stream, and was entangled in a section I had not before seen. Should I risk this dangerous jump, or try to regain the woods on the west shore, make a fire, and have only hunger to endure while waiting for a new day? I had already crossed so broad a tangle of dangerous ice that I saw it would be difficult to get back to the woods through the storm; while the ice just beyond the present barrier seemed more promising, and the east shore was now perhaps about as near as the west. I was therefore eager to go on; but this wide jump was a tremendous obstacle. At length, because of the dangers already behind me, I determined to venture against those that might be ahead, jumped, and landed well, but with so little to spare that I more than ever dreaded being compelled to take that jump back from the lower side. Stickeen followed, making nothing of it. But within a distance of a few hundred yards we were stopped again by the widest crevasse yet encountered. Of course I made haste to explore it, hoping all might yet be well. About three fourths of a mile up-stream it united with the one we had just crossed, as I feared it would. Then, tracing it down, I found it joined the other great crevasse at the lower end, maintaining a width of forty to fifty feet. We were on an island about two miles long and from one hundred to three hundred yards wide, with two barely possible ways of escape—one by the way we came, the other by an almost inaccessible sliver-bridge that crossed the larger crevasse from near the middle of the island. After tracing the brink, I ran back to the sliver-bridge and cautiously studied it. Crevasses caused by strains from variations of the rate of motion of different parts of the glacier and by convexities in the channel are mere cracks when they first open,— so narrow as hardly to admit the blade of a pocket-knife,—and widen gradually, according to the extent of the strain. Now some of these cracks are interrupted like the cracks in wood, and, in opening, the strip of ice between overlapping ends is dragged out; and if the flow of the glacier there is such that no strain is made on the sliver, it maintains a continuous connection between the sides, just as the two sides of a slivered crack in wood that is being split are connected. Some crevasses remain open for years, and by the melting of their sides continue to increase in width long after the opening strain has ceased, while the sliver-bridges, level on top at first, and perfectly safe, are at length melted to thin, knife-edged blades, the upper portion being most exposed to the weather; and since the exposure is greatest in the middle, they at length curve downward like the cables of suspension-bridges. This one was evidently very old, for it had been wasted until it was the worst bridge I ever saw. The width of the crevasse was here about fifty feet, and the sliver, crossing diagonally, was about seventy feet long, was depressed twenty-five or thirty feet in the middle, and the up-curving ends were attached to the sides eight or ten feet below the surface of the glacier. Getting down the nearly vertical wall to the end of it and up the other side were the main difficulties, and they seemed all but insurmountable. Of the many perils encountered in my years of wandering in mountain altitudes, none seemed so plain and stern and merciless as this. And it was presented when we were wet to the skin and hungry, the sky was dark with snow, and the night near, and we had to fear the snow in our eyes and the disturbing action of the wind in any movement we might make. But we were forced to face it. It was a tremendous necessity.

Beginning not immediately above the sunken end of the bridge, but a little to one side, I cut nice hollows on the brink for my knees to rest in; then, leaning over, with my short-handled ax cut a step sixteen or eighteen inches below, which, on account of the sheerness of the wall, was shallow. That step, however, was well made; its floor sloped slightly inward, and formed a good hold for my heels. Then, slipping cautiously upon it, and crouching as low as possible, with my left side twisted toward the wall, I steadied myself with my left hand in a slight notch, while with the right I cut other steps and notches in succession, guarding against glinting of the ax, for life or death was in every stroke, and in the niceness of finish of every foothold. After the end of the bridge was reached, it was a delicate thing to poise on a little platform which I had chipped on its up-curving end, and, bending over the slippery surface, get astride of it. Crossing was easy, cutting off the sharp edge with careful strokes, and hitching forward a few inches at a time, keeping my balance with my knees pressed against its sides. The tremendous abyss on each side I studiously ignored. The surface of that blue sliver was then all the world. But the most trying part of the adventure was, after working my way across inch by inch, to rise from the safe position astride that slippery strip of ice, and to cut a ladder in the face of the wall—chipping, climbing, holding on with feet and fingers in mere notches. At such times one's whole body is eye, and common skill and fortitude are replaced by power beyond our call or knowledge. Never before had I been so long under deadly strain. How I got up the cliff at the end of the bridge I never could tell. The thing seemed to have been done by somebody else. I never have had contempt of death, though in the course of my explorations I oftentimes felt that to meet one's fate on a mountain, in a grand cañon, or in the heart of a crystal glacier would be blessed as compared with death from disease, a mean accident in a street, or from a sniff of sewer-gas. But the sweetest, cleanest death, set thus calmly and glaringly clear before us, is hard enough to face, even though we feel gratefully sure that we have already had happiness enough for a dozen lives.

But poor Stickeen, the wee, silky, sleekit beastie— think of him! When I had decided to try the bridge, and while I was on my knees cutting away the rounded brow, he came behind me, pushed his head past my shoulder, looked down and across, scanned the sliver and its approaches with his queer eyes, then looked me in the face with a startled air of surprise and concern, and began to mutter and whine, saying as plainly as if speaking with words, "Surely you are not going to try that awful place?" This was the first time I had seen him gaze deliberately into a crevasse or into my face with a speaking look. That he should have recognized and appreciated the danger at the first glance showed wonderful sagacity. Never before had the quick, daring midget seemed to know that ice was slippery, or that there was such a thing as danger anywhere. His looks and the tones of his voice when he began to complain and speak his fears were so human that I unconsciously talked to him as I would to a boy, and in trying to calm his fears perhaps in some measure moderated my own. "Hush your fears, my boy," I said; "we will get across safe, though it is not going to be easy. No right way is

easy in this rough world. We must risk our lives to
save them. At the worst we can only slip; and then
how grand a grave we shall have! And by and by our
nice bones will do good in the terminal moraine."
But my sermon was far from reassuring him; he
began to cry, and after taking another piercing look
at the tremendous gulf, ran away in desperate excitement, seeking some other crossing. By the time he
got back, baffled, of course, I had made a step or two.
I dared not look back, but he made himself heard;
and when he saw that I was certainly crossing, he
cried aloud in despair. The danger was enough to
daunt anybody, but it seems wonderful that he
should have been able to weigh and appreciate it so
justly. No mountaineer could have seen it more
quickly or judged it more wisely, discriminating
between real and apparent peril.

After I had gained the other side he howled
louder than ever, and after running back and forth
in vain search for a way of escape, he would return
to the brink of the crevasse above the bridge, moan-
ing and groaning as if in the bitterness of death.
Could this be the silent, philosophic Stickeen? I
shouted encouragement, telling him the bridge was
not so bad as it looked, that I had left it flat for his
feet, and he could walk it easily. But he was afraid to
try it. Strange that so small an animal should be
capable of such big, wise fears! I called again and
again in a reassuring tone to come on and fear

nothing; that he could come if he would only try. Then he would hush for a moment, look again at the bridge, and shout his unshakable conviction that he could never, never come that way; then lie back in despair, as if howling: "Oh-o-o, what a place! No-o-o; I can never go-o-o down there!" His natural composure and courage had vanished utterly in a tumultuous storm of fear. Had the danger been less, his distress would have seemed ridiculous. But in this gulf—a huge, yawning sepulcher big enough to hold everybody in the territory—lay the shadow of death, and his heartrending cries might well have called Heaven to his help. Perhaps they did. So hidden before, he was transparent now, and one could see the workings of his mind like the movements of a clock out of its case. His voice and gestures were perfectly human, and his hopes and fears unmistakable, while he seemed to understand every word of mine. I was troubled at the thought of leaving him. It seemed impossible to get him to venture. To compel him to try by fear of being left, I started off as if leaving him to his fate, and disappeared back of a hummock; but this did no good, for he only lay down and cried. So after hiding a few minutes, I went back to the brink of the crevasse, and in a severe tone of voice shouted across to him that now I must certainly leave him—I could wait no longer; and that if he would not come, all I could promise was that I would return

to seek him next day. I warned him that if he went
back to the woods the wolves would kill him, and
finished by urging him once more by words and
gestures to come on. He knew very well what I
meant, and at last, with the courage of despair,
hushed and breathless, he lay down on the brink in
the hollow I had made for my knees, pressed his
body against the ice to get the advantage of the friction, gazed into the first step, put his little feet
together, and slid them slowly down into it, bunch-
ing all four in it, and almost standing on his head.
Then, without lifting them, as well as I could see
through the snow, he slowly worked them over the
edge of the step, and down into the next and the
next in succession in the same way, and gained the
bridge. Then lifting his feet with the regularity and
slowness of the vibrations of a seconds' pendulum,
as if counting and measuring one, two, three, holding himself in dainty poise, and giving separate
attention to each little step, he gained the foot of the
cliff, at the top of which I was kneeling to give him
a lift should he get within reach. Here he halted in
dead silence, and it was here I feared he might fail,
for dogs are poor climbers. I had no cord. If I had
had one, I would have dropped a noose over his
head and hauled him up. But while I was thinking
whether an available cord might be made out of
clothing, he was looking keenly into the series of
notched steps and finger-holds of the ice-ladder I

had made, as if counting them and fixing the position of each one in his mind. Then suddenly up he came, with a nervy, springy rush, hooking his paws into the notches and steps so quickly that I could not see how it was done, and whizzed past my head, safe at last!

And now came a scene! "Well done, well done, little boy! Brave boy!" I cried, trying to catch and caress him; but he would not be caught. Never before or since have I seen anything like so passionate a revulsion from the depths of despair to uncontrollable, exultant, triumphant joy. He flashed and darted hither and thither as if fairly demented, screaming and shouting, swirling round and round in giddy loops and circles like a leaf in a whirlwind, lying down and rolling over and over, sidewise and heels over head, pouring forth a tumultuous flood of hysterical cries and sobs and gasping mutterings. And when I ran up to him to shake him, fearing he might die of joy, he flashed off two or three hundred yards, his feet in a mist of motion; then, turning suddenly, he came back in wild rushes, and launched himself at my face, almost knocking me down, all the time screeching and screaming and shouting as if saying, "Saved! saved! saved!" Then away again, dropping suddenly at times with his feet in the air, trembling, and fairly sobbing. Such passionate emotion was enough to kill him. Moses' stately song of triumph after escaping the Egyptians and the Red Sea was nothing to it. Who could have guessed the capacity of the dull, enduring little fellow for all that most stirs this mortal frame? Nobody could have helped crying with him.

But there is nothing like work for toning down either excessive fear or joy. So I ran ahead, calling him, in as gruff a voice as I could command, to come on and stop his nonsense, for we had far to go, and it would soon be dark. Neither of us feared another trial like this. Heaven would surely count one enough for a lifetime. The ice ahead was gashed by thousands of crevasses, but they were common ones. The joy of deliverance burned in us like fire, and we ran without fatigue, every muscle, with immense rebound, glorying in its strength. Stickeen flew across everything in his way, and not till dark did he settle into his normal fox-like, gliding trot. At last the mountains crowned with spruce came in sight, looming faintly in the gloaming, and we soon felt the solid rock beneath our feet, and were safe. Then came weariness. We stumbled down along the lateral moraine in the dark, over rocks and tree-trunks, through the bushes and devil-club thickets and mossy logs and boulders of the woods where we had sheltered ourselves in the morning. Then out on the level mud-slope of the terminal moraine. Danger had vanished, and so had our strength. We reached camp about ten o'clock, and found a big fire and a big supper. A party of Hoona Indians had visited Mr. Young, bringing a gift of porpoise-meat and wild strawberries, and hunter Joe had brought in a wild goat. But we lay down, too tired to eat much, and soon fell into a troubled sleep. The man who said, "The harder the toil the sweeter the rest," never was profoundly tired. Stickeen kept springing up and muttering in his sleep, no doubt dreaming that he was still on the brink of the crevasse; and so did I—that night and many others, long afterward, when I was nervous and overtired.

Thereafter Stickeen was a changed dog. During the rest of the trip, instead of holding aloof, he would come to me at night, when all was quiet about the camp-fire, and rest his head on my knee, with a look of devotion, as if I were his god. And often, as he caught my eye, he seemed to be trying to say, "Wasn't that an awful time we had together on the glacier?"

None of his old friends know what finally became of him. When my work for the season was done I departed for California, and never saw the dear little fellow again. Mr. Young wrote me that in the summer of 1883 he was stolen by a tourist at Fort Wrangel, and taken away on a steamer. His fate is wrapped in mystery. If alive he is very old. Most likely he has left this world—crossed the last crevasse—and gone to another. But he will not be forgotten. Come what may, to me Stickeen is immortal.

The Boat Journey

SIR ERNEST SHACKLETON

Excerpted from Shackleton's book South, *"The Boat Journey" is the account of the heroic journey made by Shackleton and five members of his crew to seek relief and supplies for his ice-locked ship* Endurance. *In an Antarctic expedition in 1914, the* Endurance *was locked in a sea of ice and drifted for ten months before eventually being crushed. Shackleton led the twenty-seven men of his ship's company to camps on ice floes for five months and finally landed on the uninhabited Elephant Island in the South Shetland Islands. With no rescue seemingly possible, cut off from the outside world, Shackleton makes the decision to try a desperate voyage in an open boat with five men over 800 miles of icy, stormy ocean to seek assistance. The twenty-two men left behind on Elephant Island will have to survive in the meantime. And if Shackleton and his companions are lost at sea, the Elephant Island group will likely never be found.*

The increasing sea made it necessary for us to drag the boats farther up the beach. This was a task for all hands, and after much labour we got the boats into safe positions among

the rocks and made fast the painters to big boulders.
Then I discussed with Wild and Worsley the chances
of reaching South Georgia before the winter locked
the sea against us. Some effort had to be made to
secure relief. Privation and exposure had left their
mark on the party, and the health and mental condition of several men were causing me serious anxiety.
Blackborrow's feet, which had been frost-bitten during the boat journey, were in a bad way, and the two
doctors feared that an operation would be necessary.
They told me that the toes would have to be ampu-
tated unless animation could be restored within a
short period. Then the food-supply was a vital consideration. We had left ten cases of provisions in the
crevice of the rocks at our first camping-place on
the island. An examination of our stores showed that
we had full rations for the whole party for a period
of five weeks. The rations could be spread over three
months on a reduced allowance and probably would
be supplemented by seals and sea-elephants to some
extent. I did not dare to count with full confidence
on supplies of meat and blubber, for the animals
seemed to have deserted the beach and the winter
was near. Our stocks included three seals and two
and a half skins (with blubber attached). We were
mainly dependent on the blubber for fuel, and, after
making a preliminary survey of the situation, I
decided that the party must be limited to one hot
meal a day.

A boat journey in search of relief was necessary and must not be delayed. That conclusion was forced upon me. The nearest port where assistance could certainly be secured was Port Stanley, in the Falkland Islands, 540 miles away, but we could scarcely hope to beat up against the prevailing northwesterly wind in a frail and weakened boat with a small sail area. South Georgia was over 800 miles away, but lay in the area of the west winds, and I could count upon finding whalers at any of the whaling-stations on the east coast. A boat party might make the voyage and be back with relief within a month, provided that the sea was clear of ice and the boat survive the great seas. It was not difficult to decide that South Georgia must be the objective, and I proceeded to plan ways and means. The hazards of a boat journey across 800 miles of stormy sub-Antarctic ocean were obvious, but I calculated that at worst the venture would add nothing to the risks of the men left on the island. There would be fewer mouths to feed during the winter and the boat would not require to take more than one month's provisions for six men, for if we did not make South Georgia in that time we were sure to go under. A consideration that had weight with me was that there was no chance at all of any search being made for us on Elephant Island.

The case required to be argued in some detail, since all hands knew that the perils of the proposed journey were extreme. The risk was justified solely by our urgent need of assistance. The ocean south of Cape Horn in the middle of May is known to be the most tempestuous storm-swept area of water in the world. The weather then is unsettled, the skies are dull and overcast, and the gales are almost unceasing. We had to face these conditions in a small and weather-beaten boat, already strained by the work of the months that had passed. Worsley and Wild realized that the attempt must be made, and they both asked to be allowed to accompany me on the voyage. I told Wild at once that he would have to stay behind. I relied upon him to hold the party together while I was away and to make the best of his way to Deception Island with the men in the spring in the event of our failure to bring help. Worsley I would take with me, for I had a very high opinion of his accuracy and quickness as a navigator, and especially in the snapping and working out of positions in difficult circumstances—an opinion that was only enhanced during the actual journey. Four other men would be required, and I decided to call for volunteers, although, as a matter of fact, I pretty well knew which of the people I would select. Crean I proposed to leave on the island as a right-hand man for Wild, but he begged so hard to be allowed to come in the boat that, after consultation with Wild, I promised to take him. I called the men together, explained my plan, and asked for volunteers. Many came forward at once. Some were not fit enough for the work that would have to be done, and others would not have been much use in the boat since they were not seasoned sailors, though the experiences of recent months entitled them to some consideration as seafaring men. McIlroy and Macklin were both anxious to go but realized that their duty lay on the island with the sick men. They suggested that I should take Blackborrow in order that he might have shelter and warmth as quickly as possible, but I had to veto this idea. It would be hard enough for fit men to live in the boat. Indeed, I did not see how a sick man, lying helpless in the bottom of the boat, could possibly survive in the heavy weather we were sure to encounter. I finally selected McNeish, McCarthy, and Vincent in addition to Worsley and Crean. The crew seemed a strong one, and as I looked at the men I felt confidence increasing.

The decision made, I walked through the blizzard with Worsley and Wild to examine the *James Caird*. The 20-ft. boat had never looked big; she appeared to have shrunk in some mysterious way when I viewed her in the light of our new undertaking. She was an ordinary ship's whaler, fairly strong, but showing signs of the strains she had endured since the crushing of the *Endurance*. Where she was holed in leaving the pack was, fortunately, about the waterline and easily patched. Standing beside her, we glanced at the fringe of the storm-swept, tumultuous sea that formed our path. Clearly, our voyage would be a big adventure. I called the carpenter and asked him if he could do anything to make the boat more seaworthy. He first inquired if he was to go with me, and seemed quite pleased when I said "Yes." He was over fifty years of age and not altogether fit, but he had a good knowledge of sailing-boats and was very quick. McCarthy said that he could contrive some sort of covering for the *James Caird* if he might use the lids of the cases and the four sledge-runners that we had lashed inside the boat for use in the event of a landing on Graham Land at Wilhelmina Bay. This bay, at one time the goal of our desire, had been left behind in the course of our drift, but we had retained the runners. The carpenter proposed to complete the covering with some of our canvas, and he set about making his plans at once.

Noon had passed and the gale was more severe than ever. We could not proceed with our preparations that day. The tents were suffering in the wind and the sea was rising. We made our way to the snow-slope at the shoreward end of the spit, with the intention of digging a hole in the snow large enough to provide shelter for the party. I had an idea that Wild and his men might camp there during my absence, since it seemed impossible that the tents could hold together for many more days against the attacks of the wind; but an examination of the spot indicated that any hole we could dig probably would be filled quickly by the drift. At dark, about 5 P.M.,

we all turned in, after a supper consisting of a pannikin of hot milk, one of our precious biscuits, and
a cold penguin leg each.

The gale was stronger than ever on the following
morning (April 20). No work could be done.
Blizzard and snow, snow and blizzard, sudden lulls
and fierce returns. During the lulls we could see on
the far horizon to the northeast bergs of all shapes
and sizes driving along before the gale, and the sinister appearance of the swift-moving masses made us
thankful indeed that, instead of battling with the
storm amid the ice, we were required only to face
the drift from the glaciers and the inland heights.
The gusts might throw us off our feet, but at least we
fell on solid ground and not on the rocking floes.
Two seals came up on the beach that day, one of
them within ten yards of my tent. So urgent was our
need of food and blubber that I called all hands and
organized a line of beaters instead of simply walking
up to the seal and hitting it on the nose. We were
prepared to fall upon this seal *en masse* if it attempted to escape. The kill was made with a pick-handle,
and in a few minutes five days' food and six days'
fuel were stowed in a place of safety among the
boulders above high-water mark. During this day
the cook, who had worked well on the floe and
throughout the boat journey, suddenly collapsed. I
happened to be at the galley at the moment and saw
him fall. I pulled him down the slope to his tent and

pushed him into its shelter with orders to his tent-mates to keep him in his sleeping-bag until I allowed him to come out or the doctors said he was fit enough. Then I took out to replace the cook one of the men who had expressed a desire to lie down and die. The task of keeping the galley fire alight was both difficult and strenuous, and it took his thoughts away from the chances of immediate dissolution. In fact, I found him a little later gravely concerned over the drying of a naturally not over-clean pair of socks which were hung up in close proximity to our evening milk. Occupation had brought his thoughts back to the ordinary cares of life.

There was a lull in the bad weather on April 21, and the carpenter started to collect material for the decking of the *James Caird*. He fitted the mast of the *Stancomb Wills* fore and aft inside the *James Caird* as a hog-back and thus strengthened the keel with the object of preventing our boat "hogging"—that is, buckling in heavy seas. He had not sufficient wood to provide a deck, but by using the sledge-runners and box-lids he made a framework extending from the forecastle aft to a well. It was a patched-up affair, but it provided a base for a canvas covering. We had a bolt of canvas frozen stiff, and this material had to be cut and then thawed out over the blubber-stove, foot by foot, in order that it might be sewn into the form of a cover. When it had been nailed and screwed into position it certainly gave an appearance of safety to the boat, though I had an uneasy feeling that it bore a strong likeness to stage scenery, which may look like a granite wall and is in fact nothing better than canvas and lath. As events proved, the covering served its purpose well. We certainly could not have lived through the voyage without it.

Another fierce gale was blowing on April 22, interfering with our preparations for the voyage. The cooker from No. 5 tent came adrift in a gust, and, although it was chased to the water's edge, it disappeared for good. Blackborrow's feet were giving him much pain, and McIlroy and Macklin thought it would be necessary for them to operate soon. They were under the impression then that they had no chloroform, but they found some subsequently in the medicine-chest after we had left. Some cases of stores left on a rock off the spit on the day of our arrival were retrieved during this day. We were setting aside stores for the boat journey and choosing the essential equipment from the scanty stock at our disposal. Two ten-gallon casks had to be filled with water melted down from ice collected at the foot of the glacier. This was a rather slow business. The blubber-stove was kept going all night, and the watchmen emptied the water into the casks from the pot in which the ice was melted. A working party started to dig a hole in the snow-slope about forty feet above sea-level with the object of providing a site for a camp. They made fairly good progress at first, but the snow drifted down unceasingly from the inland ice, and in the end the party had to give up the project.

The weather was fine on April 23, and we hurried forward our preparations. It was on this day I decided finally that the crew for the *James Caird* should consist of Worsley, Crean, McNeish, McCarthy, Vincent, and myself. A storm came on about noon, with driving snow and heavy squalls. Occasionally the air would clear for a few minutes, and we could see a line of pack-ice, five miles out, driving across from west to east. This sight increased my anxiety to get away quickly. Winter was advancing, and soon the pack might close completely round the island and stay our departure for days or even for weeks, I did not think that ice would remain around Elephant Island continuously during the winter, since the strong winds and fast currents would keep it in motion. We had noticed ice and bergs going past at the rate of four or five knots. A certain amount of ice was held up about the end of our spit, but the sea was clear where the boat would have to be launched.

Worsley, Wild, and I climbed to the summit of the seaward rocks and examined the ice from a better vantage-point than the beach offered. The belt of pack outside appeared to be sufficiently broken for our purposes, and I decided that, unless the conditions forbade it, we would make a start in the *James Caird* on the following morning. Obviously the pack might close at any time. This decision made, I spent the rest of the day looking over the boat, gear, and stores, and discussing plans with Worsley and Wild.

Our last night on the solid ground of Elephant Island was cold and uncomfortable. We turned out at dawn and had breakfast. Then we launched the *Stancomb Wills* and loaded her with stores, gear, and ballast, which would be transferred to the *James Caird* when the heavier boat had been launched. The ballast consisted of bags made from blankets and filled with sand, making a total weight of about 1000 lb. In addition we had gathered a number of round boulders and about 250 lb. of ice, which would supplement our two casks of water.

The stores taken in the *James Caird,* which would last six men for one month, were as follows:

30 boxes of matches.
6½ gallons paraffin.
1 tin methylated spirit.
10 boxes of flamers.
1 box of blue lights.
2 Primus stoves with spare parts and prickers.
1 Nansen aluminum cooker.
6 sleeping-bags.
A few spare socks.
A few candles and some blubber-oil in an oil-bag.
Food:
3 cases sledging rations = 300 rations.

2 cases nut food = 200".

2 cases biscuits = 600 biscuits.

1 case lump sugar.

30 packets of Trumilk.

1 tin of Bovril cubes.

1 tin of Cerebos salt.

36 gallons of water.

112 lb. of ice.

Instruments:

Sextant. Sea-anchor.

Binoculars. Charts.

Prismatic compass. Aneroid.

The swell was slight when the *Stancomb Wills* was launched and the boat got under way without any difficulty; but half an hour later, when we were pulling down the *James Caird,* the swell increased suddenly. Apparently the movement of the ice outside had made an opening and allowed the sea to run in without being blanketed by the line of pack. The swell made things difficult. Many of us got wet to the waist while dragging the boat out—a serious matter in that climate. When the *James Caird* was afloat in the surf she nearly capsized among the rocks before we could get her clear, and Vincent and the carpenter, who were on the deck, were thrown into the water. This was really bad luck, for the two men would have small chance of drying their clothes after we had got under way. Hurley, who had

the eye of the professional photographer for "incidents," secured a picture of the upset, and I firmly
believe that he would have liked the two unfortunate
men to remain in the water until he could get a
"snap" at close quarters; but we hauled them out
immediately, regardless of his feelings.

The *James Caird* was soon clear of the breakers.
We used all the available ropes as a long painter to
prevent her drifting away to the north-east, and then
the *Stancomb Wills* came alongside, transferred her
load, and went back to the shore for more. As she
was being beached this time the sea took her stern
and half filled her with water. She had to be turned
over and emptied before the return journey could be
made. Every member of the crew of the *Stancomb
Wills* was wet to the skin. The water-casks were
towed behind the *Stancomb Wills* on this second
journey, and the swell, which was increasing rapidly,
drove the boat on to the rocks, where one of the
casks was slightly stove in. This accident proved later
to be a serious one, since some sea-water had entered
the cask and the contents were now brackish.

By midday the *James Caird* was ready for the voyage. Vincent and the carpenter had secured some dry
clothes by exchange with members of the shore
party (I heard afterwards that it was a full fortnight
before the soaked garments were finally dried), and
the boat's crew was standing by waiting for the order
to cast off. A moderate westerly breeze was blowing.

I went ashore in the *Stancomb Wills* and had a last word with Wild, who was remaining in full command, with directions as to his course of action in the event of our failure to bring relief, but I practically left the whole situation and scope of action and decision to his own judgment, secure in the knowledge that he would act wisely. I told him that I trusted the party to him and said good-bye to the men. Then we pushed off for the last time, and within a few minutes I was aboard the *James Caird*. The crew of the *Stancomb Wills* shook hands with us as the boats bumped together and offered us the last good wishes. Then, setting our jib, we cut the painter and moved away to the north-east. The men who were staying behind made a pathetic little group on the beach, with the grim heights of the island behind them and the sea seething at their feet, but they waved to us and gave three hearty cheers. There was hope in their hearts and they trusted us to bring the help that they needed.

I had all sails set, and the *James Caird* quickly dipped the beach and its line of dark figures. The westerly wind took us rapidly to the line of pack, and as we entered it I stood up with my arm around the mast, directing the steering, so as to avoid the great lumps of ice that were flung about in the heave of the sea. The pack thickened and we were forced to turn almost due east, running before the wind towards a gap I had seen in the morning from the high ground. I could not see the gap now, but we had come out on its bearing and I was prepared to find that it had been influenced by the easterly drift. At four o'clock in the afternoon we found the channel, much narrower than it had seemed in the morning but still navigable. Dropping sail, we rowed through without touching the ice anywhere, and by 5:30 P.M. we were clear of the pack with open water before us. We passed one more piece of ice in the darkness an hour later, but the pack lay behind, and with fair wind swelling the sails we steered our little craft through the night, our hopes centred on our distant goal. The swell was very heavy now, and when the time came for our first evening meal we found great difficulty in keeping the Primus lamp alight and preventing the hoosh splashing out of the pot. Three men were needed to attend to the cooking, one man holding the lamp and two men guarding the aluminum cooking-pot, which had to be lifted clear of the Primus whenever the movement of the boat threatened to cause a disaster. Then the lamp had to be protected from water, for sprays were coming over the bows and our flimsy decking was by no means water-tight. All these operations were conducted in the confined space under the decking, where the men lay or knelt and adjusted themselves as best they could to the angles of our cases and ballast. It was uncomfortable, but we found consolation in the reflection that without the decking we could not have used the cooker at all.

The tale of the next sixteen days is one of supreme strife amid heaving waters. The sub-Antarctic Ocean lived up to its evil winter reputation. I decided to run north for at least two days while the wind held and so get into warmer weather before turning to the east and laying a course for South Georgia. We took two-hourly spells at the tiller. The men who were not on watch crawled into the sodden sleeping-bags and tried to forget their troubles for a period; but there was no comfort in the boat. The bags and cases seemed to be alive in the unfailing knack of presenting their most uncomfortable angles to our rest-seeking bodies. A man might imagine for a moment that he had found a position of ease, but always discovered quickly that some unyielding point was impinging on muscle or bone. The first night aboard the boat was one of acute discomfort for us all, and we were heartily glad when the dawn came and we could set about the preparation of a hot breakfast.

This record of the voyage to South Georgia is based upon scanty notes made day by day. The notes dealt usually with the bare facts of distances, positions, and weather, but our memories retained the incidents of the passing days in a period never to be forgotten. By running north for the first two days I hoped to get warmer weather and also to avoid lines of pack that might be extending beyond the main body. We needed all the advantage that we could

obtain from the higher latitude for sailing on the
great circle, but we had to be cautious regarding possible ice-streams. Cramped in our narrow quarters
and continually wet by the spray, we suffered severely from cold throughout the journey. We fought the
seas and the winds and at the same time had a daily
struggle to keep ourselves alive. At times we were in
dire peril. Generally we were upheld by the knowledge that we were making progress towards the land
where we would be, but there were days and nights
when we lay hove to, drifting across the storm-
whitened seas and watching, with eyes interested
rather than apprehensive, the uprearing masses of
water, flung to and fro by Nature in the pride of her
strength. Deep seemed the valleys when we lay
between the reeling seas. High were the hills when
we perched momentarily on the tops of giant
combers. Nearly always there were gales. So small
was our boat and so great were the seas that often
our sail flapped idly in the calm between the crests
of two waves. Then we would climb the next slope
and catch the full fury of the gale where the wool-
like whiteness of the breaking water surged around
us. We had our moments of laughter—rare, it is
true, but hearty enough. Even when cracked lips
and swollen mouths checked the outward and visible signs of amusement we could see a joke of the
primitive kind. Man's sense of humour is always
most easily stirred by the petty misfortunes of his

neighbours, and I shall never forget Worsley's efforts on one occasion to place the hot aluminum stand on top of the Primus stove after it had fallen off in an extra heavy roll. With his frost-bitten fingers he picked it up, dropped it, picked it up again, and toyed with it gingerly as though it were some fragile article of lady's wear. We laughed, or rather gurgled with laughter.

The wind came up strong and worked into a gale from the north-west on the third day out. We stood away to the east. The increasing seas discovered the weaknesses of our decking. The continuous blows shifted the box-lids and sledge-runners so that the canvas sagged down and accumulated water. Then icy trickles, distinct from the driving sprays, poured fore and aft into the boat. The nails that the carpenter had extracted from cases at Elephant Island and used to fasten down the battens were too short to make firm the decking. We did what we could to secure it, but our means were very limited, and the water continued to enter the boat at a dozen points. Much baling was necessary, and nothing that we could do prevented our gear from becoming sodden. The searching runnels from the canvas were really more unpleasant than the sudden definite douches of the sprays. Lying under the thwarts during watches below, we tried vainly to avoid them. There were no dry places in the boat, and at last we simply covered our heads with our Burberrys and

endured the all-pervading water. The baling was
work for the watch. Real rest we had none. The
perpetual motion of the boat made repose impossible; we were cold, sore, and anxious. We moved on
hands and knees in the semi-darkness of the day
under the decking. The darkness was complete by 6
P.M. and not until 7 A.M. of the following day could
we see one another under the thwarts. We had a few
scraps of candle, and they were preserved carefully in
order that we might have light at meal-times. There
was one fairly dry spot in the boat, under the solid
original decking at the bows, and we managed to
protect some of our biscuit from the salt water; but
I do not think any of us got the taste of salt out of
our mouths during the voyage.

The difficulty of movement in the boat would
have had its humorous side if it had not involved us
in so many aches and pains. We had to crawl under
the thwarts in order to move along the boat, and our
knees suffered considerably. When a watch turned
out it was necessary for me to direct each man by
name when and where to move, since if all hands
had crawled about at the same time the result would
have been dire confusion and many bruises. Then
there was the trim of the boat to be considered. The
order of the watch was four hours on and four hours
off, three men to the watch. One man had the tiller-
ropes, the second man attended to the sail, and the
third baled for all he was worth. Sometimes when

the water in the boat had been reduced to reasonable proportions, our pump could be used. This
pump, which Hurley had made from the Flinders
bar case of our ship's standard compass, was quite
effective, though its capacity was not large. The man
who was attending the sail could pump into the big
outer cooker, which was lifted and emptied overboard when filled. We had a device by which the
water could go direct from the pump into the sea
through a hole in the gunwale, but this hole had to
be blocked at an early stage of the voyage, since we
found that it admitted water when the boat rolled.

While a new watch was shivering in the wind and
spray, the men who had been relieved groped hurriedly among the soaked sleeping-bags and tried to
steal a little of the warmth created by the last occu-
pants; but it was not always possible for us to find
even this comfort when we went off watch. The
boulders that we had taken aboard for ballast had to
be shifted continually in order to trim the boat and
give access to the pump, which became choked with
hairs from the moulting sleeping-bags and
finneskoe. The four reindeer-skin sleeping-bags
shed their hair freely owing to the continuous wetting, and soon became quite bald in appearance. The
moving of the boulders was weary and painful
work. We came to know every one of the stones by
sight and touch, and I have vivid memories of their
angular peculiarities even to-day. They might have

been of considerable interest as geological specimens to a scientific man under happier conditions.
As ballast they were useful. As weights to be moved
about in cramped quarters they were simply
appalling. They spared no portion of our poor bodies. Another of our troubles, worth mention here,
was the chafing of our legs by our wet clothes,
which had not been changed now for seven months.
The insides of our thighs were rubbed raw, and the
one tube of Hazeline cream in our medicine-chest
did not go far in alleviating our pain, which was
increased by the bite of the salt water. We thought
at the time that we never slept. The fact was that we
would doze off uncomfortably, to be aroused quickly by some new ache or another call to effort. My
own share of the general unpleasantness was accen-
tuated by a finely developed bout of sciatica. I had
become possessor of this originally on the floe several months earlier.

Our meals were regular in spite of the gales.
Attention to this point was essential, since the conditions of the voyage made increasing calls upon our
vitality. Breakfast, at 8 A.M., consisted of a pannikin
of hot hoosh made from Bovril sledging ration, two
biscuits, and some lumps of sugar. Lunch came at 1
P.M., and comprised Bovril sledging ration, eaten
raw, and a pannikin of hot milk for each man. Tea,
at 5 P.M., had the same menu. Then during the night
we had a hot drink, generally of milk. The meals

were the bright beacons in those cold and stormy days. The glow of warmth and comfort produced by the food and drink made optimists of us all. We had two tins of Virol, which we were keeping for an emergency; but, finding ourselves in need of an oil-lamp to eke out our supply of candles, we emptied one of the tins in the manner that most appealed to us, and fitted it with a wick made by shredding a bit of canvas. When this lamp was filled with oil it gave a certain amount of light, though it was easily blown out, and was of great assistance to us at night. We were fairly well off as regarded fuel, since we had 6 1/2 gallons of petroleum.

A severe south-westerly gale on the fourth day out forced us to heave to. I would have liked to have run before the wind, but the sea was very high and the *James Caird* was in danger of broaching to and swamping. The delay was vexatious, since up to that time we had been making sixty or seventy miles a day; good going with our limited sail area. We hove to under double-reefed mainsail and our little jigger, and waited for the gale to blow itself out. During that afternoon we saw bits of wreckage, the remains probably of some unfortunate vessel that had failed to weather the strong gales south of Cape Horn. The weather conditions did not improve, and on the fifth day out the gale was so fierce that we were compelled to take in the double-reefed mainsail and hoist our small jib instead. We put out a sea-anchor to keep the *James Caird*'s head up to the sea. This anchor consisted of a triangular canvas bag fastened to the end of the painter and allowed to stream out from the bows. The boat was high enough to catch the wind, and, as she drifted to leeward, the drag of the anchor kept her head to windward. Thus our boat took most of the seas more or less end on. Even then the crests of the waves often would curl right over us and we shipped a great deal of water, which necessitated unceasing baling and pumping. Looking out abeam, we would see a hollow like a tunnel formed as the crest of a big wave toppled over on to the swelling body of water. A thousand times it appeared as though the *James Caird* must be engulfed; but the boat lived. The south-westerly gale had its birthplace above the Antarctic Continent, and its freezing breath lowered the temperature far towards zero. The sprays froze upon the boat and gave bows, sides, and decking a heavy coat of mail. This accumulation of ice reduced the buoyancy of the boat, and to that extent was an added peril; but it possessed a notable advantage from one point of view. The water ceased to drop and trickle from the canvas, and the spray came in solely at the well in the after part of the boat. We could not allow the load of ice to grow beyond a certain point, and in turns we crawled about the decking forward, chipping and picking at it with the available tools.

When daylight came on the morning of the sixth day out we saw and felt that the *James Caird* had lost her resiliency. She was not rising to the oncoming seas. The weight of the ice that had formed in her and upon her during the night was having its effect, and she was becoming more like a log than a boat. The situation called for immediate action. We first broke away the spare oars, which were encased in ice and frozen to the sides of the boat, and threw them overboard. We retained two oars for use when we got inshore. Two of the fur sleeping-bags went over the side; they were thoroughly wet, weighing probably 40 lb. each, and they had frozen stiff during the night. Three men constituted the watch below, and when a man went down it was better to turn into the wet bag just vacated by another man than to thaw out a frozen bag with the heat of his unfortunate body. We now had four bags, three in use and one for emergency use in case a member of the party should break down permanently. The reduction of weight relieved the boat to some extent, and vigorous chipping and scraping did more. We had to be very careful not to put axe or knife through the frozen canvas of the decking as we crawled over it, but gradually we got rid of a lot of ice. The *James Caird* lifted to the endless waves as though she lived again.

About 11 A.M. the boat suddenly fell off into the trough of the sea. The painter had parted and the sea-anchor had gone. This was serious. The *James*

Caird went away to leeward, and we had no chance at all of recovering the anchor and our valuable rope, which had been our only means of keeping the boat's head up to the seas without the risk of hoisting sail in a gale. Now we had to set the sail and trust to its holding. While the *James Caird* rolled heavily in the trough, we beat the frozen canvas until the bulk of the ice had cracked off it and then hoisted it. The frozen gear worked protestingly, but after a struggle our little craft came up to the wind again, and we breathed more freely. Skin frost-bites were troubling us, and we had developed large blisters on our fingers and hands. I shall always carry the scar of one of these frost-bites on my left hand, which became badly inflamed after the skin had burst and the cold had bitten deeply.

We held the boat up to the gale during that day, enduring as best we could discomforts that amounted to pain. The boat tossed interminably on the big waves under grey, threatening skies. Our thoughts did not embrace much more than the necessities of the hour. Every surge of the sea was an enemy to be watched and circumvented. We ate our scanty meals, treated our frost-bites, and hoped for the improved conditions that the morrow might bring. Night fell early, and in the lagging hours of darkness we were cheered by a change for the better in the weather. The wind dropped, the snow-squalls became less frequent, and the sea moderated. When the morning of the seventh day dawned there was not much wind. We shook the reef out of the sail and laid our course once more for South Georgia. The sun came out bright and clear, and presently Worsley got a snap for longitude. We hoped that the sky would remain clear until noon, so that we could get the latitude. We had been six days out without an observation, and our dead reckoning naturally was uncertain. The boat must have presented a strange appearance that morning. All hands basked in the sun. We hung our sleeping-bags to the mast and spread our socks and other gear all over the deck. Some of the ice had melted off the *James Caird* in the morning after the gale began to slacken, and dry patches were appearing in the decking. Porpoises came blowing round the boat, and Cape pigeons wheeled and swooped within a few feet of us. These little black-and-white birds have an air of friendliness that is not possessed by the great circling albatross. They had looked grey against the swaying sea during the storm as they darted about over our heads and uttered their plaintive cries. The albatrosses, of the black or sooty variety, had watched with hard, bright eyes, and seemed to have a quite impersonal interest in our struggle to keep afloat amid the battering seas. In addition to the Cape pigeons an occasional stormy petrel flashed overhead. Then there was a small bird, unknown to me, that appeared always to be in a fussy, bustling state, quite out of keeping with the surroundings. It irritated me. It had practically no tail, and it flitted about vaguely as though in search of the lost member. I used to find myself wishing it would find its tail and have done with the silly fluttering.

We revelled in the warmth of the sun that day. Life was not so bad, after all. We felt we were well on our way. Our gear was drying, and we could have a hot meal in comparative comfort. The swell was still heavy, but it was not breaking and the boat rode easily. At noon Worsley balanced himself on the gunwale and clung with one hand to the stay of the mainmast while he got a snap of the sun. The result was more than encouraging. We had done over 380 miles and were getting on for half-way to South Georgia. It looked as though we were going to get through.

The wind freshened to a good stiff breeze during the afternoon, and the *James Caird* made satisfactory progress. I had not realized until the sunlight came how small our boat really was. There was some influence in the light and warmth, some hint of happier days, that made us revive memories of other voyages, when we had stout decks beneath our feet, unlimited food at our command, and pleasant cabins for our ease. Now we clung to a battered little boat, "alone, alone, all, all alone, alone on a wide, wide sea." So low in the water were we that each succeeding swell cut off our view of the sky-line. We were a tiny speck in the vast vista of the sea—the ocean that is open to all and merciful to none, that threatens even when it seems to yield, and that is pitiless always to weakness. For a moment the consciousness of the forces arrayed against us would be almost overwhelming. Then hope and confidence would rise again as our boat rose to a wave and tossed aside the crest in a sparkling shower like the play of prismatic colours at the foot of a waterfall. My double-barrelled gun and some cartridges had been stowed aboard the boat as an emergency precaution against a shortage of food, but we were not disposed to destroy our little neighbours, the Cape pigeons, even for the sake of fresh meat. We might have shot an albatross, but the wandering king of the ocean aroused in us something of the feeling that inspired, too late, the Ancient Mariner. So the gun remained among the stores and sleeping-bags in the narrow quarters beneath our leaking deck, and the birds followed us unmolested.

The eighth, ninth, and tenth days of the voyage had few features worthy of special note. The wind blew hard during those days, and the strain of navigating the boat was unceasing, but always we made some advance towards our goal. No bergs showed on our horizon, and we knew that we were clear of the ice-fields. Each day brought its little round of troubles, but also compensation in the form of food and growing hope. We felt that we were going to succeed. The odds against us had been great, but we were winning through. We still suffered severely from the cold, for, though the temperature was rising, our vitality was declining owing to shortage of food, exposure, and the necessity of maintaining our cramped positions day and night. I found that it was now absolutely necessary to prepare hot milk for all hands during the night, in order to sustain life till dawn. This meant lighting the Primus lamp in the darkness and involved an increased drain on our small store of matches. It was the rule that one match must serve when the Primus was being lit. We had no lamp for the compass and during the early days of the voyage we would strike a match when the steersman wanted to see the course at night; but later the necessity for strict economy impressed itself upon us, and the practice of striking matches at night was stopped. We had one water-tight tin of matches. I had stowed away in a pocket, in readiness for a sunny day, a lens from one of the telescopes, but this was of no use during the voyage. The sun seldom shone upon us. The glass of the compass got broken one night, and we contrived to mend it with adhesive tape from the medicine-chest. One of the memories that comes to me from those days is of Crean singing at the tiller. He always sang while he was steering, and nobody ever discovered what the song was. It was devoid of tune and as monotonous as the chanting of a Buddhist monk at his prayers; yet somehow it was cheerful. In moments of inspiration Crean would attempt "The Wearing of the Green."

On the tenth night Worsley could not straighten his body after his spell at the tiller. He was thoroughly cramped, and we had to drag him beneath the decking and massage him before he could unbend himself and get into a sleeping-bag. A hard north-westerly gale came up on the eleventh day (May 5) and shifted to the south-west in the late afternoon. The sky was overcast and occasional snow-squalls added to the discomfort produced by a tremendous cross-sea—the worst, I thought, that we had experienced. At midnight I was at the tiller and suddenly noticed a line of clear sky between the south and south-west. I called to the other men that the sky was clearing, and then a moment later I realized that what I had seen was not a rift in the clouds but the white crest of an enormous wave. During twenty-six years' experience of the ocean in all its moods I had not encountered a wave so gigantic. It was a mighty upheaval of the ocean, a thing quite apart from the big white-capped seas that had been our tireless enemies for many days. I shouted, "For God's sake, hold on! It's got us!" Then came a moment of suspense that seemed drawn out into hours. White surged the foam of the breaking sea around us. We felt our boat lifted and flung forward like a cork in breaking surf. We were in a seething chaos of tortured water; but somehow the boat lived through it, half-full of water, sagging to the dead weight and shuddering under the blow. We baled with the energy of men fighting for life, flinging the water over the sides with every receptacle that came to our hands, and after ten minutes of uncertainty we felt the boat renew her life beneath us. She floated again and ceased to lurch drunkenly as though dazed by the attack of the sea. Earnestly we hoped that never again would we encounter such a wave.

The conditions in the boat, uncomfortable before, had been made worse by the deluge of water. All our gear was thoroughly wet again. Our cooking-stove had been floating about in the bottom of the boat, and portions of our last hoosh seemed to have permeated everything. Not until 3 A.M., when we were all chilled almost to the limit of endurance, did we manage to get the stove alight and make ourselves hot drinks. The carpenter was suffering particularly, but he showed grit and spirit. Vincent had for the past week ceased to be an active member of the crew, and I could not easily account for his collapse. Physically he was one of the strongest men in the boat. He was a young man, he had served on North Sea trawlers, and he should have been able to bear hardships better than McCarthy, who, not so strong, was always happy.

The weather was better on the following day (May 6), and we got a glimpse of the sun. Worsley's observation showed that we were not more than a hundred miles from the northwest corner of South Georgia. Two more days with a favourable wind and

we would sight the promised land. I hoped that
there would be no delay, for our supply of water was
running very low. The hot drink at night was essential, but I decided that the daily allowance of water
must be cut down to half a pint per man. The lumps
of ice we had taken aboard had gone long ago. We
were dependent upon the water we had brought
from Elephant Island, and our thirst was increased by
the fact that we were now using the brackish water
in the breaker that had been slightly stove in in the
surf when the boat was being loaded. Some sea-
water had entered at that time.

Thirst took possession of us. I dared not permit
the allowance of water to be increased since an
unfavourable wind might drive us away from the
island and lengthen our voyage by many days. Lack
of water is always the most severe privation that men
can be condemned to endure, and we found, as during our earlier boat voyage, that the salt water in our
clothing and the salt spray that lashed our faces made
our thirst grow quickly to a burning pain. I had to
be very firm in refusing to allow any one to antici-
pate the morrow's allowance, which I was sometimes
begged to do. We did the necessary work dully and
hoped for the land. I had altered the course to the
east so as to make sure of our striking the island,
which would have been impossible to regain if we
had run past the northern end. The course was laid
on our scrap of chart for a point some thirty miles

down the coast. That day and the following day passed for us in a sort of nightmare. Our mouths were dry and our tongues were swollen. The wind was still strong and the heavy sea forced us to navigate carefully, but any thought of our peril from the waves was buried beneath the consciousness of our raging thirst. The bright moments were those when we each received our one mug of hot milk during the long, bitter watches of the night. Things were bad for us in those days, but the end was coming. The morning of May 8 broke thick and stormy, with squalls from the north-west. We searched the waters ahead for a sign of land, and though we could see nothing more than had met our eyes for many days, we were cheered by a sense that the goal was near at hand. About ten o'clock that morning we passed a little bit of kelp, a glad signal of the proximity of land. An hour later we saw two shags sitting on a big mass of kelp, and knew then that we must be within ten or fifteen miles of the shore. These birds are as sure an indication of the proximity of land as a lighthouse is, for they never venture far to sea. We gazed ahead with increasing eagerness, and at 12:30 P.M., through a rift in the clouds, McCarthy caught a glimpse of the black cliffs of South Georgia, just fourteen days after our departure from Elephant Island. It was a glad moment. Thirst-ridden, chilled, and weak as we were, happiness irradiated us. The job was nearly done.

We stood in towards the shore to look for a landing-place, and presently we could see the green tussock-grass on the ledges above the surf-beaten rocks. Ahead of us and to the south, blind rollers showed the presence of uncharted reefs along the coast. Here and there the hungry rocks were close to the surface, and over them the great waves broke, swirling viciously and spouting thirty and forty feet into the air. The rocky coast appeared to descend sheer to the sea. Our need of water and rest was well-nigh desperate, but to have attempted a landing at that time would have been suicidal. Night was drawing near, and the weather indications were not favourable. There was nothing for it but to haul off till the following morning, so we stood away on the starboard tack until we had made what appeared to be a safe offing. Then we hove to in the high westerly swell. The hours passed slowly as we waited the dawn, which would herald, we fondly hoped, the last stage of our journey. Our thirst was a torment and we could scarcely touch our food; the cold seemed to strike right through our weakened bodies. At 5 A.M. the wind shifted to the north-west and quickly increased to one of the worst hurricanes any of us had ever experienced. A great cross-sea was running, and the wind simply shrieked as it tore the tops off the waves and converted the whole seascape into a haze of driving spray. Down into valleys, up to tossing heights, straining until her seams opened, swung our little boat, brave still but labouring heavily. We knew that the wind and set of the sea was driving us ashore, but we could do nothing. The dawn showed us a storm-torn ocean, and the morning passed without bringing us a sight of the land; but at 1 P.M., through a rift in the flying mists, we got a glimpse of the huge crags of the island and realized that our position had become desperate. We were on a dead lee shore, and we could gauge our approach to the unseen cliffs by the roar of the breakers against the sheer walls of rock. I ordered the double-reefed mainsail to be set in the hope that we might claw off, and this attempt increased the strain upon the boat. The *James Caird* was bumping heavily, and the water was pouring in everywhere. Our thirst was forgotten in the realization of our imminent danger, as we baled unceasingly, and adjusted our weights from time to time; occasional glimpses showed that the shore was nearer. I knew that Annewkow Island lay to the south of us, but our small and badly marked chart showed uncertain reefs in the passage between the island and the mainland, and I dared not trust it, though as a last resort we could try to lie under the lee of the island. The afternoon wore away as we edged down the coast, with the thunder of the breakers in our ears. The approach of evening found us still some distance from Annewkow Island, and, dimly in the twilight, we could see a snow-capped mountain looming above us. The chance of surviving the night, with the driving gale and the implacable sea forcing us on to the lee shore, seemed small. I think most of us had a feeling that the end was very near. Just after 6 P.M., in the dark, as the boat was in the yeasty backwash from the seas flung from this iron-bound coast, then, just when things looked their worst, they changed for the best. I have marvelled often at the thin line that divides success from failure and the sudden turn that leads from apparently certain disaster to comparative safety. The wind suddenly shifted, and we were free once more to make an offing. Almost as soon as the gale eased, the pin that locked the mast to the thwart fell out. It must have been on the point of doing this throughout the hurricane, and if it had gone nothing could have saved us; the mast would have snapped like a carrot. Our backstays had carried away once before when iced up and were not too strongly fastened now. We were thankful indeed for the mercy that had held that pin in its place throughout the hurricane.

We stood off shore again, tired almost to the point of apathy. Our water had long been finished. The last was about a pint of hairy liquid, which we strained through a bit of gauze from the medicine-chest. The pangs of thirst attacked us with redoubled intensity, and I felt that we must make a landing on the following day at almost any hazard. The night wore on. We were very tired. We longed for day. When at last the dawn came on the morning of May

10 there was practically no wind, but a high cross-sea was running. We made slow progress towards the shore. About 8 A.M. the wind backed to the north-west and threatened another blow. We had sighted in the meantime a big indentation which I thought must be King Haakon Bay, and I decided that we must land there. We set the bows of the boat towards the bay and ran before the freshening gale. Soon we had angry reefs on either side. Great glaciers came down to the sea and offered no landing-place. The sea spouted on the reefs and thundered against the shore. About noon we sighted a line of jagged reef, like blackened teeth, that seemed to bar the entrance to the bay. Inside, comparatively smooth water stretched eight or nine miles to the head of the bay. A gap in the reef appeared, and we made for it. But the fates had another rebuff for us. The wind shifted and blew from the east right out of the bay. We could see the way through the reef, but we could not approach it directly. That afternoon we bore up, tacking five times in the strong wind. The last tack enabled us to get through, and at last we were in the wide mouth of the bay. Dusk was approaching. A small cove, with a boulder-strewn beach guarded by a reef, made a break in the cliffs on the south side of the bay, and we turned in that direction. I stood in the bows directing the steering as we ran through the kelp and made the passage of the reef. The entrance was so narrow that we had to take in

the oars, and the swell was piling itself right over the reef into the cove; but in a minute or two we were inside, and in the gathering darkness the *James Caird* ran in on a swell and touched the beach. I sprang ashore with the short painter and held on when the boat went out with the backward surge. When the *James Caird* came in again three of the men got ashore, and they held the painter while I climbed some rocks with another line. A slip on the wet rocks twenty feet up nearly closed my part of the story just at the moment when we were achieving safety. A jagged piece of rock held me and at the same time bruised me sorely. However, I made fast the line, and in a few minutes we were all safe on the beach, with the boat floating in the surging water just off the shore. We heard a gurgling sound that was sweet music in our ears, and, peering around, found a stream of fresh water almost at our feet. A moment later we were down on our knees drinking the pure, ice-cold water in long draughts that put new life into us. It was a splendid moment.

The next thing was to get the stores and ballast out of the boat, in order that we might secure her for the night. We carried the stores and gear above high-water mark and threw out the bags of sand and the boulders that we knew so well. Then we attempted to pull the empty boat up the beach, and discovered by this effort how weak we had become. Our united strength was not sufficient to get the *James Caird*

clear of the water. Time after time we pulled together, but without avail. I saw that it would be necessary to have food and rest before we beached the
boat. We made fast a line to a heavy boulder and set
a watch to fend the *James Caird* off the rocks of the
beach. Then I sent Crean round to the left side of
the cove, about thirty yards away, where I had
noticed a little cave as we were running in. He could
not see much in the darkness, but reported that the
place certainly promised some shelter. We carried
the sleeping-bags round and found a mere hollow in
the rock-face, with a shingle floor sloping at a steep
angle to the sea. There we prepared a hot meal, and
when the food was finished I ordered the men to
turn in. The time was now about 8 P.M., and I took
the first watch beside the *James Caird,* which was still
afloat in the tossing water just off the beach.

Fending the *James Caird* off the rocks in the darkness was awkward work. The boat would have
bumped dangerously if allowed to ride in with the
waves that drove into the cove. I found a flat rock for
my feet, which were in a bad way owing to cold,
wetness, and lack of exercise in the boat, and during
the next few hours I laboured to keep the *James
Caird* clear of the beach. Occasionally I had to rush
into the seething water. Then, as a wave receded, I
let the boat out on the alpine rope so as to avoid a
sudden jerk. The heavy painter had been lost when
the sea-anchor went adrift. The *James Caird* could be

seen but dimly in the cove, where the high black cliffs made the darkness almost complete, and the strain upon one's attention was great. After several hours had passed I found that my desire for sleep was becoming irresistible, and at 1 A.M. I called Crean. I could hear him groaning as he stumbled over the sharp rocks on his way down the beach. While he was taking charge of the *James Caird* she got adrift, and we had some anxious moments. Fortunately, she went across towards the cave and we secured her unharmed. The loss or destruction of the boat at this stage would have been a very serious matter, since we probably would have found it impossible to leave the cove except by sea. The cliffs and glaciers around offered no practicable path towards the head of the bay. I arranged for one-hour watches during the remainder of the night and then took Crean's place among the sleeping men and got some sleep before the dawn came.

The sea went down in the early hours of the morning (May 11), and after sunrise we were able to set about getting the boat ashore, first bracing ourselves for the task with another meal. We were all weak still. We cut off the topsides and took out all the movable gear. Then we waited for Byron's "great ninth wave," and when it lifted the *James Caird* in we held her and, by dint of great exertion, worked her round broadside to the sea. Inch by inch we dragged her up until we reached the fringe of the tussock-grass and knew that the boat was above high-water mark. The rise of the tide was about five feet, and at spring tide the water must have reached almost to the edge of the tussock-grass. The completion of this job removed our immediate anxieties, and we were free to examine our surroundings and plan the next move. The day was bright and clear.

King Haakon Bay is an eight-mile sound penetrating the coast of South Georgia in an easterly direction. We had noticed that the northern and southern sides of the sound were formed by steep mountain-ranges, their flanks furrowed by mighty glaciers, the outlets of the great ice-sheet of the interior. It was obvious that these glaciers and the precipitous slopes of the mountains barred our way inland from the cove. We must sail to the head of the sound. Swirling clouds and mist-wreaths had obscured our view of the sound when we were entering, but glimpses of snow-slopes had given us hope that an overland journey could be begun from that point. A few patches of very rough, tussocky land, dotted with little tarns, lay between the glaciers along the foot of the mountains, which were heavily scarred with scree-slopes. Several magnificent peaks and crags gazed out across their snowy domains to the sparkling waters of the sound.

Our cove lay a little inside the southern headland of King Haakon Bay. A narrow break in the cliffs, which were about a hundred feet high at this point,

formed the entrance to the cove. The cliffs continued inside the cove on each side and merged into a
hill which descended at a steep slope to the boulder
beach. The slope, which carried tussock-grass, was
not continuous. It eased at two points into little
peaty swamp-terraces dotted with frozen pools and
drained by two small streams. Our cave was a recess
in the cliff on the left-hand end of the beach. The
rocky face of the cliff was undercut at this point, and
the shingle thrown up by the waves formed a steep
slope, which we reduced to about one in six by
scraping the stones away from the inside. Later we
strewed the rough floor with the dead, nearly dry
underleaves of the tussock-grass, so as to form a
slightly soft bed for our sleeping-bags. Water had
trickled down the face of the cliff and formed long
icicles, which hung down in front of the cave to the
length of about fifteen feet. These icicles provided
shelter, and when we had spread our sails below
them, with the assistance of oars, we had quarters
that, in the circumstances, had to be regarded as reasonably comfortable. The camp at least was dry, and
we moved our gear there with confidence. We built
a fireplace and arranged our sleeping-bags and blankets around it. The cave was about 8 ft. deep and 12
ft. wide at the entrance.

While the camp was being arranged Crean and I
climbed the tussock slope behind the beach and
reached the top of a headland overlooking the

sound. There we found the nests of albatrosses, and, much to our delight, the nests contained young birds. The fledgelings were fat and lusty, and we had no hesitation about deciding that they were destined to die at an early age. Our most pressing anxiety at this stage was a shortage of fuel for the cooker. We had rations for ten more days, and we knew now that we could get birds for food; but if we were to have hot meals we must secure fuel. The store of petroleum carried in the boat was running very low, and it seemed necessary to keep some quantity for use on the overland journey that lay ahead of us. A sea-elephant or a seal would have provided fuel as well as food, but we could see none in the neighbourhood. During the morning we started a fire in the cave with wood from the top-sides of the boat, and though the dense smoke from the damp sticks inflamed our tired eyes, the warmth and the prospect of hot food were ample compensation. Crean was cook that day, and I suggested to him that he should wear his goggles, which he happened to have brought with him. The goggles helped him a great deal as he bent over the fire and tended the stew. And what a stew it was! The young albatrosses weighed about fourteen pounds each fresh killed, and we estimated that they weighed at least six pounds each when cleaned and dressed for the pot. Four birds went into the pot for six men, with a Bovril ration for thickening. The flesh was white and succulent, and the bones, not fully formed, almost melted in our mouths. That was a memorable meal. When we had eaten our fill, we dried our tobacco in the embers of the fire and smoked contentedly. We made an attempt to dry our clothes, which were soaked with salt water, but did not meet with much success. We could not afford to have a fire except for cooking purposes until blubber or driftwood had come our way.

The final stage of the journey had still to be attempted. I realized that the condition of the party generally, and particularly of McNeish and Vincent, would prevent us putting to sea again except under pressure of dire necessity. Our boat, moreover, had been weakened by the cutting away of the topsides, and I doubted if we could weather the island. We were still 150 miles away from Stromness whaling-station by sea. The alternative was to attempt the crossing of the island. If we could not get over, then we must try to secure enough food and fuel to keep us alive through the winter, but this possibility was scarcely thinkable. Over on Elephant Island twenty-two men were waiting for the relief that we alone could secure for them. Their plight was worse than ours. We must push on somehow. Several days must elapse before our strength would be sufficiently recovered to allow us to row or sail the last nine miles up to the head of the bay. In the meantime we could make what preparations were possible and dry our clothes by taking advantage of every scrap of heat from the fires we lit for the cooking of our meals. We turned in early that night, and I remember that I dreamed of the great wave and aroused my companions with a shout of warning as I saw with half-awakened eyes the towering cliff on the opposite side of the cove.

Shortly before midnight a gale sprang up suddenly from the north-east with rain and sleet showers. It brought quantities of glacier-ice into the cove, and by 2 A.M. (May 12) our little harbour was filled with ice, which surged to and fro in the swell and pushed its way on to the beach. We had solid rock beneath our feet and could watch without anxiety. When daylight came rain was falling heavily, and the temperature was the highest we had experienced for many months. The icicles overhanging our cave were melting down in streams and we had to move smartly when passing in and out lest we should be struck by falling lumps. A fragment weighing fifteen or twenty pounds crashed down while we were having breakfast. We found that a big hole had been burned in the bottom of Worsley's reindeer sleeping-bag during the night. Worsley had been awakened by a burning sensation in his feet, and had asked the men near him if his bag was all right; they looked and could see nothing wrong. We were all superficially frost-bitten about the feet, and this condition caused the extremities to burn painfully, while at the same time sensation was lost in the skin. Worsley thought that the uncomfortable heat of his feet was due to the frost-bites, and he stayed in his bag and presently went to sleep again. He discovered when he turned out in the morning that the tussock-grass which we had laid on the floor of the cave had smouldered outwards from the fire and had actually burned a large hole in the bag beneath his feet. Fortunately, his feet were not harmed.

Our party spent a quiet day, attending to clothing and gear, checking stores, eating and resting. Some more of the young albatrosses made a noble end in our pot. The birds were nesting on a small plateau above the right-hand end of our beach. We had previously discovered that when we were landing from the boat on the night of May 10 we had lost the rudder. The *James Caird* had been bumping heavily astern as we were scrambling ashore, and evidently the rudder was then knocked off. A careful search of the beach and the rocks within our reach failed to reveal the missing article. This was a serious loss, even if the voyage to the head of the sound could be made in good weather. At dusk the ice in the cove was rearing and crashing on the beach. It had forced up a ridge of stones close to where the *James Caird* lay at the edge of the tussock-grass. Some pieces of ice were driven right up to the canvas wall at the front of our cave. Fragments lodged within two feet of Vincent, who had the lowest sleeping-place, and within four feet of our fire. Crean and McCarthy had brought down six more of the young albatrosses in the afternoon, so we were well supplied with fresh food. The air temperature that night probably was not lower than 38° or 40° Fahr., and we were rendered uncomfortable in our cramped sleeping quarters by the unaccustomed warmth. Our feelings towards our neighbours underwent a change. When the temperature was below 20° Fahr. we could not get too close to one another—every man wanted to cuddle against his neighbour; but let the temperature rise a few degrees and the warmth of another man's body ceased to be a blessing. The ice and the waves had a voice of menace that night, but I heard it only in my dreams.

The bay was still filled with ice on the morning of Saturday, May 13, but the tide took it all away in the afternoon. Then a strange thing happened. The rudder, with all the broad Atlantic to sail in and the coasts of two continents to search for a resting-place, came bobbing back into our cove. With anxious eyes we watched it as it advanced, receded again, and then advanced once more under the capricious influence of wind and wave. Nearer and nearer it came as we waited on the shore, oars in hand, and at last we were able to seize it. Surely a remarkable salvage! The day was bright and clear; our clothes were drying and our strength was returning. Running water made a musical sound down the tussock slope and among the boulders. We carried our blankets up the hill and tried to dry them in the breeze 300 ft. above sea-level. In the afternoon we began to prepare the *James Caird* for the journey to the head of King Haakon Bay. A noon observation on this day gave our latitude as 54° 10' 47" S., but according to the German chart the position should have been 54° 12'S. Probably Worsley's observation was the more accurate. We were able to keep the fire alight until we went to sleep that night, for while climbing the rocks above the cove I had seen at the foot of a cliff a broken spar, which had been thrown up by the waves. We could reach this spar by climbing down the cliff, and with a reverse supply of fuel thus in sight we could afford to burn the fragments of the *James Caird*'s topsides more freely.

During the morning of this day (May 13) Worsley and I tramped across the hills in a north-easterly direction with the object of getting a view of the sound and possibly gathering some information that would be useful to us in the next stage of our journey. It was exhausting work, but after covering about 2½ miles in two hours, we were able to look east, up the bay. We could not see very much of the country that we would have to cross in order to reach the whaling-station on the other side of the island. We had passed several brooks and frozen tarns, and at a point where we had to take to the beach on the shore of the sound we found some wreckage—an 18-ft. pine-spar (probably part of a ship's topmast), several pieces of timber, and a little model of a ship's hull, evidently a child's toy. We wondered what tragedy that pitiful little plaything indicated. We encountered also some gentoo penguins and a young sea-elephant, which Worsley killed.

When we got back to the cave at 3 P.M., tired, hungry, but rather pleased with ourselves, we found a splendid meal of stewed albatross chicken waiting for us. We had carried a quantity of blubber and the sea-elephant's liver in our blouses, and we produced our treasures as a surprise for the men. Rough climbing on the way back to camp had nearly persuaded us to throw the stuff away, but we had held on (regardless of the condition of our already sorely tried clothing), and had our reward at the camp. The long bay had been a magnificent sight, even to eyes that had dwelt on grandeur long enough and were hungry for the simple, familiar things of everyday life. Its green-blue waters were being beaten to fury by the north-westerly gale. The mountains, "stern peaks that dared the stars," peered through the mists, and between them huge glaciers poured down from the great ice-slopes and -fields that lay behind. We counted twelve glaciers and heard every few minutes the reverberating roar caused by masses of ice calving from the parent streams.

On May 14 we made our preparations for an early start on the following day if the weather held fair. We expected to be able to pick up the remains of the sea-elephant on our way up the sound. All hands were recovering from the chafing caused by our wet clothes during the boat journey. The insides of our legs had suffered severely, and for some time after landing in the cove we found movement extremely uncomfortable. We paid our last visit to the nests of the albatrosses, which were situated on a little undulating plateau above the cave amid tussocks, snow-patches, and little frozen tarns. Each nest consisted of a mound over a foot high of tussock-grass, roots, and a little earth. The albatross lays one egg and very rarely two. The chicks, which are hatched in January, are fed on the nest by the parent birds for almost seven months before they take to the sea and fend for themselves. Up to four months of age the chicks are beautiful white masses of downy fluff, but when we arrived on the scene their plumage was almost complete. Very often one of the parent birds was on guard near the nest. We did not enjoy attacking these birds, but our hunger knew no law. They tasted so very good and assisted our recuperation to such an extent that each time we killed one of them we felt a little less remorseful.

May 15 was a great day. We made our hoosh at 7:30 A.M. Then we loaded up the boat and gave her a flying launch down the steep beach into the surf. Heavy rain had fallen in the night and a gusty north-westerly wind was now blowing, with misty showers. The *James Caird* headed to the sea as if anxious to face the battle of the waves once more. We passed through the narrow mouth of the cove with the ugly rocks and waving kelp close on either side, turned to the east, and sailed merrily up the bay as the sun broke through the mists and made the tossing waters sparkle around us. We were a curious-looking party on that bright morning, but we were feeling happy. We even broke into song, and, but for our Robinson Crusoe appearance, a casual observer might have taken us for a picnic party sailing in a Norwegian fiord or one of the beautiful sounds of the west coast of New Zealand. The wind blew fresh and strong, and a small sea broke on the coast as we advanced. The surf was sufficient to have endangered the boat if we had attempted to land where the carcass of the sea-elephant was lying, so we decided to go on to the head of the bay without risking anything, particularly as we were likely to find sea-elephants on the upper beaches. The big creatures have a habit of seeking peaceful quarters protected from the waves. We had hopes, too, of finding penguins. Our expectation as far as the sea-elephants were concerned was not at fault. We heard the roar of the bulls as we neared the head of the bay, and soon afterwards saw the great unwieldy forms of the beasts lying on a shelving beach towards the bay-head. We rounded a high, glacier-worn bluff on the north side, and at 12:30 P.M. we ran the boat ashore on a low beach of sand and pebbles, with tussock growing above high-water mark. There were hundreds of sea-elephants lying about, and our anxieties with regard to food disappeared. Meat and blubber enough to feed our party for years was in sight. Our landing-place was about a mile and a half west of the north-east corner of the bay. Just east of us was a glacier-snout ending on the beach but giving a passage towards the head of the bay, except at high water or when a very heavy surf was running. A cold, drizzling rain had begun to fall, and we provided ourselves with shelter as quickly as possible. We hauled the *James Caird* up above high-water mark and turned her over just to the lee or east side of the bluff. The spot was separated from the mountain-side by a low morainic bank, rising twenty or thirty feet above sea-level. Soon we had converted the boat into a very comfortable cabin *à la* Peggotty, turfing it round with tussocks, which we dug up with knives. One side of the *James Caird* rested on stones so as to afford a low entrance, and when we had finished she looked as though she had grown there. McCarthy entered into this work with great spirit. A sea-elephant provided us with fuel and meat, and that evening found a well-fed and fair-ly contented party at rest in Peggotty Camp.

Our camp, as I have said, lay on the north side of King Haakon Bay near the head. Our path towards the whaling-stations led round the seaward end of the snouted glacier on the east side of the camp and up a snow-slope that appeared to lead to a pass in the great Allardyce Range, which runs north-west and south-east and forms the main backbone of South Georgia.

The range dipped opposite the bay into a well-defined pass from east to west. An ice-sheet covered most of the interior, filling the valleys and disguising the configuration of the land, which, indeed, showed only in big rocky ridges, peaks, and nunataks. When we looked up the pass from Peggotty Camp the country to the left appeared to offer two easy paths through to the opposite coast, but we knew that the island was uninhabited at that point (Possession Bay). We had to turn our attention farther east, and it was impossible from the camp to learn much of the conditions that would confront us on the overland journey. I planned to climb to the pass and then be guided by the configuration of the country in the selection of a route eastward to Stromness Bay, where the whaling-stations were established in the minor bays, Leith, Husvik, and Stromness. A range of mountains with precipitous slopes, forbidding peaks, and large glaciers lay immediately to the south of King Haakon Bay and seemed to form a continuation of the main range. Between this secondary range and the pass above our camp a great snow-upland sloped up to the inland ice-sheet and reached a rocky ridge that stretched athwart our path and seemed to bar the way. This ridge was a right-angled offshoot from the main ridge. Its chief features were four rocky peaks with spaces between that looked from a distance as though they might prove to be passes.

The weather was bad on Tuesday, May 16, and we stayed under the boat nearly all day. The quarters were cramped but gave full protection from the weather, and we regarded our little cabin with a great deal of satisfaction. Abundant meals of sea-elephant steak and liver increased our contentment. McNeish reported during the day that he had seen rats feeding on the scraps, but this interesting statement was not verified. One would not expect to find rats at such a spot, but there was a bare possibility that they had landed from a wreck and managed to survive the very rigorous conditions.

A fresh west-south-westerly breeze was blowing on the following morning (Wednesday, May 17), with misty squalls, sleet, and rain. I took Worsley with me on a pioneer journey to the west with the object of examining the country to be traversed at the beginning of the overland journey. We went round the seaward end of the snouted glacier, and after tramping about a mile over stony ground and snow-coated debris, we crossed some big ridges of scree and moraines. We found that there was good going for a sledge as far as the north-east corner of the bay, but did not get much information regarding the conditions farther on owing to the view becoming obscured by a snow-squall. We waited a quarter of an hour for the weather to clear but were forced to turn back without having seen more of the country. I had satisfied myself, however, that we could reach a good snow-slope leading apparently to the inland ice. Worsley reckoned from the chart that the distance from our camp to Husvik, on an east magnetic course, was seventeen geographical miles, but we could not expect to follow a direct line. The carpenter started making a sledge for use on the overland journey. The materials at his disposal were limited in quantity and scarcely suitable in quality.

We overhauled our gear on Thursday, May 18, and hauled our sledge to the lower edge of the snouted glacier. The vehicle proved heavy and cumbrous. We had to lift it empty over bare patches of rock along the shore, and I realized that it would be too heavy for three men to manage amid the snow-plains, glaciers, and peaks of the interior. Worsley and Crean were coming with me, and after consultation we decided to leave the sleeping-bags behind us and make the journey in very light marching order. We would take three days' provisions for each man in the form of sledging ration and biscuit. The food was to be packed in three socks, so that each member of the party could carry his own supply. Then we were to take the Primus lamp filled with oil, the small cooker, the carpenter's adze (for use as an ice-axe), and the alpine rope, which made a total length of fifty feet when knotted. We might have to lower ourselves down steep slopes or cross crevassed glaciers. The filled lamp would provide six hot meals, which would consist of sledging ration boiled up with biscuit. There were two boxes of matches left, one full and the other partially used. We left the full box with the men at the camp and took the second box, which contained forty-eight matches. I was unfortunate as regarded footgear, since I had given away my heavy Burberry boots on the floe, and had now a comparatively light pair in poor condition. The carpenter assisted me by putting several screws in the sole of each boot with the object of providing a grip on the ice. The screws came out of the *James Caird*.

We turned in early that night, but sleep did not come to me. My mind was busy with the task of the following day. The weather was clear and the outlook for an early start in the morning was good. We were going to leave a weak party behind us in the camp. Vincent was still in the same condition, and he could not march. McNeish was pretty well broken up. The two men were not capable of managing for themselves and McCarthy must stay to look after them. He might have a difficult task if we failed to reach the whaling-station. The distance to Husvik, according to the chart, was no more than seventeen geographical miles in a direct line, but we had very scanty knowledge of the conditions of the interior. No man had ever penetrated a mile from the coast of South Georgia at any point, and the whalers I knew regarded the country as inaccessible. During that day, while we were walking to the snouted glacier, we had seen three wild duck flying towards the head of the bay from the eastward.

I hoped that the presence of these birds indicated tussock-land and not snow-fields and glaciers in the interior, but the hope was not a very bright one.

We turned out at 2 A.M. on the Friday morning and had our hoosh ready an hour later. The full moon was shining in a practically cloudless sky, its rays reflected gloriously from the pinnacles and crevassed ice of the adjacent glaciers. The huge peaks of the mountains stood in bold relief against the sky and threw dark shadows on the waters of the sound. There was no need for delay, and we made a start as soon as we had eaten our meal. McNeish walked about 200 yds. with us; he could do no more. Then we said good-bye and he turned back to the camp. The first task was to get round the edge of the snouted glacier, which had points like fingers projecting towards the sea. The waves were reaching the points of these fingers, and we had to rush from one recess to another when the waters receded. We soon reached the east side of the glacier and noticed its great activity at this point. Changes had occurred within the preceding twenty-four hours. Some huge pieces had broken off, and the masses of mud and stone that were being driven before the advancing ice showed movement. The glacier was like a gigantic plough driving irresistibly towards the sea.

Lying on the beach beyond the glacier was wreckage that told of many ill-fated ships. We noticed stanchions of teak-wood, liberally carved, that must have come from ships of the older type; iron-bound timbers with the iron almost rusted through; battered barrels and all the usual debris of the ocean. We had difficulties and anxieties of our own, but as we passed the graveyard of the sea we thought of the many tragedies written in the wave-worn fragments of lost vessels. We did not pause, and soon we were ascending a snow-slope, heading due east on the last lap of our long trail.

The snow-surface was disappointing. Two days before we had been able to move rapidly on hard, packed snow; now we sank over our ankles at each step and progress was slow. After two hours' steady climbing we were 2500 ft. above sea-level. The weather continued fine and calm, and as the ridges drew nearer and the western coast of the island spread out below, the bright moonlight showed us that the interior was broken tremendously. High peaks, impassable cliffs, steep snow-slopes, and sharply descending glaciers were prominent features in all directions, with stretches of snow-plain overlaying the ice-sheet of the interior. The slope we were ascending mounted to a ridge and our course lay direct to the top. The moon, which proved a good friend during this journey, threw a long shadow at one point and told us that the surface was broken in our path. Warned in time, we avoided a huge hole capable of swallowing an army. The bay was now about three miles away, and the continued roaring of a big glacier at the head of the bay came to our ears. This glacier, which we had noticed during the stay at Peggotty Camp, seemed to be calving almost continuously.

I had hoped to get a view of the country ahead of us from the top of the slope, but as the surface became more level beneath our feet, a thick fog drifted down. The moon became obscured and produced a diffused light that was more trying than darkness, since it illuminated the fog without guiding our steps. We roped ourselves together as a precaution against holes, crevasses, and precipices, and I broke trail through the soft snow. With almost the full length of the rope between myself and the last man we were able to steer an approximately straight course, since, if I veered to the right or the left when marching into the blank wall of the fog, the last man on the rope could shout a direction. So, like a ship with its "port," "starboard," "steady," we tramped through the fog for the next two hours.

Then, as daylight came, the fog thinned and lifted, and from an elevation of about 3000 ft. we looked down on what seemed to be a huge frozen lake with its farther shores still obscured by the fog. We halted there to eat a bit of biscuit while we discussed whether we would go down and cross the flat surface of the lake, or keep on the ridge we had already reached. I decided to go down, since the lake lay on our course. After an hour of comparatively easy travel through the snow we noticed the thin beginnings of crevasses. Soon they were increasing in size and showing

fractures, indicating that we were travelling on a glacier. As the daylight brightened the fog dissipated; the
lake could be seen more clearly, but still we could not
discover its east shore. A little later the fog lifted completely, and then we saw that our lake stretched to the
horizon, and realized suddenly that we were looking
down upon the open sea on the east coast of the
island. The slight pulsation at the shore showed that
the sea was not even frozen; it was the bad light that
had deceived us. Evidently we were at the top of
Possession Bay, and the island at that point could not
be more than five miles across from the head of King
Haakon Bay. Our rough chart was inaccurate. There
was nothing for it but to start up the glacier again.
That was about seven o'clock in the morning, and by
nine o'clock we had more than recovered our lost
ground. We regained the ridge and then struck south-
east, for the chart showed that two more bays indent-
ed the coast before Stromness. It was comforting to
realize that we would have the eastern water in sight
during our journey, although we could see there was
no way around the shoreline owing to steep cliffs and
glaciers. Men lived in houses lit by electric light on
the east coast. News of the outside world waited us
there, and, above all, the east coast meant for us the
means of rescuing the twenty-two men we had left
on Elephant Island.

Battle with the Giant Octopus

VICTOR HUGO

Just as Gilliatt was making up his mind to resign himself to sea-urchins and sea-chestnuts, a splash was made at his feet.

A huge crab, frightened by his approach, had just dropped into the water. The crab did not sink so deeply that Gilliatt lost sight of it.

Gilliatt set out on a run after the crab along the base of the reef. The crab sought to escape.

Suddenly, he was no longer in sight.

The crab had just hidden in some crevice under the rock.

Gilliatt clung to the projections of the rock, and thrust forward his head to get a look under the overhanging cliff.

There was in fact a cavity there. The crab must have taken refuge in it.

It was something more than a crevice. It was a sort of porch.

The sea entered beneath this porch, but was not deep. The bottom was visible, covered with stones. These stones were smooth and clothed with algae, which indicated that they were never dry. They resembled the tops of children's heads covered with green hair.

Gilliatt took his knife in his teeth, climbed down with his hands and feet from the top of the cliff, and leaped into the water. It reached almost to his shoulders.

He passed under the porch. He entered a much worn corridor in the form of a rude pointed arch overhead. The walls were smooth and polished. He no longer saw the crab. He kept his foothold, and advanced through the diminishing light. He began to be unable to distinguish objects.

After about fifteen paces, the vault above him came to an end. He was out of the corridor. He had here more space, and consequently more light; and besides, the pupils of his eyes were now dilated: he saw with tolerable clearness. He had a surprise.

He was just re-entering that strange cave which he had visited a month previously.

Only he had returned to it by way of the sea.

That arch which he had then seen submerged was the one through which he had just passed. It was accessible at certain low tides.

His eyes became accustomed to the place. He saw better and better. He was astounded. He had found again that extraordinary palace of shadows, that vault, those pillars, those purple and blood-like stains, that jewel-like vegetation, and at the end that crypt, almost a sanctuary, and that stone which was almost an altar.

He had not taken much notice of these details; but he carried the general effect in his mind, and he beheld it again.

Opposite him, at a certain height in the cliff, he saw the crevice through which he had made his entrance on the first occasion, and which, from the point where he now stood, seemed inaccessible.

He beheld again, near the pointed arch, those low and obscure grottoes, a sort of caverns within the cavern, which he had already observed from a distance. Now he was close to them. The one nearest to him was dry and easily accessible.

Still nearer than that opening he noticed a horizontal fissure in the granite above the level of the water. The crab was probably there. He thrust in his hand as far as he could and began to grope in this hole of shadows.

All at once he felt himself seized by the arm.

What he felt at that moment was indescribable horror.

Something thin, rough, flat, slimy, adhesive, and living, had just wound itself round his bare arm in the dark. It crept up towards his breast. It was like the pressure of a leather thong and the thrust of a gimlet. In less than a second an indescribable spiral form had passed around his wrist and his elbow, and reached to his shoulder. The point burrowed under his armpit.

Gilliatt threw himself backwards, but could hardly move. He was as though nailed to the spot; with his left hand, which remained free, he took his knife, which he held between his teeth, and holding the knife with his hand he braced himself against the rock, in a desperate effort to withdraw his arm. He only succeeded in disturbing the ligature a little, which resumed its pressure. It was as supple as leather, as solid as steel, as cold as night.

A second thong, narrow and pointed, issued from the crevice of the rock. It was like a tongue from the jaws of a monster. It licked Gilliatt's naked form in a terrible fashion, and suddenly stretching out, immensely long and thin, it applied itself to his skin and surrounded his whole body. At the same time, unheard-of suffering, which was comparable to nothing he had previously known, swelled Gilliatt's contracted muscles. He felt in his skin round and horrible perforations; it seemed to him that innumerable lips were fastened to his flesh and were seeking to drink his blood.

A third thong undulated outside the rock, felt of Gilliatt, and lashed his sides like a cord. It fixed itself there.

Anguish is mute when at its highest point. Gilliatt

did not utter a cry. There was light enough for him to see the repulsive forms adhering to him.

A fourth ligature, this one as swift as a dart, leaped towards his belly and rolled itself around there.

Impossible either to tear or to cut away these shiny thongs which adhered closely to Gilliatt's body, and by a number of points. Each one of those points was the seat of frightful and peculiar pain. It was what would be experienced if one were being swallowed simultaneously by a throng of mouths which were too small.

A fifth prolongation leaped from the hole. It superimposed itself upon the others, and folded over Gilliatt's chest. Compression was added to horror; Gilliatt could hardly breathe.

These thongs, pointed at their extremity, spread out gradually like the blades of swords towards the hilt. All five evidently belonged to the same centre. They crept and crawled over Gilliatt. He felt these strange points of pressure, which seemed to him to be mouths, changing their places.

Suddenly a large, round, flat, slimy mass emerged from the lower part of the crevice.

It was the centre; the five thongs were attached to it like spokes to a hub; on the opposite side of this foul disk could be distinguished the beginnings of three other tentacles, which remained under the slope of the rock. In the middle of this sliminess there were two eyes gazing. The eyes were fixed on Gilliatt.

Gilliatt recognized the octopus (*devil-fish*).

To believe in the octopus, one must have seen it.

Compared with it, the hydras of old are laughable.

At certain moments one is tempted to think that the intangible forms which float through our vision encounter in the realms of the possible, certain magnetic centers to which their lineaments cling, and that from these obscure fixations of the living dream, beings spring forth. The unknown has the marvelous at its disposal, and it makes use of it to compose the monster. Orpheus, Homer, and Hesiod were only able to make the Chimaera: God made the octopus.

When God wills it, he excels in the execrable. . . .

All ideals being admitted, if terror be an object, the octopus is a masterpiece.

The whale has enormous size, the octopus is small; the hippopotamus has a cuirass, the octopus is naked; the jararoca hisses, the octopus is dumb; the rhinoceros has a horn, the octopus has no horn; the scorpion has a sting, the octopus has no sting; the buthus has claws, the octopus has no claws; the ape has a prehensile tail, the octopus has no tail; the shark has sharp fins, the octopus has no fins; the vespertilio vampire has wings armed with barbs, the octopus has no barbs; the hedgehog has quills, the octopus has no quills; the sword-fish has a sword, the octopus has no sword; the torpedo-fish has an electric shock, the octopus has none; the toad has a virus, the octopus has no virus; the viper has a venom, the octopus has no venom; the lion has claws, the octopus has no claws; the hawk has a beak, the octopus has no beak; the crocodile has jaws, the octopus has no teeth.

The octopus has no muscular organization, no menacing cry, no breastplate, no horn, no dart, no pincers, no prehensile or bruising tail, no cutting pectoral fins, no barbed wings, no quills, no sword, no electric discharge, no virus, no venom, no claws, no beak, no teeth. Of all creatures, the octopus is the most formidably armed.

What then is the octopus? It is the cupping-glass.

In open sea reefs, where the water displays and hides all its splendors, in the hollows of unvisited rocks, in the unknown caves where vegetations, crustaceans, and shell-fish abound, beneath the deep portals of the ocean,—the swimmer who hazards himself there, led on by the beauty of the place, runs the risk of an encounter. If you have this encounter, be not curious but fly. One enters there dazzled, one emerges from thence terrified.

This is the nature of the encounter always possible among rocks in the open sea.

A grayish form undulates in the water: it is as thick as a man's arm, and about half an ell long; it is a rag; its form resembles a closed umbrella without a handle. This rag gradually advances towards you, suddenly it opens: eight radii spread out abruptly around a face which has two eyes; these radii are alive; there is some-thing of the flame in their undulation; it is a sort of wheel; unfolded, it is four or five feet in diameter. Frightful expansion. This flings itself upon you.

The hydra harpoons its victim.

This creature applies itself to its prey; covers it, and knots its long bands about it. Underneath, it is yellow-ish; on top, earth-colored: nothing can represent this inexplicable hue of dust; one would pronounce it a creature made of ashes, living in the water. In form it is spider-like, and like a chameleon in its coloring. When irritated it becomes violet in hue. Its most ter-rible quality is its softness.

Its folds strangle; its contact paralyzes.

It has an aspect of scurvy and gangrene. It is disease embodied in monstrosity.

It is not to be torn away. It adheres closely to its prey. How? By a vacuum. Its eight antennae, large at the root, gradually taper off and end in needles. Underneath each one of them are arranged two rows of decreasing pustules, the largest near the head, the smallest ones at the tip. Each row consists of twenty-five; there are fifty pustules to each antenna, and the whole creature has four hundred of them. These pus-tules are cupping-glasses.

These cupping-glasses are cylindrical, horny, livid cartilages. On the large species they gradually diminish from the diameter of a five-franc piece to the size of a lentil. These fragments of tubes are thrust out from the animal and retire into it. They can be inserted into the prey for more than an inch.

This sucking apparatus has all the delicacy of a key-board. It rises, then retreats. It obeys the slightest wish of the animal. The most exquisite sensibilities cannot equal the contractibility of these suckers, always proportioned to the internal movements of the creature and to the external circumstances. This dragon is like a sensitive-plant.

This is the monster which mariners call the poulp, which science calls the cephalopod, and which legend calls the kraken. English sailors call it the "devil-fish." They also call it the "blood-sucker." In the Channel Islands it is called the *pieuvre*.

It is very rare in Guernsey, very small in Jersey, very large and quite frequent in Sark.

A print from Sonnini's edition of Buffon represents an octopus crushing a frigate. Denis Montfort thinks that the octopus of the high latitudes is really strong enough to sink a ship. Bory Saint Vincent denies this, but admits that in our latitudes it does attack man. Go to Sark and they will show you, near Brecq-Hou, the hollow in the rock where, a few years ago, an octopus seized and drowned a lobster-fisher.

Péron and Lamarck are mistaken when they doubt whether the octopus can swim, since it has no fins.

He who writes these lines has seen with his own eyes at Sark, in the caves called the Shops, an octopus swimming and chasing a bather. When killed and measured it was found to be four English feet in spread, and four hundred suckers could be counted. The dying monster thrust them out convulsively.

According to Denis Montfort, one of those observers whose strong gift of intuition causes them to descend or to ascend even to magianism, the octopus has almost the passions of a man; the octopus hates. In fact, in the absolute, to be hideous is to hate.

The misshapen struggles under a necessity of elimination, and this consequently renders it hostile.

The octopus when swimming remains, so to speak, in its sheath. It swims with all its folds held close. Let the reader picture to himself a sewed-up sleeve with a closed fist inside of it. This fist, which is the head, pushes through the water, and advances with a vague, undulating movement. Its two eyes, though large, are not very distinct, being the color of the water.

The octopus on the chase or lying in wait, hides; it contracts, it condenses itself; it reduces itself to the simplest possible expression. It confounds itself with the shadow. It looks like a ripple of the waves. It resembles everything except something living.

The octopus is a hypocrite. When one pays no heed to it, suddenly it opens.

A glutinous mass possessed of a will—what more frightful? Glue filled with hatred.

It is in the most beautiful azure of the limpid water that this hideous, voracious star of the sea arises.

It gives no warning of its approach, which renders it more terrible. Almost always, when one sees it, one is already caught.

At night, however, and in breeding season, it is phosphorescent. This terror has its passions. It awaits the nuptial hour. It adorns itself, it lights up, it illuminates itself; and from the summit of a rock one can see it beneath, in the shadowy depths, spread out in a pallid irradiation,—a spectre sun.

It has no bones, it has no blood, it has no flesh. It is flabby. There is nothing in it. It is a skin. One can turn its eight tentacles wrong side out, like the fingers of a glove.

It has a single orifice in the centre of its radiation. Is this one hole the vent? Is it the mouth? It is both.

The same aperture fulfills both functions. The entrance is the exit.

The whole creature is cold.

The carnarius of the Mediterranean is repulsive. An odious contact has this animated gelatine, which envelops the swimmer, into which the hands sink, where the nails scratch, which one rends without killing and tears off without pulling away, a sort of flowing and tenacious being which slips between one's fingers; but no horror equals the sudden appearance of the octopus,—Medusa served by eight serpents.

No grasp equals the embrace of the cephalopod.

It is the pneumatic machine attacking you. You have to deal with a vacuum furnished with paws. Neither scratches nor bites; an indescribable scarification. A bite if formidable, but less so than a suction. A claw is nothing beside the cupping-glass. The claw means the beast entering into your flesh; the cupping-glass means yourself entering into the beast.

Your muscles swell, your fibres writhe, your skin cracks under the foul weight, your blood spurts forth and mingles frightfully with the lymph of the mollusk. The creature superimposes itself upon you by a thousand mouths; the hydra incorporates itself with the man; the man amalgamates himself with the hydra. You form but one. This dream is upon you. The tiger can only devour you; the octopus, oh horror! breathes you in. It draws you to it, and into it; and bound, ensnared, powerless, you feel yourself slowly emptied into that frightful pond, which is the monster itself.

Beyond the terrible, being devoured alive, is the inexpressible, being drunk alive. . .

Such was the creature in whose power Gilliatt had been for several moments.

This monster was the inhabitant of that grotto. It was the frightful genius of the place. A sort of sombre demon of the water.

All these magnificences had horror for their centre.

A month previously, on the day when for the first time Gilliatt had made his way into the grotto, the dark outline, of which he had caught a glimpse in the ripples of the water, was this octopus.

This was its home.

When Gilliatt, entering that cave for the second time in pursuit of the crab, had perceived the crevices in which he thought the crab had taken refuge, the octopus was lying in wait in that hole.

Can the reader picture that lying in wait?

Not a bird would dare to brood, not an egg would dare to hatch, not a flower would dare to open, not a breast would dare to give suck, not a heart would dare to love, not a spirit would dare to take flight, if one meditated on the sinister shapes patiently lying in ambush in the abyss.

Gilliatt had thrust his arm into the hole; the octopus had seized it.

It held it.

He was the fly for this spider.

Gilliatt stood in water to his waist, his feet clinging to the slippery roundness of the stones, his right arm grasped and subdued by the flat coils of the octopus's thongs, and his body almost hidden by the folds and crossings of that horrible bandage. Of the eight arms of the octopus, three adhered to the rock while five adhered to Gilliatt. In this manner, clamped on one side to the granite, on the other to the man, it chained Gilliatt to the rock. Gilliatt had two hundred and fifty suckers upon him. A combination of anguish and disgust. To be crushed in a gigantic fist, whose elastic fingers, nearly a metre in length, are inwardly full of living pustules which ransack your flesh.

As we have said, one cannot tear one's self away from the octopus. If one attempts it, one is but the more surely bound. It only clings the closer. Its efforts increase in proportion to yours. A greater struggle produces a greater constriction.

Gilliatt had but one resource,—his knife.

He had only his left hand free; but as the reader knows, he could make powerful use of it. It might have been said of him that he had two right hands.

His open knife was in his hand.

The tentacles of an octopus cannot be cut off; they are leathery and difficult to sever, they slip away from under the blade. Moreover, the superposition is such that a cut into these thongs would attack your own flesh.

The octopus is formidable; nevertheless there is a way of getting away from it. The fishermen of Sark are acquainted with it; any one who has seen them executing abrupt movements at sea knows it. Porpoises also know it: they have a way of biting the cuttlefish which cuts off its head. Hence all the headless squids and cuttlefish which are met with on the open sea.

The octopus is in fact vulnerable only in the head. Gilliatt was not ignorant of this fact.

He had never seen an octopus of this size. He found himself seized at the outset by one of the larger species. Any other man would have been terrified.

In the case of the octopus as in that of the bull, there is a certain moment at which to seize it: it is the instant when the bull lowers his neck, it is the instant when the octopus thrusts forward its head—a sudden movement. He who misses that juncture is lost.

All that we have related lasted but a few minutes. But Gilliatt felt the suction of the two hundred and fifty cupping-glasses increasing.

The octopus is cunning. It tries to stupefy its prey in the first place. It seizes, then waits as long as it can.

Gilliatt held his knife. The suction increased.

He gazed at the octopus, which stared at him.

All at once the creature detached its sixth tentacle from the rock, and launching it at him, attempted to seize his left arm.

At the same time it thrust its head forward swiftly. A second more and its mouth would have been applied to Gilliatt's breast. Gilliatt, wounded in the flank and with both arms pinioned, would have been a dead man.

But Gilliatt was on his guard. Being watched, he watched.

He avoided the tentacle, and at the moment when the creature was about to bite his breast, his armed fist descended on the monster.

Two convulsions in opposite directions ensued: that of Gilliatt and that of the octopus.

It was like the conflict of two flashes of lightning.

Gilliatt plunged the point of his knife into the flat, viscous mass, and with a twisting movement, similar to the flourish of a whip, describing a circle around the two eyes, he tore out the head as one wrenches out a tooth.

It was finished.

The whole creature dropped.

It resembled a sheet detaching itself. The air-pump destroyed, the vacuum no longer existed. The four hundred suckers released their hold, simultaneously, of the rock and the man.

It sank to the bottom.

Gilliatt, panting with the combat, could perceive on the rocks at his feet two shapeless, gelatinous masses, the head on one side, the rest on the other. We say "the rest," because one could not say the body.

Gilliatt however, fearing some convulsive return of agony, retreated beyond the reach of the tentacles.

But the monster was really dead.

Gilliatt closed his knife.

It was time that Gilliatt killed the octopus. He was almost strangled; his right arm and his body were violet in hue; more than two hundred swellings were outlined upon them; the blood spurted from some of them here and there. The remedy for these wounds is salt water: Gilliatt plunged into it. At the same time he rubbed himself with the palm of his hand. The swelling subsided under this friction.

Encounter with the Blackfeet

OSBORNE RUSSELL

For an authentic, highly readable account of what being a mountain man was like in the Rockies during the halcyon fur-trade years, 1834-1843, you need look no further than this amazing book. In a manuscript now skillfully edited by Aubrey Haines, Osborne Russell describes the life of the mountain man with great clarity and detail. The terrain, the wildlife, the Indians are superbly pictured, just as Russell and the first white men to enter the High Rockies saw them. Russell, born in 1814 in Maine, passed away in 1892 while living in California. Most mountain men did not fare nearly so well and "went under" while living the life they loved. In this excerpt you'll see one of the reasons why as Russell and his companions explore the area that is Yellowstone Park today.

Aug 22 we left this Stream and travelled along the foot of the mountain at the edge of the plain about 20 Mls west cours and encamped at a spring. The next day we crossed the Yellowstone river and travelled up it on the west side to the mouth of Gardnes fork where we staid the next day 25th We travelled to "Gardners hole" then altered our cousre SE crossing the eastern point of the valley and encamping on a small branch among the pines 26 We encamped on the YellowStone in the big plain below the lake The next day we went to the lake and set our traps on a branch running into it near the outlet on the NE side 28th after visiting my traps I returned to the Camp where after stopping about an hour or two I took my rifle and sauntered down the shore of the Lake among the [scattered] groves of tall pines until tired of walking about (the day being very warm) I took a bath in the lake for probably half an hour and returned to camp about 4 ockk PM Two of my comrades observed let us take a walk among the pines and kill an Elk and started off whilst the other was laying asleep— Sometime after they were gone I went to a bale of dried meat which had been spread in the Sun 30 or 40 feet from the place where we slept here I pulled off my powder horn and bullet pouch laid them on a log drew my butcher knife and began to cut We were encamped about a half a mile from the Lake on a stream running into it in a S.W. direction thro. a prarie bottom about a quarter of a mile wide On each side of this valley arose a bench of land about 20 ft high running paralell with the stheam and covered with pines On this bench we were encamped on the SE side of the stream The pines immediately behind us was thickly intermingled with logs and fallen trees—After eating a few [minutes] I arose and kindled a fire filled my tobacco pipe and sat down to smoke My comrade whose name was White was still sleeping. Presently I cast my eyes towards the horses which were feeding in the Valley and discovered the heads of some Indians who were gliding round under the bench within 30 steps of me I jumped to my rifle and aroused White and looking towards my powder horn and bullet pouch it was already in the hands of an Indian and we were completely surrounded We cocked our rifles and started thro. their ranks into the woods which seemed to be completely filled with Blackfeet who rent the air with their horrid yells. on presenting our rifles they opened a space about 20 ft. wide thro. which we plunged about the fourth jump an arrow struck White on the right hip joint I hastily told him to pull it out and I spoke another arrow struck me in the same place but they did not retard our progress At length another arrow striking thro. my right leg above the knee benumbed the flesh so that I fell with my breast across a log. The Indian who shot me was within 8 ft and made a Spring towards me with his uplifted battle axe: I made a leap and avoided the blow and kept hopping from log to log thro. a shower of arrows which flew around us like hail, lodging in the pines and logs. After we had passed them about 10 paces we wheeled about and took [aim] at them They then began to dodge behind the trees and shoot their guns we then ran and hopped about 50 yards further in the logs and bushes and made a stand—I was very faint from the loss of blood and we set down among the logs determined to kill the two foremost when they came up and then die like men we rested our rifles across a log White aiming at the foremost and Myself at the second I whispered to him that when they turned their eyes toward us to pull trigger. About 20 of them passed by us within 15 feet without casting a glance towards us another file came round on the [opposite] side within 20 or 30 paces closing with the first a few rods beyond us and all turning to the right the next minute were out of our sight among the bushes They were all well armed with fusees, bows & battle axes We sat still until the rustling among the bushes had died away then arose and after looking carefully around us White asked in a whisper how far it was to the lake I replied pointing to the SE about a quarter of a mile. I was nearly fainting from the loss of blood and the want of water We hobbled along 40 or 50 rods and I was obliged to sit down a few minutes then go a little further and rest again. we managed in this way until we reached the bank of the lake Our next object was to obtain some of the water as the bank was very steep and high. White had been perfectly calm and deliberate until now his conversation became wild hurried and despairing he observed "I cannot go down to that water for I am wounded all over I shall die" I told him to sit down while I crawled down and brought some in my hat. This I effected with a great deal of difficulty. We then hobbled along the border of the Lake for a mile and a half when it grew dark and we stopped. We could still hear the shouting of the Savages over their booty. We stopped under a large pine near the lake and I told White I could go no further "Oh said he let us go up into the pines and find a spring" I replied there was no spring within a Mile of us which I knew to be a fact. Well said he if you stop here I shall make a fire Make as much as you please I replied angrily This is a poor time now to undertake to frighten me into measurs. I then started to the water crawling on my hands and one knee and returned in about an hour with some in my hat. While I was at this he had kindled a small fire and taking a draught of water from the hat he exclaimed Oh dear we shall die here, we shall never get out of these mountains, Well said I if you persist in thinking so you will die but I can crawl from this place upon my hands and one knee and Kill 2 or 3 Elk and make a shelter of the skins dry the meat until we get able to travel. In this manner I persuaded him that we were not in half so bad a Situation as we might be altho. he was not in half so bad a situation as I expected for on examining I found only a slight wound from an arrow on his hip bone but he was not so much to blame as he was a young man who had been brot up in Missouri the pet of the family and had never done or learned much of anything but horseracing and gambling whilst under the care of his parents (if care it can be called). I pulled off an old piece of a coat made of Blanket (as he was entirely without clothing except his hat and shirt) Set myself in a leaning position against a tree ever and anon gathering such leaves and rubbish as I could reach without altering the position of My body to keep up a little fire in this manner miserably spent the night. The next morning Aug 29th I could not arise without assistance When White procured me a couple of sticks for crutches by the help of which I hobbled to a small grove of pines about 60 yds distant. We had scarcely entered the grove when we heard a dog barking and Indians singing and talking. The sound seemed to be approaching us. They at length came near to where we were to the number of 60 Then commenced shooting at a large bank of elk that was swimming in the lake killed 4 of them dragged them to shore and butchered them which occupied about 3 hours. They then packed the meat in small bundles on their backs and travelled up along the rocky shore about a mile and encamped. We then left our hiding place crept into the thick pines about 50 yds distant and started in the direction of our encampment in the hope of finding our comrades My leg was very much swelled and painful but I managed to get along slowly on my crutches by Whites carrying my rifle when we were within about 60 rods of the encampment we discovered the Canadian hunting round among the trees as tho he was looking for a trail we approached him within 30 ft before he saw us and he was so much agitated by fear that he knew not whether to run or stand still. On being asked where Elbridge was he said they came to the Camp the night before at sunset the Indians pursued them into the woods where they separated and he saw him no more. At the encampment I found a sack of salt—everything else the Indians had carried away or cut to pieces They had built 7 large Conical forts near the spot from which we supposed their number to have been 70 or 80 part of whom had returned to their Village with the horses and plunder. We left the place heaping curses on the head of the Blackfoot nation which neither injured them or alleviated our distress We followed down the shores of the lake and stopped for the night My companions threw some logs and rubbish together forming a kind of shelter from the night breeze but in the night it took fire (the logs being pitch pine) the blaze ran to the tops of the trees we removed a short distance built another fire and laid by it until Morning We then made a raft of dry poles and crossed the outlet upon it. We then went to a small grove of pines nearby and made a fire where we stopped the remainder of the day in hopes that Elbridge would see our signals and come to us for we left directions on a tree at the encampment which route we would take. In the meantime the Cannadian went to hunt something to eat but without success. I had bathed my wounds in Salt water and made a salve of Beavers Oil and Castoreum which I applied to them This had eased the pain and drawn out the swelling in a great measure. The next morning I felt very stiff and sore but we were obliged to travel or starve as we had eaten nothing since our defeat and game was very scarce on the West side of the Lake and morover the Cannadian had got such a fright we could not prevail on him to go out of our sight to hunt So on we truged slowly and after getting warm I could bear half my weight on my lame leg but it was bent considerably and swelled so much that my Knee joint was stiff. About 10 oclk the Cannadian killed a couple of small Ducks which served us for breakfast. after eating them we pursued our journey. At 12 oclk it began to rain but we still kept on until the Sun was 2 hours high in the evening when the weather clearing away we encamped at some hot springs and killed a couple of geese. Whilst we were eating them a Deer came swimming along in the lake within about 100 yards of the shore we fired several shots at him but the water glancing the balls he remained unhurt and apparently unalarmed but still Kept swimming to and fro in the Lake in front of us for an hour and then started along up close to the shore.

The hunter went to watch it in order to kill it when it should come ashore but as he was lying in wait for the Deer a Doe Elk came to the water to Drink and he killed her but the Deer was still out in the lake swimming to and fro till dark. Now we had aplenty of meat and drink but [were] almost destitute of clothing I had on a par of trowsers and a cotton shirt which were completely drenched with the rain. We made a sort of shelter from the wind of pine branches and built a large fire of pitch Knots in front of it, so that we were burning on one side and freezing on the other alternately all night. The next morning we cut some of the Elk meat in thin slices and cooked it slowly over a fire then packed it in bundles strung them on our backs and started by this time I could carry my own rifle and limp along half as fast as a man could walk but when my foot touched against the logs or brush the pain in my leg was very severe We left the lake at the hot springs and travelled thro. the thick pines over a low ridge of land thro. the snow and rain together but we travelled by the wind about 8 Mls in a SW direction when we came to a Lake about 12 Mls in circumference which is the head spring of the right branch of Lewis fork. Here we found a dry spot near a number of hot springs under some thick pines our hunter had Killed a Deer on the way and I took the skin wrapped it around me and felt prouder of my Mantle than a Monarch with his imperial robes. This night I slept more than 4 hours which was more than I had slept at any one time since I was wounded and arose the next morning much refreshed These Springs are similar to those on the Madison and among these as well as those Sulphur is found in its purity in large quantities on the surface of the ground. We travelled along the Shore on the south side about 5 Mls in an East direction fell in with a large band of Elk killed two fat Does and took some of the meat. We then left the lake and travelled due South over a rough broken country covered with thick pines for about 12 Mls when we came to the fork again which ran thro. a narrow prarie bottom followed drown it about six miles and encamped at the forks We had passed up the left hand fork on the 9th of July on horse back in good health and spirits and came down on the right on the 31st of Aug. on foot with weary limbs and sorrowful countenances. We built a fire and laid down to rest, but I could not sleep more than 15 or 20 minutes at a time the night was so very cold. We had plenty of Meat however and made Mocasins of raw Elk hide The next day we crossed the stream and travelled down near to Jacksons Lake on the West side then took up a small branch in a West direction to the head. We then had the Teton mountain to cross which looked like a laborious undertaking as it was steep and the top covered with snow. We arrived at the summit how-ever with a great deal of difficulty before sunset and after resting a few moments travelled down about a mile on the other side and stopped for the night. After spending another cold and tedious night we were descending the Mountain thro. the pines at day light and the next night reached the forks of Henrys fork of Snake river. This day was very warm but the wind blew cold at night we made a fire and gathered some dry grass to sleep on and then sat down and eat the remainder of our provisions. It was now 90 Mls to Fort Hall and we expected to see little or no game on the route but we determined to travel it in 3 days we lay down and shivered with the cold till daylight then arose and again pursued our journey towards the fork of Snake river where we arrived sun about an hour high forded the river which was nearly swimming and encamped The weather being very cold and fording the river so late at night caused me much suffering during the night Septr 4th we were on our way at day break and travelled all day thro. the high Sage and sand down Snake river We stopped at dark nearly worn out with fatigue hunger and want of sleep as we had now travelled 65 Mls in two days without eating. We sat and hovered over a small fire until another day appeared then set out as usual and travelled to within about 10 Ms of the Fort when I was seized with a cramp in my wounded leg which compelled me to stop and sit down ever 30 or 40 rods at length we discovered a half breed encamped in the Valley who furnished us with horses and went with us to the fort where we arrived about sun an hour high being naked hungry wounded sleepy and fatigued. Here again I entered a trading post after being defeated by the Indians but the treatment was quite different from that which I had received at Larameys fork in 1837 when I had been defeated by the Crows

The Fort was in charge of Mr. Courtney M. Walker who had been lately employed by the Hudsons Bay Company for that purpose He invited us into a room and ordered supper to be prepared immediately. Likewise such articles of clothing and Blankets as we called for. After dressin ourselves and giving a brief history of our defeat and sufferings supper was brot. in consisting of tea Cakes butter milk dried meat etc I eat very sparingly as I had been three days fasting but drank so much strong tea that it kept me awake till after midnight. I continued to bathe my leg in warm salt water and applied a salve which healed it in a very short time so that in 10 days I was again setting traps for Beaver.

Around the Horn

RICHARD HENRY DANA, JR.

In our first attempt to double the Cape, when we came up to the latitude of it, we were nearly seventeen hundred miles to the westward, but, in running for the Straits of Magellan, we stood so far to the eastward that we made our second attempt at a distance of not more than four or five hundred miles; and we had great hopes, by this means, to run clear of the ice; thinking that the easterly gales, which had prevailed for a long time, would have driven it to the westward. With the wind about two points free, the yards braced in a little, and two close-reefed topsails and a reefed foresail on the ship, we made great way toward the southward; and almost every watch, when we came on deck, the air seemed to grow colder, and the sea to run higher. Still we saw no ice, and had great hopes of going clear of it altogether, when, one afternoon, about three o'clock, while we were taking a *siesta* during our watch below, "All hands!" was called in a loud and fearful voice. "Tumble up here, men!—tumble up!—don't stop for your clothes—before we're upon it!" We sprang out of our berths and hurried upon deck. The loud, sharp voice of the captain was heard giving orders, as though for life or death, and we ran aft to the braces, not waiting to look ahead, for not a moment was to be lost. The helm was hard up, the after yards shaking, and the ship in the act of wearing. Slowly, with the stiff ropes and iced rigging, we swung the yards round, everything coming hard and with a creaking and rending sound, like pulling up a plank which has been frozen into the ice. The ship wore round fairly, the yards were steadied, and we stood off on the other tack, leaving behind us, directly under our larboard quarter, a large ice island, peering out of the mist, and reaching high above our tops; while astern, and on either side of the island, large tracts of field-ice were dimly seen, heaving and rolling in the sea. We were now safe, and standing to the northward; but, in a few minutes more, had it not been for the sharp lookout of the watch, we should have been fairly upon the ice, and left our ship's old bones adrift in the Southern Ocean. After standing to the northward a few hours, we wore ship, and, the wind having hauled, we stood to the southward and eastward. All night long a bright lookout was kept from every part of the deck; and whenever ice was seen on the one bow or the other the helm was shifted and the yards braced, and, by quick working of the ship, she was kept clear. The accustomed cry of "Ice ahead!"— "Ice on the lee bow!"—"Another island!" in the same tones, and with the same orders following them, seemed to bring us directly back to our old position of the week before. During our watch on deck, which was from twelve to four, the wind came out ahead, with a pelting storm of hail and sleet, and we lay hove-to, under a close-reefed fore topsail, the whole watch. During the next watch it fell calm with a drenching rain until daybreak, when the wind came out to the westward, and the weather cleared up, and showed us the whole ocean, in the course which we should have steered, had it not been for the head wind and calm, completely blocked up with ice. Here, then, our progress was stopped, and we wore ship, and once more stood to the northward and eastward; not for the Straits of Magellan, but to make another attempt to double the Cape, still farther to the eastward; for the captain was determined to get round if perseverance could do it, and the third time, he said, never failed.

With a fair wind we soon ran clear of the field-ice, and by noon had only the stray islands floating far and near upon the ocean. The sun was out bright, the sea of a deep blue, fringed with the white foam of the waves, which ran high before a strong southwester; our solitary ship tore on through the open water as though glad to be out of her confinement; and the ice islands lay scattered here and there, of various sizes and shapes, reflecting the bright rays of the sun, and drifting slowly northward before the gale. It was a contrast to much that we had lately seen, and a spectacle not only of beauty, but of life; for it required but little fancy to imagine these islands to be animate masses which had broken loose from the "thrilling regions of thick-ribbed ice," and were working their way, by wind and current, some alone, and some in fleets, to milder climes. No pencil has ever yet given anything like the true effect of an iceberg. In a picture, they are huge, uncouth masses, stuck in the sea, while their chief beauty and grandeur—their slow, stately motion, the whirling of the snow about their summits, and the fearful groaning and cracking of their parts—the picture cannot give. This is the large iceberg,—while the small and distant islands, floating on the smooth sea, in the light of a clear day, look like little floating fairy isles of sapphire.

From a northeast course we gradually hauled to the eastward, and after sailing about two hundred miles, which brought us as near to the western coast of Terra del Fuego as was safe, and having lost sight of the ice altogether,—for the third time we put the ship's head to the southward, to try the passage of the Cape. The weather continued clear and cold, with a strong gale from the westward, and we were fast getting up with the latitude of the Cape, with a prospect of soon being round. One fine afternoon, a man who had gone into the fore-top to shift the rolling tackles sung out at the top of his voice, and with evident glee, "Sail ho!" Neither land nor sail had we seen since leaving San Diego; and only those who have traversed the length of a whole ocean alone can imagine what an excitement such an announcement produced on board. "Sail ho!" shouted the cook, jumping out of his galley; "Sail ho!" shouted a man, throwing back the slide of the scuttle, to the watch below, who were soon out of their berths and on deck; and "Sail ho!" shouted the captain down the companion-way to the passenger in the cabin. Beside the pleasure of seeing a ship and human beings in so desolate a place, it was important for us to speak a vessel, to learn whether there was ice to the eastward, and to ascertain the longitude; for we had no chronometer, and had been drifting about so long that we had nearly lost our reckoning; and opportunities for lunar observations are not frequent or sure in such a place as Cape Horn. For these various reasons the excitement in our little community was running high, and conjectures were made, and everything thought of for which the captain would hail, when the man aloft sung out— "Another sail, large on the weather bow!" This was a little odd, but so much the better, and did not shake our faith in their being sails. At length the man in the top hailed, and said he believed it was land, after all. "Land in your eye!" said the mate, who was looking through the telescope; "they are ice islands, if I can see a hole through a ladder"; and a few moments showed the mate to be right; and all our expectations fled; and instead of what we most wished to see we had what we most dreaded, and what we hoped we had seen the last of. We soon, however, left these astern, having passed within about two miles of them, and at sundown the horizon was clear in all directions.

Having a fine wind, we were soon up with and passed the latitude of the Cape, and, having stood far enough to the southward to give it a wide berth, we began to stand to the eastward, with a good prospect of being round and steering to the northward, on the other side, in a very few days. But ill luck seemed to have lighted upon us. Not four hours had we been standing on in this course before it fell dead calm, and in half in hour it clouded up, a few straggling blasts, with spits of snow and sleet, came from the eastward, and in an hour more we lay hove-to under a close-reefed main topsail, drifting bodily off to leeward before the fiercest storm that we had yet felt, blowing dead ahead, from the eastward. It seemed as though the genius of the place had been roused at finding that we had nearly slipped through his fingers, and had come down upon us with ten-fold fury. The sailors said that every blast, as it shook the shrouds, and whistled through the rigging, said to the old ship, "No, you don't!"—"No, you don't!"

For eight days we lay drifting about in this man-ner. Sometimes—generally towards noon—it fell calm; once or twice a round copper ball showed itself for a few moments in the place where the sun ought to have been, and a puff or two came from the westward, giving some hope that a fair wind had come at last. During the first two days we made sail for these puffs, shaking the reefs out of the topsails and boarding the tacks of the courses; but finding that it only made work for us when the gale set in again, it was soon given up, and we lay-to under our close-reefs. We had less snow and hail than when we were farther to the westward, but we had an abundance of what is worse to a sailor in cold weather,—drenching rain. Snow is blinding, and very bad when coming upon a coast, but, for gen-uine discomfort, give me rain with freezing weath-er. A snowstorm is exciting, and it does not wet through the clothes (a fact important to a sailor); but a constant rain there is no escaping from. It wets to the skin, and makes all protection vain. We had long ago run through all our dry clothes, and as sailors have no other way of drying them than by the sun, we had nothing to do but to put on those which were the least wet. At the end of each watch, when we came below, we took off our clothes and wrung them out; two taking hold of a pair of trousers, one at each end,—and jackets in the same way. Stockings, mittens, and all, were wrung out also, and then hung up to drain and chafe dry against the bulkheads. Then, feeling of all our clothes, we picked out those which were the least wet, and put them on, so as to be ready for a call, and turned-in, covered ourselves up with blankets, and slept until three knocks on the scuttle and the dismal sound of "All Starbowlines ahoy! Eight bells, there below! Do you hear the news?" drawled out from on deck, and the sulky answer of "Aye, aye!" from below, sent us up again.

On deck all was dark, and either a dead calm, with the rain pouring steadily down, or, more generally, a violent gale dead ahead, with rain pelting horizontally, and occasional variations of hail and sleet; decks afloat with water swashing from side to side, and constantly wet feet, for boots could not be wrung out like drawers, and no composition could stand the constant soaking. In fact, wet and cold feet are inevitable in such weather, and are not the least of those items which go to make up the grand total of the discomforts of a winter passage round Cape Horn. Few words were spoken between the watches as they shifted; the wheel was relieved, the mate took his place on the quarter-deck, the lookouts in the bows; and each man had his narrow space to

walk fore and aft in, or rather to swing himself forward and back in, from one belaying-pin to another, for the decks were too slippery with ice and water
to allow of much walking. To make a walk, which is
absolutely necessary to pass away the time, one of us
hit upon the expedient of sanding the decks; and
afterwards, whenever the rain was not so violent as
to wash it off, the weather-side of the quarter-deck,
and a part of the waist and forecastle were sprinkled
with the sand which we had on board for holyston-
ing, and thus we made a good promenade, where we
walked fore and aft, two and two, hour after hour, in
our long, dull, and comfortless watches. The bells
seemed to be an hour or two apart, instead of half
an hour, and an age to elapse before the welcome
sound of eight bells. The sole object was to make
the time pass on. Any change was sought for which
would break the monotony of the time; and even
the two hours' trick at the wheel, which came round
to us in turn, once in every other watch, was looked
upon as a relief. The never-failing resource of long
yarns, which eke out many a watch, seemed to have
failed us now; for we had been so long together that
we had heard each other's stories told over and over
again till we had them by heart; each one knew the
whole history of each of the others, and we were
fairly and literally talked out. Singing and joking we
were in no humor for; and, in fact, any sound of
mirth or laughter would have struck strangely upon

our ears, and would not have been tolerated any
more than whistling or a wind instrument. The last
resort, that of speculating upon the future, seemed
now to fail us; for our discouraging situation, and the
danger we were really in (as we expected every day
to find ourselves drifted back among the ice),
"clapped a stopper" upon all that. From saying
"*when* we get home," we began insensibly to alter it
to "*if* we get home," and at last the subject was
dropped by a tacit consent.

In this state of things, a new light was struck out,
and a new field opened, by a change in the watch.
One of our watch was laid up for two or three days
by a bad hand (for in cold weather the least cut or
bruise ripens into a sore), and his place was supplied
by the carpenter. This was a windfall, and there was
a contest who should have the carpenter to walk
with him. As "Chips" was a man of some little edu-
cation, and he and I had had a good deal of inter-
course with each other, he fell in with me in my
walk. He was a Fin, but spoke English well, and gave
me long accounts of his country,—the customs, the
trade, the towns, what little he knew of the government (I found he was no friend of Russia), his voyages, his first arrival in America, his marriage and
courtship; he had married a countrywoman of his, a
dress-maker, whom he met with in Boston. I had
very little to tell him of my quiet, sedentary life at
home; and in spite of our best efforts, which had

protracted these yarns through five or six watches, we fairly talked each other out, and I turned him over to another man in the watch, and put myself upon my own resources.

I commenced a deliberate system of time-killing, which united some profit with a cheering up of the heavy hours. As soon as I came on deck, and took my place and regular walk, I began with repeating over to myself in regular order a string of matters which I had in my memory,—the multiplication table and the tables of weights and measures; the Kanaka numerals; then the States of the Union, with their capitals; the counties of England, with their shire towns, and the kings of England in their order, and other things. This carried me through my facts, and, being repeated deliberately, with long intervals, often eked out the first two bells. Then came the Ten Commandments, the thirty-ninth chapter of Job, and a few other passages from Scripture. The next in the order, which I seldom varied from, came Cowper's Castaway, which was a great favorite with me; its solemn measure and gloomy character, as well as the incident it was founded upon, making it well suited to a lonely watch at sea. Then his lines to Mary, his address to the Jackdaw, and a short extract from Table Talk (I abounded in Cowper, for I happened to have a volume of his poems in my chest); "Ille et nefasto" from Horace, and Goethe's Erl König. After I had got through these, I allowed myself a more general range among everything that I could remember, both in prose and verse. In this way, with an occasional break by relieving the wheel, heaving the log, and going to the scuttle-butt for a drink of water, the longest watch was passed away; and I was so regular in my silent recitations that, if there was no interruption by ship's duty, I could tell very nearly the number of bells by my progress.

Our watches below were no more varied than the watch on deck. All washing, sewing, and reading was given up, and we did nothing but eat, sleep, and stand our watch, leading what might be called a Cape Horn life. The forecastle was too uncomfortable to sit up in; and whenever we were below, we were in our berths. To prevent the rain and the sea-water which broke over the bows from washing down, we were obliged to keep the scuttle closed, so that the forecastle was nearly air-tight. In this little, wet, leaky hole, we were all quartered, in an atmosphere so bad that our lamp, which swung in the middle from the beams, sometimes actually burned blue, with a large circle of foul air about it. Still, I was never in better health than after three weeks of this life. I gained a great deal of flesh, and we all ate like horses. At every watch when we came below, before turning in, the bread barge and beef kid were overhauled. Each man drank his quart of hot tea night and morning, and glad enough we were to get it; for no nectar and ambrosia were sweeter to the lazy immortals than was a pot of hot tea, a hard biscuit, and a slice of cold salt beef to us after a watch on deck. To be sure, we were mere animals, and, had this life lasted a year instead of a month, we should have been little better than the ropes in the ship. Not a razor, nor a brush, nor a drop of water, except the rain and the spray, had come near us all the time; for we were on an allowance of fresh water; and who would strip and wash himself in salt water on deck, in the snow and ice, with the thermometer at zero?

After about eight days of constant easterly gales, the wind hauled occasionally a little to the southward, and blew hard, which, as we were well to the southward, allowed us to brace in a little, and stand on under all the sail we could carry. These turns lasted but a short while, and sooner or later it set in again from the old quarter; yet at each time we made something, and were gradually edging along to the eastward. One night, after one of these shifts of the wind, and when all hands had been up a great part of the time, our watch was left on deck, with the mainsail hanging in the buntlines, ready to be set if necessary. It came on to blow worse and worse, with hail and snow beating like so many furies upon the ship, it being as dark and thick as night could make it. The mainsail was blowing and slatting with a noise like thunder, when the captain came on deck and ordered it to be furled. The mate was about to call all hands, when the captain stopped him, and said that the men would be beaten out if they were called up so often; that, as our watch must stay on deck, it might as well be doing that as anything else. Accordingly, we went upon the yard; and never shall I forget that piece of work. Our watch had been so reduced by sickness, and by some having been left in California, that, with one man at the wheel, we had only the third mate and three beside myself to go aloft; so that at most we could only attempt to furl one yard-arm at a time. We manned the weather yard-arm, and set to work to make a furl of it. Our lower masts being short, and our yards very square, the sail had a head of nearly fifty feet, and a short leech, made still shorter by the deep reef which was in it, which brought the clew away out on the quarters of the yard, and made a bunt nearly as square as the mizzen royal yard. Beside this difficulty, the yard over which we lay was cased with ice, the gaskets and rope of the foot and leech of the sail as stiff and hard as a piece of leather hose, and the sail itself about as pliable as though it had been made of sheets of sheathing copper. It blew a perfect hurricane, with alternate blasts of snow, hail, and rain. We had to *fist* the sail with bare hands. No one could trust himself to mittens, for if he slipped he was a gone man. All the boats were hoisted in on deck, and there was nothing to be lowered for him. We had need of every finger God had given us. Several times we got the sail upon the yard, but it blew away again before we could secure it. It required men to lie over the yard to pass each turn of the gaskets, and when they were passed it was almost impossible to knot them so that they would hold. Frequently we were obliged to leave off altogether and take to beating our hands upon the sail to keep them from freezing. After some time—which seemed forever—we got the weather side stowed after a fashion, and went over to leeward for another trial. This was still worse, for the body of the sail had been blown over to leeward, and, as the yard was a-cock-bill by the lying over of the vessel, we had to light it all up to windward. When the yard-arms were furled, the bunt was all adrift again, which made more work for us. We got all secure at last, but we had been nearly an hour and a half upon the yard, and it seemed an age. It had just struck five bells when we went up, and eight were struck soon after we came down. This may seem slow work; but considering the state of everything, and that we had only five men to a sail with just half as many square yards of canvas in it as the mainsail of the Independence, sixty-gun ship, which musters seven hundred men at her quarters, it is not wonderful that we were no quicker about it. We were glad enough to get on deck, and still more to go below. The oldest sailor in the watch said, as he went down, "I shall never forget that main yard; it beats all my going a-fishing. Fun is fun, but furling one yard-arm of a course at a time, off Cape Horn, is no better than man-killing."

During the greater part of the next two days, the wind was pretty steady from the southward. We had evidently made great progress, and had good hope of being soon up with the Cape, if we were not there already. We could put but little confidence in our reckoning, as there had been no opportunities for an observation, and we had drifted too much to allow of our dead reckoning being anywhere near the mark. If it would clear off enough to give a chance for an observation, or if we could make land, we should know where we were; and upon these, and the chances of falling in with a sail from the east-ward, we depended almost entirely.

Friday, July 22d. This day we had a steady gale from the southward, and stood on under close sail, with the yards eased a little by the weather braces, the clouds lifting a little, and showing signs of break-ing away. In the afternoon, I was below with Mr. Hatch, the third mate, and two others, filling the bread locker in the steerage from the casks, when a bright gleam of sunshine broke out and shone down the companion-way, and through the skylight, light-ing up everything below, and sending a warm glow through the hearts of all. It was a sight we had not seen for weeks,—an omen, a godsend. Even the roughest and hardest face acknowledged its influ-ence. Just at that moment we heard a loud shout from all parts of the deck, and the mate called out down the companion-way to the captain, who was sitting in the cabin. What he said we could not distinguish, but the captain kicked over his chair, and was on deck at one jump. We could not tell what it was; and, anxious as we were to know, the discipline of the ship would not allow of our leaving our places. Yet, as we were not called, we knew there was no danger. We hurried to get through with our job, when, seeing the steward's black face peering out of the pantry, Mr. Hatch hailed him to know what was the matter. "Lan' o, to be sure, sir! No you hear 'em sing out, 'Lan o?' De cap'em say 'im Cape Horn!'"

This gave us a new start, and we were soon through our work and on deck; and there lay the land, fair upon the larboard beam, and slowly edging away upon the quarter. All hands were busy looking at it,—the captain and mates from the quarter-deck, the cook from his galley, and the sailors from the forecastle; and even Mr. Nuttall, the passenger, who had kept in his shell for nearly a month, and hardly been seen by anybody, and whom we had almost forgotten was on board, came out like a butterfly, and was hopping round as bright as a bird.

The land was the island of Staten Land, just to the eastward of Cape Horn; and a more desolate-looking spot I never wish to set eyes upon,—bare, broken, and girt with rocks and ice, with here and there, between the rocks and broken hillocks, a little stunted vegetation of shrubs. It was a place well suited to stand at the junction of the two oceans, beyond the reach of human cultivation, and encounter the blasts and snows of a perpetual winter. Yet, dismal as it was, it was a pleasant sight to us; not only as being the first land we had seen, but because it told us that we had passed the Cape,—were in the Atlantic,—and that, with twenty-four hours of this breeze, we might bid defiance to the Southern Ocean. It told us, too, our latitude and longitude better than any observation; and the captain now knew where we were, as well as if we were off the end of Long Wharf.

In the general joy, Mr. Nuttall said he should like to go ashore upon the island and examine a spot which probably no human being had ever set foot upon; but the captain intimated that he would see the island, specimens and all, in—another place, before he would get out a boat or delay the ship one moment for him.

We left the island gradually astern; and at sundown had the Atlantic Ocean clear before us.

The Worst Journey
in the World

APSLEY CHERRY-GARRARD

In an introduction to this story in my previous book The Greatest
Survival Stories Ever Told, *I think I set the stage for the reader in
the most helpful way. With your permission, I am repeating what I
said here:*

Apsley Cherry-Garrard was a member of the Antarctic
search party that in November, 1912 discovered the bodies
of Robert Falcon Scott and his companions in the remnants
of the snow-covered tent where they had perished of
exhaustion and starvation. Englishman Scott and his men
had failed in their attempt to be the first to reach the South
Pole (Norwegian explorer Roald Admundsen had beaten
them), then met their doom undertaking the 800-mile trek
back to the expedition's permanent base in the McMurdo
Sound area.

Even though it was undertaken in what was summer
in the Antarctic, Scott's journey was a terrible ordeal of
pushing along on skis while man-hauling their sledges of

supplies. Eventually, the survivors of the trek huddled in their tent, unable to go a step further in the terrible storms that had hounded them since their retreat from the Pole began. Ironically, a depot cache of fuel and food was only a few miles away.

Apsley Cherry-Garrard, a young volunteer for the Scott expedition that had begun in 1910, was not with the final Scott party but made a separate Antarctic trek with three men that rivals the Scott experience for hardships endured, but ended without the loss of life. Cherry-Garrard's The Worst Journey in the World *is an account not only of his own experience, but of Scott's experiences as well. Using Scott's journals found in the tent with the bodies, Cherry-Garrard describes what happened to Scott and his companions on their terrible retreat from the Pole. The text of this excerpt from the book picks up the action on January 19, after Scott, Wilson, Bowers, and Oates had made the overwhelmingly bitter discovery that the Norwegians had beaten them to the Pole. Now, defeated, they have begun their second battle: To return to the safety of the expedition base camp 800 miles away.*

No matter whether you're reading about Cherry-Garrard's personal ordeal, or his account of what Scott and his men endured, The Worst Journey in the World *ranks as a classic in survival literature.*

All the joy had gone from their sledging. They were hungry, they were cold, the pulling was heavy, and two of them were not fit. As long ago as 14 January Scott wrote that Oates was feeling the cold and fatigue more than the others and again he refers to the matter on 20 January. On 19 January Wilson wrote: 'We get our hairy faces and mouths dreadfully iced up on the march, and often one's hands very cold indeed holding ski-sticks. Evans, who cut his knuckle some days ago at the last depot, has a lot of pus in it tonight.' January 20: 'Evans has got 4 or 5 of his finger-tips badly blistered by the cold. Titus also his nose and cheeks—al[so] Evans and Bowers.' January 28: 'Evans has a number of badly blistered finger-ends which he got at the Pole. Titus' big toe is turning blue-black.' January 31: 'Evans' finger-nails all coming off, very raw and sore.' February 4: 'Evans is feeling the cold a lot, always getting frost-bitten. Titus' toes are blackening, and his nose and cheeks are dead yellow. Dressing Evans' fingers every other day with boric vaseline: they are quite sweet still.' February 5: 'Evans' fingers suppurating. Nose very bad [hard] and rotten-looking.'

Scott was getting alarmed about Evans, who 'has dislodged two finger-nails tonight; his hands are really bad, and, to my surprise, he shows signs of losing heart over it. He hasn't been cheerful since the accident.' 'The party is not improving in condition, especially Evans, who is becoming rather dull and incapable.' 'Evans' nose is almost as bad as his fingers. He is a good deal crocked up.'

Bowers's diary, quoted above, finished on 25 January, on which day they picked up their One and a Half Degree Depot. 'I shall sleep much better with our provision bag full again,' wrote Scott that night. 'Bowers got another rating sight tonight—it was wonderful how he managed to observe in such a horribly cold wind.' They marched 16 miles the next day, but got off the outward track, which was crooked. On 27 January they did 14 miles on a 'very bad surface of deep-cut sastrugi all day, until late in the afternoon when we began to get out of them.' 'By Jove, this is tremendous labour,' said Scott.

They were getting into the better surfaces again: 15.7 miles for 28 January, 'a fine day and a good march on very decent surface.' On 29 January Bowers wrote his last full day's diary:

> Our record march today. With a good breeze and improving surface we were soon in among the double tracks where the supporting party left us. Then we picked up the memorable camp where I transferred to the advance party. How glad I was to change over. The camp was much drifted up and immense sastrugi were

everywhere, S.S.E. in direction and S.E. We did 10.4 miles before lunch. I was breaking back on sledge and controlling; it was beastly cold and my hands were perished. In the afternoon I put on my dogskin mitts and was far more comfortable. A stiff breeze with drift continues: temperature -25°. Thank God our days of having to face it are over. We completed 19.5 miles [22 statute] this evening, and so are only 29 miles from our precious [Three Degree] Depot. It will be bad luck indeed if we do not get there in a march and a half anyhow.

Nineteen miles again on 30 January, but during the previous day's march Wilson had strained a tendon in his leg. 'I got a nasty bruise on the Tib[ialis] ant[icus] which gave me great pain all the afternoon.' 'My left leg exceedingly painful all day, so I gave Birdie my ski and hobbled alongside the sledge on foot. The whole of the Tibialis anticus is swollen and tight, and full of teno synovitis, and the skin red and oedematous over the skin. But we made a very fine march with the help of a brisk breeze.' January 31:

Again walking by the sledge with swollen leg but not nearly so painful. We had 5.8 miles to go to reach our Three Degree Depot. Picked this up with a week's provision and a line from Evans, and then for lunch an extra biscuit each, making 4 for lunch and 1/10 whack of butter extra as well. Afternoon we passed cairn where Birdie's ski had been left. These we picked up and came on till 7:30 P.M. when the wind which had been very light all day dropped, and with temp. -20° it felt delightfully warm and sunny and clear. We have 1/10 extra pemmican in the hoosh now also. My leg pretty swollen again tonight.

They travelled 13.5 miles that day, and 15.7 on the next. 'My leg much more comfortable, gave me no pain, and I was able to pull all day, holding on to the sledge. Still some oedema. We came down a hundred feet or so today on a fairly steep gradient.'

They were now approaching the crevassed surfaces and the ice-falls which mark the entrance to the Beardmore Glacier, and 2 February was marked by another accident, this time to Scott.

On a very slippery surface I came an awful 'purler' on my shoulder. It is horribly sore tonight and another sick person added to our tent—three out of five injured, and the most troublesome surfaces to come. We shall be lucky if we get through without serious injury. Wilson's leg is better, but might easily get bad again, and Evans' fingers. . . . We have managed to get off 17 miles. The extra food is certainly helping us, but we are getting pretty hungry. The weather is already a trifle warmer, the altitude lower and only 80 miles or so to Mount Darwin. It is time we were off the summit—Pray God another four days will see us pretty

well clear of it. Our bags are getting very wet and we
ought to have more sleep.

They had been spending some time in finding the
old tracks. But they had a good landfall for the depot
at the top of the glacier and on 3 February they
decided to push on due north, and to worry no
more for the present about tracks and cairns. They
did 16 miles that day. Wilson's diary runs:

> Sunny and breezy again. Came down a series of slopes,
> and finished the day going up one. Enormous deep-
> cut sastrugi and drifts and shiny egg-shell surface.
> Wind all S.E.E.ly Today at about 11 P.M. we got our
> first sight again of mountain peaks on our eastern
> horizon. . . . We crossed the outmost line of crevassed
> ridge top today, the first on our return.
>
> *February 4.* 18 miles. Clear cloudless blue sky, sur-
> face drift. During forenoon we came down gradual
> descent including 2 or 3 irregular terrace slopes, on
> crest of one of which were a good many crevasses.
> Southernmost were just big enough for Scott and
> Evans to fall in to their waists, and very deceptively
> covered up. They ran east and west. Those nearer the
> crest were the ordinary broad street-like crevasses, well
> lidded. In the afternoon we again came to a crest,
> before descending, with street crevasses, and one we
> crossed had a huge hole where the lid had fallen in, big
> enough for a horse and cart to go down. We have a

great number of mountain tops on our right and south of our beam as we go due north now. We are now camped just below a great crevassed mound, on a mountain top evidently.

February 5. 18.2 miles. We had a difficult day, getting in amongst a frightful chaos of broad chasm-like crevasses. We kept too far east and had to wind in and out amongst them and cross a multitude of bridges. We then bore west a bit and got on better all the afternoon and got round a good deal of the upper disturbances of the falls here.

[Scott wrote: 'We are camped in a very disturbed region, but the wind has fallen very light here, and our camp is comfortable for the first time for many weeks.']

February 6. 15 miles. We again had a forenoon of trying to cut corners. Got in amongst great chasms running E. and W. and had to come out again. We then again kept west and downhill over tremendous sastrugi, with a slight breeze, very cold. In afternoon, continued bearing more and more towards Mount Darwin: we got round one of the main lines of ice-fall and looked back up to it. . . . Very cold march: many crevasses: I walking by the sledge on foot found a good many: the others all on ski.

February 7. 15.5 miles. Clear day again and we made a tedious march in the forenoon along a flat or two, and down a long slope: and then in the afternoon we had a very fresh breeze, and very fast run down long slopes covered with big sastrugi. It was a strenuous job steering and checking behind by the sledge. We reached the Upper Glacier Depot by 7.30 P.M. and found everything right.

This was the end of the plateau: the beginning of the glacier. Their hard time should be over so far as the weather was concerned. Wilson notes how fine the land looked as they approached it: 'The colour of the Dominion Range rock is in the main all brown madder or dark reddish chocolate, but there are numerous bands of yellow rock scattered amongst it. I think it is composed of dolerite and sandstone as on the W. side.'

The condition of the party was of course giving anxiety: how much it is impossible to say. A good deal was to be hoped from the warm weather ahead. Scott and Bowers were probably the fittest men. Scott's shoulder soon mended and 'Bowers is splendid, full of energy and bustle all the time.' Wilson was feeling the cold more than either of them now. His leg was not yet well enough to wear ski. Oates had suffered from a cold foot for some time. Evans, however, was the only man whom Scott seems to have been worried about. 'His cuts and wounds suppurate, his nose looks very bad, and altogether he shows considerable signs of being played out.' . . .

'Well, we have come through our seven weeks' ice-cap journey and most of us are fit, but I think another week might have had a very bad effect on P.O. Evans, who is going steadily down-hill.' They had all been having extra food which had helped them much, though they complained of hunger and want of sleep. Directly they got into the warmer weather on the glacier their food satisfied them, 'but we must march to keep on the full ration, and we want rest, yet we shall pull through all right, D.V. We are by no means worn out.'

There are no germs in the Antarctic, save for a few isolated specimens which almost certainly come down from civilization in the upper air currents. You can sleep all night in a wet bag and clothing, and sledge all day in a mail of ice, and you will not catch a cold nor get any aches. You can get deficiency diseases, like scurvy, for inland this is a deficiency country, without vitamins. You can also get poisoned if you allow your food to remain thawed out too long, and if you do not cover the provisions in a depot with enough snow the sun will get at them, even though the air temperature is far below freezing. But it is not easy to become diseased.

On the other hand, once something does go wrong it is the deuce and all to get it right: especially cuts. And the isolation of the polar traveller may place him in most difficult circumstances. There are no ambulances and hospitals, and a man on a sledge is a very

serious weight. Practically any man who undertakes
big polar journeys must face the possibility of having
to commit suicide to save his companions, and the
difficulty of this must not be overrated, for it is in
some ways more desirable to die than to live, if things
are bad enough: we got to that stage on the Winter
Journey. I remember discussing this question with
Bowers, who had a scheme of doing himself in with
a pick-axe if necessity arose, though how he could
have accomplished it I don't know: or, as he said,
there might be a crevasse and at any rate there was the
medical case. I was horrified at the time: I had never
faced the thing out with myself like that.

They left the Upper Glacier Depot under Mount
Darwin on 8 February. This day they collected the
most important of those geological specimens to
which, at Wilson's special request, they clung to the
end, and which were mostly collected by him.
Mount Darwin and Buckley Island, which are really
the tops of high mountains, stick out of the ice at the
top of the glacier, and the course ran near to both of
them, but not actually up against them. Shackleton
found coal on Buckley Island, and it was clear that
the place was of great geological importance, for it
was one of the only places in the Antarctic where
fossils could be found, so far as we knew. The ice-falls
stretched away as far as you could see towards the
mountains which bound the glacier on either side,
and as you looked upwards towards Buckley Island

they were like a long breaking wave. One of the great difficulties about the Beardmore was that you saw the ice-falls as you went up, and avoided them, but coming down you knew nothing of their where-abouts until you fell into the middle of pressure and crevasses, and then it was almost impossible to say whether you should go right or left to get out.

Evans was unable to pull this day, and was detached from the sledge, but this was not necessarily a very serious sign: Shackleton on his return journey was not able to pull at this place. Wilson wrote as follows:

February 8, Mt. Buckley Cliffs. A very busy day. We had a very cold forenoon march, blowing like blazes from the S. Birdie detached and went on ski to Mt. Darwin and collected some dolerite, the only rock he could see on the Nunatak, which was the nearest. We got into a sort of crusted surface where the snow broke through nearly to our knees and the sledge-runner also. I thought at first we were all on a thinly bridged crevasse. We then came on east a bit, and gradually got worse and worse going over an ice-fall, having great trouble to prevent sledge taking charge, but eventually got down and then made N.W. or N. into the land, and camped right by the moraine under the great sandstone cliffs of Mt. Buckley, out of the wind and quite warm again: it was a wonderful change. After lunch we all geologized on till supper, and I was very late turning in, examining the moraine after supper. Socks, all strewn over the rocks, dried splendidly. Magnificent Beacon sandstone cliffs. Masses of limestone in the moraine, and dolerite crags in various places. Coal seams at all heights in the sandstone cliffs, and lumps of weathered coal with fossil vegetable. Had a regular field-day and got some splendid things in the short time.

February 9, Moraine visit. We made our way along down the moraine, and at the end of Mt. Buckley [I] unhitched and had half an hour over the rocks and again got some good things written up in sketch-book. We then left the moraine and made a very good march on rough blue ice all day with very small and scarce scraps of névé, on one of which we camped for the night with a rather overcast foggy sky, which cleared to bright sun in the night. We are all thoroughly enjoying temps. of +10° or thereabouts now, with no wind instead of the summit winds which are incessant with temp. –20°.

February 10. ?16 m. We made a very good forenoon march from 10 to 2.45 towards the Cloudmaker. Weather overcast generally obscured everything in snowfall fog, starting with crystals of large size. . . . We had to camp after 2½ hours' afternoon march as it got too thick to see anything and we were going downhill on blue ice. . .

The next day in bad lights and on a bad surface they fell into the same pressure which both the other returning parties experienced. Like them they were in the middle of it before they realized.

Then came the fatal decision to steer east. We went on for 6 hours, hoping to do a good distance, which I suppose we did, but for the last hour or two we pressed on into a regular trap. Getting on to a good surface we did not reduce our lunch meal, and thought all going well, but half an hour after lunch we got into worst ice mess I have ever been in. For three hours we plunged on on ski, first thinking we were too much to the right, then too much to the left; meanwhile the disturbance got worse and my spirits received a very rude shock. There were times when it seemed almost impossible to find a way out of the awful turmoil in which we found ourselves. . . .

The turmoil changed in character, irregular crevassed surface giving way to huge chasms, closely packed and most difficult to cross. It was very heavy work, but we had grown desperate. We won through at 10 P.M., and I write after 12 hours on the march . . .

Wilson continues the story:

February 12. We had a good night just outside the ice-falls and disturbances, and a small breakfast of tea, thin hoosh and biscuit, and began the forenoon by a decent bit of travelling on rubbly blue ice in crampons: then plunged into an ice-fall and wandered about in it for hours and hours.

February 13. We had one biscuit and some tea after a night's sleep on very hard and irregular blue ice amongst the ice-fall crevasses. No snow on the tent, only ski, etc. Got away at 10 A.M. and by 2 P.M. found the depot, having had a good march over hard rough blue ice. Only 1/2 hour in the disturbance of yesterday. The weather was very thick, snowing and overcast, could only just see the points of bearing for depot. However, we got there, tired and hungry, and camped and had hoosh and tea and 3 biscuits each. Then away again with our three and a half days' food from this red flag depot and off down by the Cloudmaker moraine. We travelled about 4 hours on hard blue ice, and I was allowed to geologize the last hour down the two outer lines of boulders. The outer one all dolerite and quartz rocks, the inner all dolerite and sandstone. . . . We camped on the inner line of boulders, weather clearing all the afternoon.

Meanwhile both Wilson and Bowers had been badly snow-blind, though Wilson does not mention it in his diary; and this night Scott says Evans had no power to assist with camping work. A good march followed on 14 February, but

there is no getting away from the fact that we are not pulling strong. Probably none of us: Wilson's leg still troubles him and he doesn't like to trust himself on ski; but the worst case is Evans, who is giving us serious anxiety. This morning he suddenly disclosed a huge blister on his foot. It delayed us on the march, when he had to have his crampon readjusted. Sometimes I feel he is going from bad to worse, but I trust he will pick up again when we come to steady work on ski like this afternoon. He is hungry and so is Wilson. We can't risk opening out our food again, and as cook at present I am serving something under full allowance. We are inclined to get slack and slow with our camping arrangement, and small delays increase. I have talked of the matter tonight and hope for improvement. We cannot do distance without the hours.

There was something wrong with this party: more wrong, I mean, than was justified by the tremendous journey they had already experienced. Except for the blizzard at the bottom of the Beardmore and the surfaces near the Pole it had been little worse than they expected. Evans, however, who was considered by Scott to be the strongest man of the party, had already collapsed, and it is admitted that the rest of the party was becoming far from strong. There seems to be an unknown factor here somewhere.

Wilson's diary continues:

February 15. 13¾ m. geog. I got on ski again first time since damaging my leg and was on them all day for 9 hours. It was a bit painful and swelled by the evening, and every night I put on snow poultice. We are not yet abreast of Mt. Kyffin, and much discussion how far we are from the Lower Glacier Depot, probably 18 to 20 m.: and we have to reduce food again, only one biscuit tonight with a thin hoosh of pemmican. Tomorrow we have to make one day's food which remains last over the two. The weather became heavily overcast during the afternoon and then began to snow, and though we got in or 4 hours' march it was with difficulty, and we only made a bit over 5 miles. However, we are nearer the depot tonight.

February 16. 12 1/2 m. geog. Got a good start in fair weather after one biscuit and a thin breakfast, and made 7 1/2 m. in the forenoon. Again the weather became overcast and we lunched almost at our old bearing on Kyffin of lunch Dec. 15. All the afternoon the weather became thick and thicker and after 3 1/2 hours Evans collapsed, sick and giddy, and unable to walk even by the sledge on ski, so we camped. Can see no land at all anywhere, but we must be getting pretty near the Pillar Rock. Evans' collapse has much to do with the fact that he has never been sick in his life and is now helpless with his hands frost-bitten. We had thin meals for lunch and supper.

February 17. The weather cleared and we got away for a clear run to the depot and had gone a good part of the way when Evans found his ski shoes coming off. He was allowed to readjust and continue to pull, but it happened again, and then again, so he was told to unhitch, get them right, and follow on and catch us up. He lagged far behind till lunch, and when we camped we had lunch, and then went back for him as he had not come up. He had fallen and had his hands frost-bitten, and we then returned for the sledge, and brought it, and fetched him in on it as he was rapidly losing the use of his legs. He was comatose when we got him into the tent, and he died without recovering consciousness that night about 10 P.M. We had a short rest for an hour or two in our bags that night, then had a meal and came on through the pressure ridges about 4 miles farther down and reached our Lower Glacier Depot. Here we camped at last, had a good meal and slept a good night's rest which we badly needed. Our depot was all right.

A very terrible day. . . . On discussing the symptoms we think he began to get weaker just before we reached the Pole, and that his downward path was accelerated first by the shock of his frost-bitten fingers, and later by falls during rough travelling on the glacier, further by his loss of all confidence in himself. Wilson thinks it certain he must have injured his brain by a fall. It is a terrible thing to lose a companion in this way, but calm reflection shows that there could not have been a better ending to the terrible anxieties of the past week. Discussion of the situation at lunch yesterday shows us what a desperate pass we were in with a sick man on our hands at such a distance from home.

Stevenson has written of a traveller whose wife slumbered by his side what time his spirit re-adventured forth in memory of days gone by. He was quite happy about it, and I suppose his travels had been peaceful, for days and nights such as these men spent coming down the Beardmore will give you nightmare after nightmare, and wake you shrieking—years after.

Of course they were shaken and weakened. But the conditions they had faced, and the time they had been out, do not in my opinion account entirely for their weakness nor for Evans's collapse, which may have had something to do with the fact that he was the biggest, heaviest and most muscular man in the party. I do not believe that this is a life for such men, who are expected to pull their weight and to support and drive a larger machine than their companions, and at the same time to eat no extra food. If, as seems likely, the ration these men were eating was not enough to support the work they were doing, then it is clear that the heaviest man will feel the deficiency sooner and more severely than others who are smaller than he. Evans must have had a most terrible time: I think it is clear from the diaries that he had suffered very greatly without complaint. At home he would have been nursed in bed: here he must march (he was pulling the day he died) until he was crawling on his frost-bitten hands and knees in the snow—horrible: most horrible perhaps for those who found him so, and sat in the tent and watched him die. I am told that simple concussion does not kill as suddenly as this: probably some clot had moved in his brain.

For one reason and another they took very nearly as long to come down the glacier with a feather-weight sledge as we had taken to go up it with full loads. Seven days' food were allowed from the Upper to the Lower Glacier Depot. Bowers told me that he thought this was running it fine. But the two supporting parties got through all right, though they both tumbled into the horrible pressure above the Cloudmaker. The Last Return Party took 7½ days: the Polar Party 10 days: the latter had been 25½ days longer on the plateau than the former. Owing to their slow progress down the glacier the Polar Party went on short rations for the first and last time until they camped on 19 March: with the exception of these days they had either their full, or more than their full ration until that date.

Until they reached the Barrier on their return journey the weather can be described neither as abnormal nor as unexpected. There were 300 statute miles (260 geo.) to be covered to One Ton Depot, and 150 statute miles (130 geo.) more from One Ton to Hut Point. They had just picked up one week's food for five men: between the Beardmore and One Ton were three more depots each with one week's food for five men. They were four men: their way was across the main body of the Barrier out of sight of land, and away from any immediate influence of the comparatively warm sea ahead of them. Nothing was known of the weather conditions in the middle of the Barrier at this time of year, and no one suspected that March conditions there were very cold. Shackleton turned homeward on 10 January: reached his Bluff Depot on 23 February, and Hut Point on 28 February.

Wilson's diary continues:

February 18. We had only five hours' sleep. We had butter and biscuit and tea when we woke up at 2 P.M., then came over the Gap entrance to the pony-slaughter camp, visiting a rock moraine of Mt. Hope on the way.

February 19. Late in getting away after making up new 10-foot sledge and digging out pony meat. We made 5 1/2 m. on a very heavy surface indeed.

This bad surface is the feature of their first homeward marches on the Barrier. From now onwards they complain always of the terrible surfaces, but a certain amount of the heavy pulling must be ascribed to their own weakness. In the low temperatures which occurred later bad surfaces were to be expected: but now the temperatures were not really low, about zero to -17°: fine clear days for the most part and, a thing to be noticed, little wind. They wanted wind, which would probably be behind them from the south. 'Oh! for a little wind,' Scott writes. 'E. Evans evidently had plenty.' He was already very anxious.

If this goes on we shall have a bad time, but I sincerely trust it is only the result of this windless area close to the coast and that, as we are making steadily outwards, we shall shortly escape it. It is perhaps premature [19 Feb.] to be anxious about covering distance. In all other respects things are improving. We have our sleeping-bags spread on the sledge and they are drying, but, above all, we have our full measure of food again. Tonight we had a sort of stew fry of pemmican and horseflesh, and voted it the best hoosh we had ever had on a sledge journey. The absence of poor Evans is a help to the commissariat, but if he had been here in a fit state we might have got along faster. I wonder what is in store for us, with some little alarm at the lateness of the season.

And on 20 February, when they made 7 miles, 'At present our sledge and ski leave deeply ploughed tracks which can be seen winding for miles behind. It is distressing, but as usual trials are forgotten when we camp, and good food is our lot. Pray God we get better travelling as we are not so fit as we were, and the season is advancing apace.' And on 21 February, 'We never won a march of 8½ miles with greater difficulty, but we can't go on like this.'

A breeze suddenly came away from S.S.E., force 4 to 6, at 11 A.M. on 22 February, and they hoisted the sail on the sledge they had just picked up. They immediately lost the tracks they were following, and failed to find the cairns and camp remains which they should have picked up if they had been on the right course, which was difficult here owing to the thick weather we had on the outward march. Bowers was sure they were too near the land and they steered out, but still failed to pick up the line on which their depots and their lives depended. Scott was convinced they were outside, not inside the line. The next morning Bowers took a round of angles, and they came to the conclusion, on slender evidence, that they were still too near the land. They had an unhappy march still off the tracks, 'but just as we decided to lunch, Bowers' wonderful sharp eyes detected an old double lunch cairn, the theodolite telescope confirmed it, and our spirits rose accordingly.' Then Wilson had another 'bad attack of snow-glare: could hardly keep a chink of eye open in goggles to see the course. Fat pony hoosh.' This day they reached the Lower Barrier Depot.

They were in evil case, but they would have been all right, these men, if the cold had not come down upon them, a bolt quite literally from the blue of a clear sky: unexpected, unforetold and fatal. The cold itself was not so tremendous until you realize that they had been out four months, that they had fought their way up the biggest glacier in the world in feet of soft snow, that they had spent seven weeks under plateau conditions or rarefied air, big winds and low temperatures, and they had watched one of their companions die—not in a bed, in a hospital or ambulance, nor suddenly, but slowly, night by night and day by day, with his hands frost-bitten and his brain going, until they must have wondered, each man in his heart, whether in such case a human being could be left to die, that four men might live. He died a natural death and they went out on to the Barrier.

Given such conditions as were expected, and the conditions for which preparation had been made, they would have come home alive and well. Some men say the weather was abnormal: there is some evidence that it was. The fact remains that the temperature dropped into the minus thirties by day and the minus forties by night. The fact also remains that there was a great lack of southerly winds, and in consequence the air near the surface was not being mixed: excessive radiation took place, and a layer of cold air formed near the ground. Crystals also formed on the surface of the snow and the wind was not enough to sweep them away. As the temperature dropped so the surface for the runners of the sledges became worse, as I explained elsewhere. They were pulling as it were through sand.

In the face of the difficulties which beset them their marches were magnificent: 11½ miles on 25 February and again on the following day: 12.2 miles on 27 February, and 11½ miles again on 28 and 29 February. If they could have kept this up they would have come through without a doubt. But I think it was about now that they suspected, and then were sure, that they could not pull through. Scott's diary, written at lunch, 2 March, is as follows:

> Misfortunes rarely come singly. We marched to the [Middle Barrier] depot fairly easily yesterday afternoon, and since that have suffered three distinct blows which have placed us in a bad position. First, we found a shortage of oil; with most rigid economy it can scarce carry us to the next depot on this surface [71 miles away]. Second, Titus Oates disclosed his feet, the toes showing very bad indeed, evidently bitten by the late temperatures. The third blow came in the night, when the wind, which we had hailed with some joy, brought dark overcast weather. It fell below -40° in the night, and this morning it took 1 1/2 hours to get our foot-gear on, but we got away before eight. We lost cairn and tracks together and made as steady as we could N. by W., but have seen nothing. Worse was to come—the surface is simply awful. In spite of strong wind and full sail we have only done 5 1/2 miles. We are in *very* Queer Street, since there is no doubt we cannot do the extra marches and feel the cold horribly.

They did nearly ten miles that day, but on 3 March they had a terrible time. 'God help us,' wrote Scott, 'we can't keep up this pulling, that is certain. Amongst ourselves we are unendingly cheerful, but what each man feels in his heart I can only guess. Putting on foot-gear in the morning is getting slower and slower, therefore every day more dangerous.

The following extracts are taken from Scott's diary.

March 4. Lunch. We are in a very tight place indeed, but none of us despondent *yet*, or at least we preserve every semblance of good cheer, but one's heart sinks as the sledge stops dead at some sastrugi behind which the surface sand lies thickly heaped. For the moment the temperature is in the -20°—an improvement which makes us much more comfortable, but a colder snap is bound to come again soon. I fear that Oates at least will weather such an event very poorly. Providence to our aid! We can expect little from man now except the possibility of extra food at the next depot. It will be real bad if we get there and find the same shortage of oil. Shall we get there? Such a short distance it would have appeared to us on the summit! I don't know what I should do if Wilson and Bowers weren't so determinedly cheerful over things.

Monday, March 5. Lunch. Regret to say going from bad to worse. We got a slant of wind yesterday afternoon, and going on 5 hours we converted our wretched morning run of 3½ miles into something over 9. We went to bed on a cup of cocoa and pemmican solid with the chill off. . . . The result is telling on all, but mainly on Oates, whose feet are in a wretched condition. One swelled up tremendously last night and he is very lame this morning. We started march on tea and pemmican as last night—we pretend to prefer the pemmican this way. Marched for 5 hours this morning over a slightly better surface covered with high moundy sastrugi. Sledge capsized twice; we pulled on foot, covering 5 1/2 miles. We are two pony marches and 4 miles from our depot. Our fuel dreadfully low and the poor Soldier nearly done. It is pathetic enough because we can do nothing for him; more hot food might do a little, but only a little, I fear. We none of us expected these terribly low temperatures, and of the rest of us, Wilson is feeling them most; mainly, I fear, from his self-sacrificing devotion in doctoring Oates' feet. We cannot help each other, each has enough to do to take care of himself. We get cold on the march when the trudging is heavy, and the wind pierces our worn garments. The others, all of them, are unendingly cheerful when in the tent. We mean to see the game through with a proper spirit, but it's tough work to be pulling harder that we ever pulled in our lives for long hours, and to feel that the progress is so slow. One can only say 'God help us!' and plod on our weary way, cold and very miserable, though outwardly cheerful. We talk of all sorts of subjects in the tent, not much of food now, since we decided to take the risk of running a full ration. We simply couldn't go hungry at this time.

Tuesday, March 6. Lunch. We did a little better with help of wind yesterday afternoon, finishing 9 1/2 miles for the day, and 27 miles from depot. But this morning things have been awful. It was warm in the night and for the first time during the journey I overslept myself by more than an hour; then we were slow with foot-gear; then, pulling with all our might (for our lives) we could scarcely advance at rate of a mile an hour; Then it grew thick and three times we had to get out of harness to search for tracks. The result is something less than 3½ miles for the forenoon. The sun is shining now and wind gone. Poor Oates is unable to pull, sits on the sledge when we are track-searching—he is wonderfully plucky, as his feet must be giving him great pain. He makes no complaint, but his spirits only come up in spurts now, and he grows more silent in the tent. We are making a spirit lamp to try and replace the primus when our oil is exhausted. . . .

Wednesday, March 7. A little worse, I fear. One of Oates' feet *very* bad this morning; he is wonderfully brave. We still talk of what we will do together at home.

We only made 6½ miles yesterday. This morning in 4½ hours we did just over 4 miles. We are 16 miles from our depot. If we only find the correct proportion of food there and this surface continues, we may get to the next depot [Mt. Hooper, 72 miles farther] but not to One Ton Camp. We hope against hope that the dogs have been to Mt. Hooper; then we might pull through. If there is a shortage of oil we can have little hope. One feels that for poor Oates the crisis is near, but none of us are improving, though we are wonderfully fit considering the really excessive work we are doing. We are only kept going by good food. No wind this morning till a chill northerly air came ahead. Sun bright and cairns showing up well. I should like to keep the track to the end.

Thursday, March 8. Lunch. Worse and worse in morning; poor Oates' left foot can never last out, and time over foot-gear something awful. Have to wait in night foot-gear for nearly an hour before I start changing, and then am generally first to be ready. Wilson's feet giving trouble now, but this mainly because he gives so much help to others. We did 4½ miles this morning and are now 8½ miles from the depot—a ridiculously small distance to feel in difficulties, yet on this surface we know we cannot equal half our marches, and that for that effort we expend nearly double the energy. The great question is: What shall we find at the depot? If the dogs have visited it we may get along a good distance, but if there is another short allowance of fuel, God help us indeed. We are in a very bad way, I fear, in any case.

Saturday, March 10. Things steadily downhill. Oates' foot worse. He has rare pluck and must know that he can never get through. He asked Wilson if he had a chance this morning, and of course Bill had to say he didn't know. In point of fact he has none. Apart from him, if he went under now, I doubt whether we could get through. With great care we might have a dog's chance, but no more. The weather conditions are awful, and our gear gets steadily more icy and difficult to manage . . .

Yesterday we marched up the depot, Mt. Hooper. Cold comfort. Shortage on our allowance all round. I don't know that any one is to blame. The dogs which would have been our salvation have evidently failed. Meares had a bad trip home I suppose.

This morning it was calm when we breakfasted, but the wind came from the W.N.W. as we broke camp. It rapidly grew in strength. After travelling for half an hour I saw that none of us could go on facing such conditions. We were forced to camp and are spending the rest of the day in a comfortless blizzard camp, wind quite foul.

Sunday, March 11. Titus Oates is very near the end, one feels. What we or he will do, God only knows. We discussed the matter after breakfast; he is a brave fine fellow and understands the situation, but he practically asked for advice. Nothing could be said but to urge him to march as long as he could. One satisfactory result to the discussion: I practically ordered Wilson to hand over the means of ending our troubles to us, so that any one of us may know how to do so. Wilson had no choice between doing so and our ransacking the medicine case. We have 30 opium tabloids apiece and he is left with a tube of morphine. So far the tragical side of our story.

The sky completely overcast when we started this morning. We could see nothing, lost the tracks, and doubtless have been swaying a good deal since—3.1 miles for the forenoon—terribly heavy dragging—expected it. Know that 6 miles is about the limit of our endurance now, if we get no help from wind or surfaces. We have 7 days' food and should be about 55 miles from One Ton Camp tonight, 6 x 7 = 42, leaving us 13 miles short of our distance, even if things get no worse. Meanwhile the season rapidly advances.

Monday, March 12. We did 6.9 miles yesterday, under our necessary average. Things are left much the same, Oates not pulling much, and now with hands as well as feet pretty well useless. We did 4 miles this morning in 4 hours 20 min.—we may hope for 3 this afternoon, 7 x 6 = 42. We shall be 47 miles from the depot. I doubt if we can possibly do it. The surface remains awful, the cold intense, and our physical condition running down. God help us! Not a breath of favourable wind for more than a week, and apparently liable to head winds at any moment.

Wednesday, March 14. No doubt about the going downhill, but everything going wrong for us. Yesterday we woke to a strong northerly wind with temp. -37°. Couldn't face it, so remained in camp til 2, then did 5 1/4 miles. Wanted to march later, but party feeling the cold badly as the breeze (N.) never took off entirely, and as the sun sank the temp. fell. Long time getting supper in dark.

This morning started with southerly breeze, set sail and passed another cairn at good speed; half-way, however, the wind shifted to W. by S. or W.S.W., blew through our wind-clothes and into our mitts. Poor Wilson horribly cold, could [not] get off ski for some time. Bowers and I practically made camp, and when we got into the tent at last we were all deadly cold. Then temp. now midday down -43° and the wind strong. We *must* go on, but now the making of every camp must be more difficult and dangerous. It must be near the end, but a pretty merciful end. Poor Oates got it again in the foot. I shudder to think what it will be like tomorrow. It is only with greatest pains rest of us keep off frost-bites. No idea there could be temperatures like this at this time of year with such winds. Truly awful outside the tent. Must fight it out to the last biscuit; but can't reduce rations.

Friday, March 16, or Saturday, 17. Lost track of dates, but think the last correct. Tragedy all along the line. At lunch, the day before yesterday, poor Titus Oates said he couldn't go on; he proposed we should leave him in his sleeping-bag. That we could not do, and we induced him to come on, on the afternoon march. In spite of its awful nature for him he struggled on and we made a few miles. At night he was worse and we knew the end had come.

Should this be found I want these facts recorded. Oates' last thoughts were of his mother, but immediately before he took pride in thinking that his regiment would be pleased with the bold way in which he met his death. We can testify to his bravery. He has borne intense suffering for weeks without complaint, and to the very last was able and willing to discuss outside subjects. He did not—would not—give up hope till the very end. He was a brave soul. This was the end. He slept through the night before last, hoping not to wake; but he woke in the morning—yesterday. It was blowing a blizzard. He said, 'I am just going outside and may be some time.' He went out into the blizzard and we have not seen him since.

I take this opportunity of saying that we have stuck to our sick companions to the last. In case of Edgar Evans, when absolutely out of food and he lay insensible, the safety of the remainder seemed to demand his abandonment, but Providence mercifully removed him at this critical moment. He died a natural death, and we did not leave him till two hours after his death. We knew that poor Oates was walking to his death, but though we tried to dissuade him, we knew it was the act of a brave man and an English gentleman. We all hope to meet the end with a similar spirit, and assuredly the end is not far.

I can only write at lunch and then only occasionally. The cold is intense, -40° at midday. My companions are unendingly cheerful, but we are all on the verge of serious frost-bites, and though we constantly talk of fetching through I don't think any one of us believes it in his heart.

We are cold on the march now, and at all times except meals. Yesterday we had to lay up for a blizzard and today we move dreadfully slowly. We are at No. 14 Pony Camp, only two pony marches from One Ton Depot. We leave here our theodolite, a camera, and Oates' sleeping-bags. Diaries, etc., and geological specimens carried at Wilson's special request, will be found with us or on our sledge.

Sunday, March 18. Today, lunch, we are 21 miles from the depot. Ill fortune presses, but better may come. We have had more wind and drift from ahead yesterday; had to stop marching; wind N.W., force 4, temp. -35°. No human being could face it, and we are worn out *nearly*.

My right foot has gone, nearly all the toes—two days ago I was proud possessor of best feet. . . . Bowers takes first place in condition, but there is not much to choose after all. The others are still confident of getting through—or pretend to be—I don't know! We have the last *half* fill of oil in our primus and a very small quantity of spirit—this alone between us and thirst. The wind is fair for the moment, and that is perhaps a fact to help. The mileage would have seemed ridiculously small on our outward journey.

Monday, March 19. Lunch. We camped with difficulty last night and were dreadfully cold till after our supper of cold pemmican and biscuit and a half pannikin of cocoa cooked over the spirit. Then, contrary to expectation, we got warm and all slept well. Today we started in the usual dragging manner. Sledge dreadfully heavy. We are 15 1/2 miles from the depot and ought to get there in three days. What progress! We have two days' food but barely a day's fuel. All our feet are getting bad—Wilson's best, my right foot worse, left all right. There is no chance to nurse one's feet till we can get hot food into us. Amputation is the least I can hope for now, but will the trouble spread? That is the serious question. The weather doesn't give us a chance—the wind from N. to N.W. and -40° temp. today.

Wednesday, March 21. Got within 11 miles of depot Monday night; had to lay up all yesterday in severe blizzard. Today forlorn hope, Wilson and Bowers going to depot for fuel.

22 and 23. Blizzard bad as ever—Wilson and Bowers unable to start—tomorrow last chance—no fuel and only one or two of food left—must be near the end. Have decided it shall be natural—we shall march for the depot with or without our effects and die in our tracks.

Thursday, March 29. Since the 21st we have had a continuous gale from W.S.W. and S.W. We had fuel to make two cups of tea apiece and bare food for two days on the 20th. Every day we have been ready to start for our depot 11 miles away, but outside the door of the tent it remains a scene of whirling drift. I do not think we can hope for any better things now. We shall stick it out to the end, but we are getting weaker, of course, and the end cannot be far.

It seems a pity, but I do not think I can write more.

R. SCOTT

Last entry. For God's sake, look after our people.

The following extracts are from letters written by Scott:

To Mrs E. A. Wilson

MY DEAR MRS WILSON. If this letter reaches you, Bill and I will have gone out together. We are very near it now and I should like you to know how splendid he was at the end—everlastingly cheerful and ready to sacrifice himself for others, never a word of blame to me for leading him into this mess. He is not suffering, luckily, at least only minor discomforts.

His eyes have a comfortable blue look of hope and his mind is peaceful with the satisfaction of his faith in regarding himself as part of the great scheme of the Almighty. I can do no more to comfort you than to tell you that he died as he lived, a brave, true man—the best of comrades and staunchest of friends.

My whole heart goes out to you in pity. Yours,

R. SCOTT

To Mrs Bowers

MY DEAR MRS BOWERS. I am afraid this will reach you after one of the heaviest blows of your life.

I write when we are very near the end of our journey, and I am finishing it in company with two gallant, noble gentlemen. One of these is your son. He had come to be one of my closest and soundest friends, and I appreciate his wonderful upright nature, his ability and energy. As the troubles have thickened his dauntless spirit ever shone brighter and he has remained cheerful, hopeful and indomitable to the end . . .

To Sir J. M. Barrie

MY DEAR BARRIE. We are pegging out in a very comfortless spot. Hoping this letter may be found and sent to you, I write a word of farewell . . . Good-bye. I am not at all afraid of the end, but sad to miss many a humble pleasure which I had planned for the future on our long marches. I may not have proved a great explorer, but we have done the greatest march ever made and come very near to great success. Good-bye, my dear friend. Yours ever,

R. SCOTT

We are in a desperate state, feet frozen, etc. No fuel and a long way from food, but it would do your heart good to be in our tent, to hear our songs and the cheery conversation as to what we will do when we get to Hut Point.

Later. We are very near the end, but have not and will not lose our good cheer. We have four days of storm in our tent and nowhere's food or fuel. We did intend to finish ourselves when things proved like this, but we have decided to die naturally in the tracks.

The following extracts are from letters written to other friends:

. . . I want to tell you that I was *not* too old for this job. It was the younger men that went under first. . . . After all we are setting a good example to our countrymen, if not by getting into a tight place, by facing it like men when we were there. We could have come through had we neglected the sick.

Wilson, the best fellow that ever stepped, has sacrificed himself again and again to the sick men of the party . . .

. . . Our journey has been the biggest on record, and nothing but the most exceptional hard luck at the end would have caused us to fail to return.

What lots and lots I could tell you of this journey. How much better has it been than lounging in too great comfort at home.

Message to the Public

The causes of the disaster are not due to faulty organization, but to misfortune in all risks which had to be undertaken.

1. The loss of pony transport in March 1911 obliged me to start later than I had intended, and obliged the limits of stuff transported to be narrowed.

2. The weather throughout the outward journey, and especially the long gale in 83°S., stopped us.

3. The soft snow in lower reaches of glacier again reduced pace.

We fought these untoward events with a will and conquered, but it cut into our provision reserve.

Every detail of our food supplies, clothing and depots made on the interior ice-sheet and over that long stretch of 700 miles to the Pole and back, worked to perfection. The advance party would have returned to the glacier in fine form and with surplus of food, but for the astonishing failure of the man whom we had least expected to fail. Edgar Evans was thought the strongest man of the party.

The Beardmore Glacier is not difficult in fine weather, but on our return we did not get a single completely fine day; this with a sick companion enormously increased our anxieties.

As I have said elsewhere, we got into frightfully rough ice and Edgar Evans received a concussion of the brain—he died a natural death, but left us a shaken party with the season unduly advanced.

But all the facts above enumerated were as nothing to the surprise which awaited us on the Barrier. I maintain that our arrangements for returning were quite adequate, and that no one in the world would have expected the temperatures and surfaces which we encountered at this time of the year. On the summit in lat. 85°-°86 we had -20°, -30°. On the Barrier in lat. 82°, 10,000 feet lower, we had -30° in the day, -47° at night pretty regularly, with continuous head-wind during our day marches. It is clear that these circumstances come on very suddenly, and our wreck is certainly due to this sudden advent of severe weather, which does not seem to have any satisfactory cause. I do not think human beings ever came through such a month as we have come through, and we should have got through in spite of the weather but for the sickening of a second companion, Captain Oates, and a shortage of fuel in our depots for which I cannot account, and finally, but for the storm which has fallen on us within 11 miles of the depot at which we hoped to secure our final supplies. Surely misfortune could scarcely have exceeded this last blow. We arrived within 11 miles of our old One Ton Camp with fuel for one last meal and food for two days. For four days we have been unable to leave the tent—the gale howling about us. We are weak, writing is difficult, but for my own sake I do not regret this journey, which has shown that Englishmen can endure hardships, help one another, and meet death with as great a fortitude as ever in the past. We took risks, we knew we took them; things have come out against us, and therefore we have no cause for complaint, but bow to the will of Providence, determined still to do our best to the last. But if we have been willing to give our lives to this enterprise, which is for the honour of our country, I appeal to our countrymen to see that those who depend on us are properly cared for.

Had we lived, I should have had a tale to tell of the hardihood, endurance, and courage of my companions which would have stirred the heart of every Englishman. These rough notes and our dead bodies must tell the tale, but surely, surely a great rich country like ours will see that those who are dependent on us are properly provided for.

R. SCOTT

On Dangerous Ground

LAMAR UNDERWOOD

The four rainbow trout finned easily to hold themselves suspended in the current, their shadows wavering over the brown pebbly streambed at a place where the Toubok River curved from the dark canyon of a spruce forest and clattered sunlit and sparkling through a field of low alder bushes. Pointed into the flow, the fish did not see or detect the enormous grizzly as it slowly emerged from the shadowed timber and walked across the sandbar to the shoals behind their position.

The great bear's muscles moved with fluid, rippling ease, so devoid of stiffness that the entire body seemed on the verge of collapse. Beneath the stumpy legs, the dry sand yielded to a depth of two inches as each footfall silently recorded the passage of the massive 1,500-pound creature. Its front feet, fifteen inches long by ten wide, bore claws that curved downward over the last half of their six-inch length. The rear feet were not as wide, their claws shorter. Tiny ears, a broad shelving forehead, and burly snout gave the bear's face a doglike appearance. The deeply dished eyes were devoid of malevolence, innocently unexpressive. Thicker and wider than the head itself, the neck led back to the prominent hump that seemed to float, unattached to the rest of the body, as the creature walked, the light upstream breeze stirring the outer frosting of silver hair and the dark brown pelt beneath.

When he reached the edge of the current, the grizzly waddled into the flow without pausing, heading directly across the rocky shoals. The trout shot upstream into a deeper pool, splinters of light as they flared through the clear water. Across the stream, the grizzly paused to shake itself. His legs and underbelly blurred with motion as luminous mist flew from the soaked fur. In a moment, he went on. Shouldering through the border of alders that grew down to the water's edge, he headed downstream.

As the great bear walked along the river, his presence had an immediate impact on the rhythm of the late-afternoon life sustained by the stream. On a hillside across the river, pine squirrels saw the bear and began to chirr in scolding, nervous alarm. A pair of ravens watched the beast approach, then flapped away, croaking as they flew. Peering from the uppermost snag of a lightning-killed white spruce, an osprey saw the bear wade directly through the bay-like depression where it had been fishing. The bird lifted into the air, caught a thermal, and circled away downstream. A hen mallard and a drake, floating on the current, bounced straight up and curved away over the spruce tops, their wings whispering.

All day the great bear had foraged opportunistically while wandering through the river valley. Once, when he was crossing a saddle of talus rock that bridged two ridges on the slopes above the stream, he had detected the powerful odor of prey in the mixture of scents his amazing nose sorted from the mountain air: dank rock, moss and lichen, wildflowers, rotting snow, pumice and sand.

For several yards he had coursed the trail over the stones like a bird dog, head down, wheezing as his nostrils flooded with scent. Rounding a rocky shoulder, he was enveloped by a cloud of odor the wind brought down from the ledges above. The bear looked up and instantly crouched into a stalk, as a band of Dall sheep ewes and lambs came into view, alert and tense, their superb vision focused on the menace before them. They watched, mesmerized for a moment, then bounded up the slope with a harsh rattling of hooves. The bear broke into a sprint for a few yards, then slowed and stopped as the weaving, bobbing forms disappeared over the ridge line. The grizzly watched the empty slope for a few moments, then turned and resumed his journey.

Later he spent two frustrating hours trying to dig a ground squirrel from its den. Barely larger than a mouse, the squirrel had screeched in mortal terror as the claws scratched and probed to within inches of its perch in a tunnel between two underground rocks. But the huge paws could not be forced into the tiny aperture. Finally, snorting with excitement, the grizzly began to dig for the tiny morsel. By the time he became bored with the pursuit and wandered on his way, the torn ground looked as if a bomb had struck.

Since copulating with a sow and then immediately leaving her two weeks before, the grizzly had become increasingly obsessed with feeding. He had been with the female for ten days, following her steady, aimless wanderings that are part of the great bears' courtship rituals, and the experience had burned away the last of the winter fat he had brought from his many weeks of semi-hibernation. Now his instincts had carried him down from the higher ranges to the fertile lower slopes, where he expected to find the tubers of wild-flowers, seed pods, plant bulbs, and other growths that composed the greater part of his diet at this time of the year. There were pea vine roots to dig, horsetail and sourdock plants to chomp down. Also, another sense of need gripped the great bear, pulling him deeper into the river valley. Usually by this time every spring, the banks of the river had provided the special food that would satisfy the craving that gnawed at him. Carrion—a moose or caribou carcass, gift of the melting winter snows—would bring the strength and satisfaction the grizzly instinctively knew he needed. The memory of such rich feeding could not be obliterated by a diet of plants, and for days the grizzly's instincts had held him close to the river. Sometimes he wandered the nearby ridges for a while, but he always came back to the current, searching expectantly along the brushy shoreline.

The great bear continued downstream, slipping in and out of the alders like some enormous shadow. When the thicket began to thin, the grizzly stopped. Across a wide expanse of muskeg that came down to the edge of the stream, open country stretched away to a distant line of timber. Closer, on one side of the muskeg, a line of willows gave way to a belt of spruce on high ground.

The bear moved into the thicket, stopped again. In every direction, the willows had been heavily browsed, the ground scarred and trampled. The scent of the beast that had fed there permeated the air like fog. The bear stepped gingerly ahead, drinking in the smell, seeking a source for the diffused odor.

Twenty yards to one side, a thick clump of brush exploded with noise and movement. A cow moose crashed through the brush and headed across the clearing, trotting in a ragged gait.

Instantly the grizzly charged.

The moose bolted in panic, nostrils flaring, eyes bulging wildly. She looked back over her shoulder just as a paw smashed into the side of her neck, breaking it with a crack that resounded over the bear's roar and the collision of the massive bodies. The bear's bulk hurtled into the cow's shoulder, breaking bones and battering muscle and sinew into pulp. One of the cow's front legs snapped under the impact, and she was thrown forward and to one side, landing on her shoulder, her head and neck flopping limply as they thudded to the ground. The grizzly bit into the flesh, sinking his fangs deep into the blood-spurting neck, shaking his head as he tightened his grip.

Gradually, the grizzly sensed the lack of movement in his prey and relaxed his hold. He stood for a moment, watching the carcass. The cow's eyes stared ahead, wide and empty, the light inside extinguished since the initial blow to the neck.

The great bear circled, sniffing and watching. Finally, he bit into the base of the neck, braced his massive shoulders, and began to pull the cow along the ground. Despite his brute strength, the grizzly could only move the body a foot or so in one continuous pull. Stopping periodically to look around and sniff the air for intruders, then bending down to gain a new purchase on his prize, the bear worked for over an hour to move his kill twenty yards from the willows. The opening where he finally stopped was closer to the spruce trees and the river but was almost identical to the spot where the moose had been struck down.

For some strange reason, however, the grizzly's instincts were satisfied now. His paws resting on the carcass, he lifted his nose, inspecting the light currents of air.

Finally he began to feed.

A pair of magpies watched from a nearby branch, keeping their distance for now but knowing their turn would come.

"I'd feel a whole lot better about leaving you here if you'd take this." The pilot clicked back the hammer of the long-barreled .44 magnum revolver. "Hell, I'll even show you how to use it." He held the gun with a two-handed combat grip, steadied his feet on the pontoons of the floatplane, and aimed across the water.

To Sam Larkin, the metallic snap of the hammer falling on an empty chamber seemed a strange sound above the lapping of the gentle waves against the rocks. He glared silently at the plane as it floated over the sun-dappled shallows, some ten yards from the level slab of stone where he and his backpacks had just been put ashore. From far down the lake, the call of a loon echoed through the stillness. The cry was at once lilting and plaintive, a cry of wildness and solitude.

The pilot lowered the handgun, opened the action, and idly spun the empty cylinder. The holster belt that sagged from his waist was lined with blunt-nosed cartridges that gleamed dully. To Larkin, the idea of lugging that grim bulk and heaviness through the Alaska wilderness for the next ten days was too depressing to contemplate. He smiled at the pilot, trying to show appreciation for his offer.

"I'll be all right," Larkin said. "I've lived in New York City for seven years without a gun. That's more dangerous than being out here."

"No it ain't," the pilot answered.

Larkin studied the man's face for a sign of levity. The eyes were cold dark slits, the other features expressionless behind a heavy reddish beard and long hair that spilled from a baseball cap with a Cessna label on the front. Larkin suspected that the pilot was very young, but he could not be certain. Whatever his age, he had handled the plane well on the flight from Anchorage, setting the single-engined 182 on the small lake with a deftness and precision that Larkin had admired. Now the pilot had become an intruder. Larkin wanted him to be on his way.

"Wilderness grizzlies just want to be left alone," Larkin said. "They'll bugger off as long as you don't do something stupid, like surprise one."

"If this is your first trip to Alaska, how come you know so much about our bears?"

"I read a lot. I've been looking forward to this for a long time."

The pilot shrugged his shoulders. He unbuckled

the gun, turned quickly, and eased gingerly along the pontoon to the cockpit. Larkin knelt on one knee and began checking the straps of his oversized backpack and a smaller shoulder pack.

The pilot carried a paddle as he came back to the front of the pontoon. Kneeling, he thrust the blade down against the brown-pebbled bottom and pushed hard to shove the plane out of the shallows. "You know," he called, "a lot of those writers have never seen a bear, 'cept in a zoo. What they write about is all made-up bullshit."

"Thanks for your help," Larkin called. "I'll be careful." He could imagine what the pilot was thinking: *This tenderfoot's gonna get his smart New York ass in deep-shit trouble.* Larkin realized that almost everything about his appearance looked new and untested: his khaki trousers and long-sleeve cotton jersey, his packs, even his boyish, lightly tanned face. His blond hair was cut short and neat. The only marks of backcountry experience about him were his well-worn boots, with leather uppers, rubber bottoms, and heavy-lugged Vibram soles—a perfect combination for the springy tundra and swampy lowlands, as well as the harder ground along the slopes of the ridges.

The plane was floating in deeper water. The pilot could no longer touch the bottom with his paddle. He stood and shouted to Larkin. "Okay, so don't surprise a grizzly. But, if you should happen to, do you know what to do?"

"Shout. Sing. Whistle. Anything to make noise and scare it way."

"No, that's all wrong!" The pilot waved his hand impatiently. "If you should happen up on a grizzly, say as close as I am to you right now, there's only one thing to do."

"What's that?" Larkin called, interested.

"The only thing you can do is to relax. Otherwise, you'll die all tensed up."

Larkin chuckled at the gag before he realized the pilot was not smiling.

"Rock Lake, ten days from now," Larkin called, getting back to business. "I'll be there."

"Don't eat all your food," the pilot shouted. "If the weather socks in, you'll have to camp at the lake till we can fly. Just sit tight."

The pilot climbed into the cockpit, slammed the door, and waved at Larkin as the electrical circuits hummed and the engine sputtered to life.

Larkin stood at the edge of the water and watched the plane taxi slowly downwind. Against the dark line of trees at the far end of the lake, the plane looked like a brightly painted toy. It made a slow U-turn and headed back toward Larkin, plowing quickly through the water. He could see white explosions of foam as the ship picked up speed. In a moment the roar of the engine was upon him and the pontoons were skimming the surface, throwing twin contrails of spray over their wakes. The plane rose slowly from the water and immediately leveled off, gathering speed. As the plane approached the shore it began to climb steeply, and was still climbing as it roared overhead and out of sight beyond the spruce hillside behind the edge of the lake.

Larkin looked at his watch. Eight P.M. here, midnight back in New York. He had left his Upper West Side apartment at six in the morning. Now, eighteen hours later, he was on a trail deep in the Alaska Range.

Larkin looked out across the water, listening for the call of the loon. Light breezes stroked the surface into wavelets that shimmered in the sunlight. Along the shoreline, the water was dark and smooth in the shadows of the low hills cupping the lake. The silence was like some strange new sound that rang in the ears. Then the loon's cry danced across the water again. Somewhere nearby, a fish swirled. Larkin felt a surge of pleasure. He was alone but not lonely.

He pulled a map from a side pocket of his backpack. The act of unfolding the map and checking his position was a formality. The curving patterns of brown, green, and blue lines had been engraved in his mind during the countless hours he had spent poring over the map in anticipation of the trip.

On the map, his landing spot was a tiny dot squeezed by flowing contour lines that marked the surrounding hills. A line indicating a trail wiggled away from where he stood and brought his finger to the serpentine course of the Toubok River, which flowed out of the Alaska Range. After hiking upstream along the river for a week, he intended to cut cross-country to Rock Lake, where the float plane would pick him up. He expected to do some superb fishing and hiking while enjoying grand views and ideal campsites all along the way. He slipped the map back into the backpack and weighed his next move. There was no need to hurry; even after the sun dipped below the horizon, it would rise again before full darkness descended. The demands that usually made him pressed for time were behind him now. Out here, he would let events flow along at their own pace. He would enjoy the view for a bit before moving toward the river to find a campsite. Despite the long hours of his journey, he felt only exhilaration.

He opened a flap of the shoulder pack and reached inside for his binoculars. He sat down on the rock shelf where the barren stone was splashed with color; lichens formed filigrees of purple, doughnuts of green, mushroom bursts of orange.

Larkin raised his knees and leaned forward to steady his elbows as he lifted the glasses. The compact but powerful 10 x 40 lenses bit into the distance and pulled startling detail into view.

Green and bright in the evening sunlight, the surrounding forest of spruce, birch, and cottonwood stretched away toward the ramparts of the Alaska Range. The spruce on the lower slopes of the mountains gave way to gulches of misty-green alder that crept up the ridges for a distance, then disappeared into the grayness of rock ledges and shale saddles. Shadowed canyons gaped alongside the slanting ridges. Above, the snow line gradually began, first in scattered pockets where the sun never reached, then in blinding white couloirs flanked by hanging curtains of glacial ice. From this jumble of stone and icy blueness, the peaks themselves erupted into the skyline, hard-etched towers looming like sentinels on the edge of the earth.

Larkin lowered the binoculars, blinking. He felt he was on the brink of some secret Eden he would be the first to enter. No glitches on the trip, perfect weather on the trail. What more could he ask?

The question produced a sudden stab of disappointment. Ted Walsh wasn't here. Sam's friend and companion of many trails and campfires had been forced to drop out of the trip, despite the fact that this trek was to have been the greatest of them all. "The finale of the carefree years," Walsh called it. Larkin was getting married later that summer.

The decision to press on alone had been an easy one for Sam. He had realized for some time that he enjoyed going solo in the wilderness.

God, he had brought a lot of stuff, Larkin thought as he reached for his backpack. He had treated himself to a new expedition-type pack with state-of-the-art features. The freeze-dried food and gear he felt he would need brought the unit to nearly sixty pounds. He braced his legs and swung the pack up to rest on an extended knee. With a quick and practiced move, he brought the load up and onto his back, pushing his arms through the shoulder straps. He staggered slightly as he wiggled into the contours of the pack's frame and reached for his waist belt.

At that moment, Larkin could not help but think of the kidding he was being spared by Ted Walsh's absence. Walsh was the absolute master of reducing weight and bulk to gossamer. Ted's tricks—such as squeezing toothpaste from the tube and carrying it wrapped in light plastic—knew no limits. In his search for lightweight, efficient gadgets he was indefatigable.

Larkin swung the strap of the kit bag over his shoulder. The bag held his fishing gear: lures and flies, lightweight fly and spinning reels, and two pack rods that broke down into twelve-inch-long sections.

He was ready to begin his journey. He looked at the lake and wondered if he would see it again. Perhaps with Susan, his bride to be, or with their children someday.

He turned to the trail, a faint trace that led up along the slope of the hillside and out of sight through the scattered spruce trees. Leaning forward against the heft of the pack, he started up the ridge. Behind him, the loon was still calling from far out on the lake.

A sudden itching sensation on the backs of his hands interrupted the pleasure Larkin was feeling. Frowning at his oversight, he slapped at the mosquitoes and reached into the shoulder pack to get some repellent.

Even paradise had its pests.

The willow thicket was quiet in the evening shadows. The magpies had ceased their quarrelling over the tidbits of flesh they could find on the ground where the grizzly had killed the moose. Smaller birds were hushed as well, leaving only the rustles of hares and ground squirrels and the swirls of rising fish. The pulse of the river world seemed to have vanished.

The carcass of the moose was almost unrecognizable now. Except for one section where a leg and hoof angled out crazily, and another where a brown patch of head lay exposed to the sky, empty baleful eyes jutting outward, the entire body was crudely covered with an assortment of brush and clumps of mossy tundra.

The great bear sprawled belly down on top of his handiwork, his legs splayed out, his head resting on a hump pushed up by the curve of the cow's shoulder. He was asleep.

Suddenly his eyes flickered, then opened wide. Without moving his head, he flared his nostrils and lifted his ears. He detected nothing that alarmed him. Then a trace of wind stirred through the willows and died away.

The grizzly slipped down from the kill without a sound and tensed into a crouch, his head thrust forward, his legs poised like springs. The sound that had awakened him was gone again. The still air held no scents that were new or threatening.

He heard the noise again, more distinct now, getting closer. Still there was no scent to send alarm through his twenty-ounce brain. But even without the message of scent, this grizzly's instincts told him the noise represented danger. He eased toward the side of the clearing, where the willows were thicker and a stand of birch trees began.

The grizzly vanished into the cover, a shadow moving within shadows.

The magpies flew down to the abandoned kill.

Sam Larkin was frustrated. He has passed up two decent campsites when he had first hit the river. Now, nearly an hour later, he was slogging through a swamp-like area where the current was hemmed in by a thick growth of alders. Forced to wade in the shallows to make any progress at all, he was sweating heavily and achingly tired. He had broken out the repellent again, and his face, hands, and hair reeked of the clammy paste of medicine and perspiration. Clouds of mosquitoes hovered in the still air. The sun had dipped behind the hills, and the breeze had died with it. Footing was difficult in the heavy shadows, and he had tripped twice, staggering and barely avoiding a headlong fall.

You're getting sloppy, Sam told himself. This is

exactly the kind of place where you have to worry about bears.

Everything he had read about the grizzly had stressed the point that the animal's relatively poor eyesight was more than offset by its superb hearing and remarkable nose. He remembered an Indian proverb from an article he had been reading on the plane only a few hours before. *The pine needle fell in the forest. The eagle saw it fall; the deer heard it fall; the bear smelled it fall.*

That was irony for you, Larkin thought. A grizzly on the cover of *In Wilderness* on the day I'm headed for Alaska.

In Wilderness was a new national magazine Ted Walsh had edited since its inception a year ago. Difficulties at the magazine had knocked Walsh out of the trip with Sam, despite the fact that Walsh had planned the entire venture. One of the magazine's regular contributors lived on the Toubok, and Walsh had mapped out a trek that would include a surprise visit to the writer's cabin, four days' hike upstream.

Even without Ted Walsh along, Sam had decided to stick to the original plan. He had always wanted to meet the writer, Jonathan Hill, whose article and photographs on the grizzly were the most recent in a series of pieces on Alaska.

Ahead, Sam could see a bend in the alders. The current was dark and smooth where it curved into view.

Okay, it's showtime, he told himself. He raised his voice in song. Bits and pieces of "Get Me to the

Church on Time" filled the air as he waded on through the dark riffles.

He broke off in mid-note, laughing. His voice sounded absurdly loud and ridiculous above the murmur of the river.

"Instead of singing, I'll settle for talking to myself," Larkin mumbled. "It'll sound a helluva lot more pleasant.

"If there're any bears around here, I hope they hear me now!" Larkin called aloud. He shuddered at the alien sound of his own voice. "This is inane," he muttered.

Larkin sloshed on around the bend. The alders seemed to be thinning out, the terrain changing. Then he saw the river pouring straight at him from a stretch of open country where the muskeg plain and stands of spruce trees formed the horizon. Beyond a point of willows on the right bank, a ramp of dry, rocky soil slanted down from the higher ground.

Larkin's spirits soared. Camp at last!

The great bear crouched in the shadows, downwind of the willow thicket. The scent of the intruder flooded his nostrils now, triggering an instinctive force that compelled him to flee. But that force was only part of the complex emotions that stirred within him. The gamy odor of the moose kill made him confused and agitated.

He watched and waited.

Within moments, the scent of the intruder became overwhelming, raging toward the grizzly like a firestorm.

The smell of the moose kill mingled with the scent of the danger. The meat provided strength, an instinctive sense of well-being.

The great bear was afraid. Yet he did not flee.

Suddenly he spotted movement. The willow branches shook, then parted.

The puny two-legged menace stood in the clearing, looking off toward the river.

Larkin had been trying to hurry. His boots made loud sucking noises as he trudged along the muddy bank where the willows grew down to the water. He paused to study the last thirty yards that separated him from the far side of the willow thicket and the beginning of the open ground. The willows seemed to be thinner up away from the bank of the river. He could see gaps in the clumps of bushes and a few scattered birches on beyond. He headed that way, expecting firmer ground.

He had to use his arms and hands to ward the thick branches from his face. The green limbs he shoved aside immediately whipped back into place, snagging on his packs. He pressed on through the tangle with dogged determination.

In a moment he broke into a clearing. To his right, away from the stream, the willows gave way to a stand of birches. Straight ahead he could see the tops of the spruces, which marked the beginning of the tundra plain. That was the spot where he wanted to make camp.

The stillness was like a kind of vapor, and his breathing was labored, as if all oxygen had been squeezed out of the air.

He stepped ahead, then stopped, listening. He had heard something.

Faint and distant, the call of a loon broke through the stillness.

Was that what he had heard? Terrific! Music for his first camp. There must be a lake somewhere over there. Loons were not river birds.

He moved along a few paces, skirting the edges of a few willow clumps that loomed in the way.

Two magpies burst into flight from off to his left, squawking as they flapped on out over the river.

Larkin gasped, startled and shaken. A feverish chill swept over him, cutting through his general discomfort of fatigue, thirst, and hunger.

Come on, for Christ's sake, his thoughts urged. Let's get to camp.

He started again, then paused in midstep, staring at the place where the magpies had jumped, his mouth wide open.

The pile of brush that held his gaze was a haphazard